THE PAULINE CANON

PAULINE STUDIES

SERIES EDITOR
Stanley E. Porter
MCMASTER DIVINITY COLLEGE
HAMILTON, ONTARIO, CANADA

VOLUME 1

THE PAULINE CANON

THE PAULINE CANON

Edited by
Stanley E. Porter

SBL
Society of Biblical Literature
Atlanta

Copyright © 2004 by Koninklijke Brill NV, Leiden,
The Netherlands

This edition published under license from Koninklijke Brill NV,
Leiden, The Netherlands by the Society of Biblical Literature.

All rights reserved. No part of this work may be reproduced or transmitted in any form or by any means, electronic or mechanical, including photocopying and recording, or by any means of any information storage or retrieval system, except as may be expressly permitted by the 1976 Copyright Act or in writing from the Publisher. Requests for permission should be addressed in writing to the Rights and Permissions Department, Koninklijke Brill NV, Leiden, The Netherlands.

Authorization to photocopy items for internal or personal use is granted by Brill provided that the appropriate fees are paid directly to The Copyright Clearance Center, 222 Rosewood Drive, Suite 910, Danvers, MA 01923, USA. Fees are subject to change.

Library of Congress Cataloging-in-Publication Data

The Pauline canon / edited by Stanley E. Porter.
    p. cm. – (Pauline studies ; ISSN 1572-4913 ; v. 1)
    Originally published: Leiden ; Boston : Brill, 2004.
    Includes bibliographical references and index.
    ISBN 978-1-58983-428-6 (paper binding : alk. paper)
  1. Bible. N.T. Epistles of Paul–Canon. 2. Bible. N.T. Epistles of Paul–Criticism, interpretation, etc. I. Title.
  BS2655.C36P38 2009
  227'012–dc22
                                      2009011934

Printed in the United States of America
on acid-free paper

John Cochrane O'Neill

1930–2003

In Memory

CONTENTS

Preface ix
Abbreviations xi

Stanley E. Porter
Introduction to the Study of the Pauline Canon 1

James W. Aageson
The Pastoral Epistles, Apostolic Authority, and the
Development of the Pauline Scriptures 5

Robert W. Wall
The Function of the Pastoral Letters within the Pauline Canon
of the New Testament: A Canonical Approach 27

M.-É. Boismard
Paul's Letter to the Laodiceans 45

Detlev Dormeyer
The Hellenistic Letter-formula and the Pauline Letter-scheme ... 59

Stanley E. Porter
When and How was the Pauline Canon Compiled?
An Assessment of Theories 95

Mark Harding
Disputed and Undisputed Letters of Paul 129

†J.C. O'Neill
Paul Wrote Some of All, but not All of Any 169

William O. Walker, Jr.
Interpolations in the Pauline Letters 189

Index of Ancient Sources 237
Index of Modern Authors 250

PREFACE

This volume has been a long time in the making—too long if you are one of the contributors, or one of those who has been looking forward to receiving this volume in aid of research or simply for scholarly or personal interest. For that delay, I apologize. However, I believe that this volume makes a significant contribution to the study of Paul, especially the canon of writings that we associate with him, and, I trust, in that regard was worth the wait. I am truly sorry that my original series co-editor, Dr. Brook W.R. Pearson of the University of Surrey Roehampton, has been unable to continue editing the series with me. I appreciate the work that he did in helping to set up the mechanics for the series, even though he is not able to see it through to completion. I wish to recognize here also the work that he did in helping to create and shape this particular volume. I wish him the very best in his other publishing endeavours.

This is the first of a series of projected volumes in the Pauline Studies Series to be published by Brill Publishers of Leiden. This volume is on the Pauline canon. Subsequent volumes currently scheduled to appear are as follows:

Volume 2: Paul and His Opponents
Volume 3: Paul the Theologian
Volume 4: Paul's World
Volume 5: Paul: Jew, Greek and Roman

I would like to invite any scholars interested in making contributions to one or more of these volumes to be in contact with me regarding submission. Contact information is provided below. The topics of the volumes are being defined and interpreted broadly, so that papers that deal, for example, with clearly related subjects, such as the Paul of the Letters and of Acts, we hope will be able to find a home in these collections of papers. Papers for the second and third volumes are already being gathered for publication, but it is not too late for possible submission. The anticipated rate of publication is one per year. We are also contemplating extending the series according to interest.

I would like to thank all of the individual authors for their worthy contributions to this first volume of essays. I would also like to thank the several people at Brill, including Louise Schoeten, Hans van der Meij, and Mattie Kuiper, who have continued to be an encouragement as this project took shape and is now finally coming to its initial fruition.

Before this volume could be completed and printed, Professor John O'Neill formerly of the University of Edinburgh, passed away. Professor O'Neill was born on 8 December 1930 in Melbourne, Australia, and died on 30 March 2003 in Edinburgh, Scotland, as the result of cancer and its complications. I know that he will be sadly missed by his family, but also by many former students and colleagues who appreciated him greatly. As a personal aside, Professor O'Neill was one of the first people to interview me for a position in New Testament, soon after his arrival at Edinburgh from Cambridge. Although I did not receive the appointment, Professor O'Neill gave me and the other unsuccessful candidate encouragement and advice to help us in the future. One of my first publications—one that I am still proud of, and that has continued to be cited in subsequent discussion—was a revised form of the presentation that I was required to give on that day. I am pleased to dedicate this volume to Professor O'Neill's worthy memory.

Stanley E. Porter

McMaster Divinity College
Hamilton, ON, Canada L8S 4K1
princpl@mcmaster.ca

ABBREVIATIONS

AARDS	American Academy of Religion Dissertation Series
AB	Anchor Bible
ABD	D.N. Freedman (ed.), *The Anchor Bible Dictionary* (6 vols.; New York: Doubleday, 1992)
ABRL	Anchor Bible Reference Library
AnBib	Analecta Biblica
ANF	*Ante-Nicene Fathers*
ANRW	*Aufstieg und Niedergang der römischen Welt*
ANTC	Abingdon New Testament Commentaries
ANTF	Arbeiten zur Neutestamentlichen Textforschung
ATR	*Anglican Theological Review*
ATRSup	*Anglican Theological Review Supplements*
BBET	Beiträge zur biblischen Exegese und Theologie
BBR	*Bulletin for Biblical Research*
BENT	Beiträge zur Einleitung in das Neue Testament
BETL	Bibliotheca ephemeridum theologicarum lovaniensium
BEvT	Beiträge zur evangelischen Theologie
Bib	*Biblica*
BibSem	The Biblical Seminar
BIS	Biblical Interpretation Supplements
BJRL	*Bulletin of the John Rylands Library*
BJS	Brown Judaic Studies
BTB	*Biblical Theology Bulletin*
BWANT	Beiträge zur Wissenschaft vom Alten und Neuen Testament
BZ	*Biblische Zeitschrift*
CahRB	Cahiers de la Revue biblique
CBQ	*Catholic Biblical Quarterly*
CBQMS	CBQ Monograph Series
ConBNT	Coniectanea biblica, New Testament
EBib	Etudes bibliques
EdF	Erträge der Forschung
ETL	*Ephemerides theologicae lovanienses*
EvT	*Evangelische Theologie*
ExpTim	*The Expository Times*
FFNT	Foundations and Facets: New Testament
FzB	Forschung zur Bibel
GBS	Guides to Biblical Scholarship
GNS	Good News Studies

GTA	Göttinger Theologische Arbeiten
HCBD	*Harper Collins Bible Dictionary*
HNTC	Harper's New Testament Commentaries
HTKNT	Herders theologischer Kommentar zum Neuen Testament
HTR	*Harvard Theological Review*
HUT	Hermeneutische Untersuchungen zur Theologie
IB	G.A. Buttrick *et al.* (eds.), *The Interpreter's Bible* (12 vols.; New York: Abingdon, 1951–57)
ICC	International Critical Commentary
IDB	G.A. Buttrick (ed.), *The Interpreter's Dictionary of the Bible* (4 vols.; Nashville, TN: Abingdon, 1962)
IDBSup	K. Crim (ed.), *Interpreter's Dictionary of the Bible: Supplementary Volume* (Nashville, TN: Abingdon, 1976)
Int	*Interpretation*
JAOS	*Journal of the American Oriental Society*
JBL	*Journal of Biblical Literature*
JBR	*Journal of Bible and Religion*
JEH	*Journal of Ecclesiastical History*
JQR	*Jewish Quarterly Review*
JR	*Journal of Religion*
JSNT	*Journal for the Study of the New Testament*
JSNTSup	JSNT Supplement Series
JTS	*Journal of Theological Studies*
LCL	Loeb Classical Library
LEC	Library of Early Christianity
NCB	New Century Bible
NICNT	New International Commentary on the New Testament
NIGTC	New International Greek Testament Commentary
NovT	*Novum Testamentum*
NovTSup	Novum Testament Supplements
NPNF	*Nicene and Post-Nicene Fathers*
NTAbh	Neutestamentliche Abhandlungen
NTC	The New Testament in Context
NTD	Das Neue Testament Deutsch
NTG	New Testament Guides
NTM	New Testament Message
NTOA	Novum Testamentum et Orbis Antiquus
NTS	*New Testament Studies*
NTT	New Testament Theology
ÖTK	Ökumenischer Taschenbuch-Kommentar
OTM	Oxford Theological Monographs
PRSt	*Perspectives in Religious Studies*
RAC	*Reallexikon für Antike und Christentum*
RB	*Revue biblique*
RHPR	*Revue de l'histoire et de philosophie religieuses*
RHR	*Revue de l'histoire des religions*

RNT	Regensburger Neues Testament
RSPT	Revue des sciences philosophiques et théologiques
SBLRBS	SBL Resources for Biblical Study
SBLSBS	SBL Sources for Biblical Study
SBLSP	SBL Seminar Papers
SBS	Stuttgarter Bibelstudien
SD	Studies and Documents
SE	*Studia Evangelica*
SNT	Studien zum Neuen Testament
SNTSMS	Society for New Testament Studies Monograph Series
SP	Sacra Pagina
SR	*Studies in Religion*
StudPat	*Studia Patristica*
TAPA	*Transactions and Proceedings of the American Philological Association*
Them	*Themelios*
TLZ	*Theologische Literaturzeitung*
TNTC	*Tyndale New Testament Commentaries*
TRE	*Theologische Realenzyklopädie*
TU	Theologische Untersuchungen
TynBul	*Tyndale Bulletin*
VC	*Vigiliae christianae*
WBC	Word Biblical Commentary
WTJ	*Westminster Theological Journal*
WUNT	Wissenschaftliche Untersuchungen zum Neuen Testament
ZBK	Zürcher Bibelkommentare
ZKG	*Zeitschrift für Kirchengeschichte*
ZNW	*Zeitschrift für die neutestamentliche Wissenschaft*
ZTK	*Zeitschrift für Theologie und Kirche*

INTRODUCTION TO THE STUDY OF THE PAULINE CANON

STANLEY E. PORTER

McMaster Divinity College
Hamilton, ON, Canada

Pauline studies are like no others in the entire area of biblical studies. The man, Paul, continues to stand at the centre of much controversy, much of it caused directly by his letters. In this volume, the subject of discussion is the canon of Paul's letters. The issue of canon has been an important and live one in recent New Testament scholarship,[1] and raises many inter-related questions especially in terms of the letters traditionally ascribed to Paul. Some of these questions are the following: Did Paul write all of the letters ascribed to him in the New Testament? If he did, can we account for how these letters were preserved and compiled into the corpus that we now have? Did he write any other letters, of which we still have direct or indirect evidence, that are not in the canon but that bear examination? If we think that he did not write all of the letters, which ones did he write? How do we know that he did or did not write these letters?

---

[1] Some of the important works on the New Testament canon include the following: B.F. Westcott, *A General Survey of the History of the Canon of the New Testament* (London: Macmillan, 7th edn, 1896 [1855]); C.R. Gregory, *Canon and Text of the New Testament* (Edinburgh: T. & T. Clark, 1907); A. Souter, *The Text and Canon of the New Testament* (rev. C.S.C. Williams; London: Duckworth, rev. edn, 1954 [1913]); H. von Campenhausen, *The Formation of the Christian Bible* (trans. J.A. Baker; Philadelphia: Fortress Press, 1972 [1968]); H.Y. Gamble, *The New Testament Canon: Its Making and Meaning* (GBS; Philadelphia: Fortress Press, 1985); B.M. Metzger, *The Canon of the New Testament* (Oxford: Clarendon Press, 1987); F.F. Bruce, *The Canon of Scripture* (Glasgow: Chapter House, 1988); L.M. McDonald, *The Formation of the Christian Biblical Canon* (Peabody, MA: Hendrickson, 1995); and L.M. McDonald and J.A. Sanders (eds.), *The Canon Debate* (Peabody, MA: Hendrickson, 2002).

What criteria can we use to discuss this issue? For those that he did not write, how do we account for their having been written and included in what is now our canonical collection as found in the New Testament? How do we account for some of the problematic juxtapositions of ideas in the letters that we do have? If we think that Paul may have written some parts of individual letters, but not all of them, how do we differentiate the parts that he wrote from the others? If Paul did not write all of the letters ascribed to him, what are the canonical, historical and even theological, implications of such a conclusion? These are the kinds of questions that are explored in the essays in this volume. As a result, this volume includes a number of papers that raise a variety of questions regarding the canon of the Pauline writings. Some of the essays are more narrowly focused in their intent, sometimes concentrating upon a single dimension related to the Pauline canon, and sometimes upon even a single letter. Others of the essays are more broadly conceived and deal with how one assesses or accounts for the process that resulted in the letters as a collection, rather than analyzing individual letters. There are also mediating positions that attempt to overcome the disjunction between authenticity and inauthenticity by exploring the complex notion of interpolation.

No collection of essays can attempt to cover all of the relevant issues in a given debate, but this volume is surprisingly wide-ranging, and even includes discussion of a number of topics that have not been as part of the mainstream of debate as the issues perhaps merit. Of course, the Pastoral Epistles come under scrutiny in this volume, as one might well expect in a discussion of the Pauline canon. The Pastoral Epistles have traditionally been the focus of much of the discussion of the Pauline canon, because they raise issues about authorship, theology, transmission and canonical process, among others. The essays by James Aageson and Rob Wall address several issues connected with the Pastorals. A consistent point of discussion over the better part of the last one-hundred years regarding the Pauline canon is the book of Ephesians. In this collection, Marie-Émile Boismard deals with the issue of the book of Ephesians and the letter of Paul to the Laodiceans, returning to the question of what possible overlap there might be between these two books. The Pauline letter-form also has bearing on questions of canon. Detlev Dormeyer utilizes recent work in letter-form and rhetorical analysis to explore issues of canon. He outlines the types of rhetorical techniques that are found in the individual letters and uses the criterion of these techniques to address questions of authorship and authenticity, and hence canonicity. Stanley Porter and Mark Harding take broader views of the full range of the Pauline letters to explore questions of authorship and canonical formation. Porter presents and discusses the major viewpoints on the formation of the Pauline canon, including assessing recent work that posits that Paul might have been a part of this process, before concluding with his own solution to the problem. Harding reaches well beyond the New Testament canon and examines a wider range of possible Pauline letters and writings that have been suggested at one time as coming from Paul, before he focuses upon the dispute over the thirteen-letter canon. The last two essays, by the late John O'Neill and William Walker, Jr., respectively, take a mediating position on the question of authenticity, by arguing that there are many interpolations in the extant Pauline letters. Rather than positing a disjunction between the letters being Pauline or not, they contend that criteria can be found by which it is possible to discuss individual interpolations within each of the letters.

The essays in this volume stand on their own as making a significant contribution to Pauline studies. It is hoped that they will add to the continuing debate regarding the canon of Paul's writings. However, it is the further hope that this volume will provide a suitable first volume in a series of volumes that explore various dimensions of Paul, who stands at the centre of the New Testament and its writings.

THE PASTORAL EPISTLES, APOSTOLIC AUTHORITY, AND THE DEVELOPMENT OF THE PAULINE SCRIPTURES

JAMES W. AAGESON

Concordia College
Moorhead, MN, USA

1. INTRODUCTION

If the Pastoral Epistles do not come directly from Paul but from someone else in the Pauline tradition,[1] a number of questions pertaining to the emergence of the Pauline writings as Scripture arise. How does the authority of Paul serve to validate the authority of the Pastoral texts? How does the attempt to emulate the authentic—and earlier—Pauline epistles shape the Pastoral Epistles? Finally, can we see already in the Pastoral Epistles something of the early movement toward the development of a body of Pauline Scriptures and ultimately a Pauline canon?[2] If, however, we conclude that the Pastorals are in fact from Paul himself, these questions undoubtedly shift, but not

---

[1] For discussions of the Pauline authorship of the Pastoral Epistles, see J. Bassler, *1 Timothy, 2 Timothy, Titus* (ANTC; Nashville: Abingdon Press, 1996), 17-30; L.R. Donelson, *Pseudepigrapha and Ethical Argument in the Pastoral Epistles* (Tübingen: Mohr Siebeck, 1986), 7-66; L.T. Johnson, *Letters to Paul's Delegates: 1 Timothy, 2 Timothy, Titus* (NTC; Valley Forge, PA: Trinity Press International, 1996), 1-36; G. Knight III, *The Pastoral Epistles: A Commentary on the Greek Text* (NIGTC; Grand Rapids: Eerdmans; Carlisle: Paternoster Press, 1992), 3-54; I.H. Marshall, 'Recent Study of the Pastoral Epistles', *Them* 23.1 (1997), 3-21; and P.H. Towner, 'Pauline Theology or Pauline Tradition in the Pastoral Epistles: The Question of Method', *TynBul* 46.2 (1995), 291-300. See also J.D. Miller's variation on the composite theory of the Pastoral Epistles, *The Pastoral Letters as Composite Documents* (SNTSMS 93; Cambridge: Cambridge University Press, 1997), 1-33.

[2] Here I observe the common distinction between the terms Scripture and canon. See H.Y. Gamble, 'Canon. New Testament', *ABD* 1 (1992), 852-61.

dramatically so in each case. The question of Pauline authority still pertains, and the issue of a developing concept of Pauline Scripture shifts only slightly. If the Pastoral Epistles are authentically Pauline, the issue of emulation does change significantly. Paul, of course, would not emulate himself, as would someone writing pseudepigraphically in the name of Paul. In either case, however, the issue of an emerging concept of Scripture is linked to the theological contour of the Pastoral Epistles, as well as to their relationship with one another and with the larger Pauline corpus.[3] The thesis to be developed here is that a Pauline concept of Scripture, the precursor to a full-fledged Pauline canon, can be detected already in the theological and literary patterns of the Pastoral Epistles.

In an earlier article on 2 Timothy,[4] I noted how Norman Petersen refocused the critical distinction between *text* and *history*, between contextual history (time of writing) and narrative world (literary construction), and applied it to the referential, narrative world of Paul as portrayed in Philemon.[5] Petersen wrote: 'In letters, as well as in narratives, we have to move from the text to its referential, narrative world, and from its narrative world to history.' [6] What we are not sure about in the case of 2 Timothy and the other Pastorals, however, is the extent to which the referential world of the texts overlaps the contextual world of the epistles. If Paul actually wrote the Pastorals, we might think—though it is not certain—that the two overlap to a greater extent than if someone else wrote in the name of Paul at a later

---

[3] As will be indicated below, I think it is most plausible to view the Pastorals as pseudepigraphic, but the argument developed here about Pauline authority and the formation of the Pauline Scriptures does not rest exclusively on this issue. Hence, it is important to recognize the questions that have prompted this discussion and how those questions shift if a different conclusion is reached on the issue of authorship.

[4] J.W. Aageson, '2 Timothy and Its Theology: In Search of a Theological Pattern', *SBL Seminar Papers 1997* (SBLSP 36; Atlanta: Scholars Press, 1997), 693-94.

[5] N.R. Petersen, *Rediscovering Paul: Philemon and the Sociology of Paul's Narrative World* (Philadelphia: Fortress Press, 1985), 1-42.

[6] Petersen, *Rediscovering Paul*, 8-9. In that same discussion, Petersen also writes: 'The only history *referred to* in a letter is its contextual history, which is the total history envisioned by the writer as relevant for the letter. However, as real as this difference between letter and narrative is, because letters refer to a world they have *referential worlds*, and these are the *narrative worlds*, from which any real-world history must be reconstructed.'

date. To establish the thesis of this essay, we must begin by identifying important theological and literary patterns in the Pastoral Epistles to see how the implied worlds of the texts are constructed, display a sense of Pauline authority, compare with each other and other Pauline texts, and begin to project a notion of an authoritative text that calls the readers and hearers to hold fast to correct teaching and to observe the proper manner of life.

2. THEOLOGY AND THE NARRATIVE WORLDS OF THE PASTORAL EPISTLES

The epistles of 1 and 2 Timothy and Titus are organized around a literary axis that runs from an implied author (Paul) to an implied reader (Timothy or Titus). In each case, the instructions, exhortations, and theological claims turn on this literary axis.[7] Furthermore, the theologies in these texts serve as a framework and foundation for the instructions and exhortations that Paul, the author, gives to Timothy and Titus. This means the theologies of the respective epistles are embedded in the narrative worlds that form the backdrop to the discussions, and at the center of these narrative worlds is this axis between the implied author (Paul) and the implied readers (Timothy or Titus). To illustrate this axis and Paul's apostolic authority, we must look in particular at the openings and closings of the three Pastoral Epistles, as well as at the opposition as it is portrayed in the respective texts.

In the beginning of the epistle to Titus, for example, Paul identifies himself as a δοῦλος θεοῦ and an ἀπόστολος Ἰησοῦ Χριστοῦ. In these words, Paul establishes his credentials as the implied author of the text. Unlike 1 Timothy, where the author is identified as an apostle of Christ according to the command of God, this greeting in Titus is extended to indicate that for which he is a slave and an apostle: the faith of the elect and knowledge of truth that is in accord with godliness (εὐσέβειαν). In contrast to 2 Timothy, where Paul indicates that his apostleship is by the will of God and for the promise of life, the author in Titus identifies faith and knowledge as the operative concepts associated with his being a slave and an apostle. The temporal sense implied in the greeting to Titus is the present time, but

---

[7] Aageson, '2 Timothy', 696-97.

this is extended into the past and the future in 1:2: '...for the hope of life eternal, which the God who does not lie promised before time began, in the proper time he revealed his word in preaching with which I was entrusted by the command of God our saviour'. Paul's work as a slave and an apostle is for the sake of the faith of the elect and knowledge of truth, but it is also done in the hope of eternal life that was promised even before time began. The activity of Paul, the apostle, is carried out with this authority and in the face of this soteriological hope. It is also noteworthy that the greetings in 1 Timothy and Titus connect σωτῆρος with God (and also Christ in Titus).[8] With this greeting, the implied author of the texts and his work are firmly situated within the larger scope of divine activity, and in that sense the greeting is highly theological. Apostolic activity and divine purpose are thoroughly overlaid in establishing the authority and Pauline legacy of the implied author.

The text of Titus ends with a conclusion (3:12-15) that is closer to 2 Timothy with its personal greetings and instructions than 1 Timothy with its virtual lack of personal comments and greetings. In 3:15, Paul sends greetings to Titus from all those who are with him and requests that Titus greet those who love 'us' in the faith. The final blessing is the same as 1 Timothy except for the inclusion of πάντων. As in 1 and 2 Timothy, Titus uses the plural form of the pronoun, ὑμῶν, which indicates that within the text itself there are markers that point to a larger implied audience in the literary world of the epistle.[9] Grace is bestowed not only on Titus but also on this wider community in Crete, according to the identification of the epistle to Titus. The inclusion of

---

[8] God is identified as saviour, or the one who saves, in Titus 1:3; 2:10; cf. 2:11; 3:4; and 3:5; whereas in 1:4; 2:13; and 3:6 Christ is identified as the saviour. Contrast the use of 'saviour' and 'save' in 1 Timothy. See the excursus in M. Dibelius and H. Conzelmann, *The Pastoral Epistles* (trans. P. Buttolph and A. Yarbro; Hermeneia; Philadelphia: Fortress Press, 1972), 100-104 and the discussions by J.M. Bassler, 'A Plethora of Epiphanies: Christology in the Pastoral Letters', *Princeton Seminary Review* 17.3 (1996), 310-25; Donelson, *Pseudepigrapha and Ethical Argument*, 135-54; L. Oberlinner, 'Die Epiphaneia des Heilswillens Gottes in Christus Jesus: Zur Grundstruktur der Christologie der Pastoralbriefe', *ZNW* 71 (1980), 192-213; and F. Young, *The Theology of the Pastoral Letters* (NTT; Cambridge: Cambridge University Press, 1994), 50-55.

[9] Bassler, *1 Timothy, 2 Timothy, Titus*, 122; B. Fiore, *The Function of Personal Example in the Socratic and Pastoral Epistles* (AnBib; Rome: Pontifical Biblical Institute, 1986), 214; Johnson, *Paul's Delegates*, 253; and Young, *Pastoral Letters*, 5.

πάντων in the conclusion to this epistle emphasizes this plural dimension all the more. In addition to the implied readers of these epistles—Timothy and Titus—there is also an implied communal audience and that suggests another literary axis for these texts. In that sense, these are not simply private letters, and the authority of the author is conveyed to a larger community as the words of these texts are read and heard again and again over time.

This larger communal context also involves opposition to Paul and the 'sound teaching' he represents in the Pastoral Epistles. Who are these opponents and what is the nature of their opposition as represented in the narrative constructions reflected in the three epistles? In 1 Tim 1:6-7, those who desire to be teachers of the law but do not understand the law are accused of engaging in meaningless chatter. This is followed in 1:8-9 with the bold assertion that the law—presumably the Jewish law—is good, which is then qualified by the claim that it is good if it is used properly. Apparently some people, probably insiders,[10] are improperly teaching and applying the law. In 4:1-5, the text illustrates further the nature of the opposition. As the spirit explicitly says, in the last times some will turn from the faith following false teachings and deceitful spirits. The error of these people's ways is that they forbid marriage and insist on abstinence from certain foods. While many have argued that this is evidence of the Gnostic or proto-Gnostic character of the opposition, the more likely explanation is that—at least on the narrative level of the text—it has to do at its core with the misapplication of the Jewish law.[11] That is most consistent with the discussion in 1:6-7, and of course does not rule out an ascetic character to the opposition.[12]

Regarding the nature of the opposition, Titus is closest to 1 Timothy. In Titus 1:10 and 1:14 the Jewish character of this opposition is explicit. The implication is that the 'circumcision' is especially problematic, though the difficulty in Crete is not limited to this group. Moreover, the problem is, as in 1 Timothy, related to what

---

[10] Bassler, *1 Timothy, 2 Timothy, and Titus*, 38 and 41 and Johnson, *Paul's Delegates*, 109.

[11] J.L. Sumney, 'A Reading of the Theology of 1 Timothy without Authorial Presuppositions' (paper presented at the Theology of the Disputed Pauline Epistles Group of the annual meeting of the SBL, New Orleans, 23-26 November 1996), 3. See also Donelson, *Pseudepigrapha and Ethical Argument*, 116-28, and Young, *Theology*, 10-11.

[12] Johnson, *Paul's Delegates*, 109.

they teach (1:11). The reference to Jewish myths in 1:14 simply reinforces the Jewish nature of the opposition in Titus. However, the reference to purity in 1:15 may also link up with a similar concern for purity in 1 Timothy regarding abstinence from marriage and food. The fact that disputes about the law are a point of contention in Crete is confirmed once again in 3:9, as Paul warns Titus to avoid senseless controversies about the law. Finally, in 3:5 it is made clear that salvation does not result from doing works of righteousness but is according to the mercy of God. On the narrative level of the text, it is clear that the core of the opposition revolves around Jewish issues and disputes about the Jewish law.[13] If these narrative representations are congruent with the actual circumstances being addressed, then we must assume that these quite distinct and separate communities are plagued by controversies over both matters of behaviour and application of the Jewish law.[14]

On the other hand, 2 Timothy is distinct from the other two epistles. In addition to the general issues of controversy, wicked passions, and persecutions leading to suffering, there are those who disrupt certain people by claiming that the resurrection has already taken place. There is no explicit reference to the Jewish character of the opposition in 2 Timothy. The personal nature of the epistle and the concern for Timothy to follow Paul's example of suffering clearly present a different view of the opponents and the perceived threat. Instead of attempting to live in harmony with the divine order, both in heaven and on earth, 2 Timothy presumes that suffering is to be expected and that Timothy ought to take up the mantle of suffering and follow in the footsteps of Paul. The opposition as a 'problem' in 2 Timothy is significantly different than that portrayed in 1 Timothy and Titus because it is generated by a different view of and orientation to the

---

[13] J.C. Beker's claim (*Heirs of Paul: Paul's Legacy in the New Testament and in the Church Today* [Minneapolis: Fortress Press, 1991], 39) that the conflict between the historical Paul and his Jewish and Judaizing opponents is replaced by a conflict between Paul and Jewish-Gnostic opponents is questionable. The Paul of the Pastorals certainly deals with his Jewish opposition in a different manner than does the Paul of the undisputed Paulines, but the claim that they are Jewish-Gnostics would only seem to create unnecessary terminological imprecision.

[14] Bassler (*1 Timothy, 2 Timothy, Titus*, 188) says that the threat arose from within Titus's community, whereas Johnson (*Paul's Delegates*, 213) thinks the opponents may be outsiders.

world beyond the community of faith.[15] Yet in each case, the fact of the opposition itself serves to situate Paul in these epistles as the defender of correct doctrine and the recipient of divine authority who stands firm in the face of those who threaten to lead the community astray. To the extent that those who receive these epistles submit to the authority and theological vision of Paul, they underscore his place in the community and validate his words.

In all three of the epistles, the claim to correct doctrine serves to present Paul as the representative of true faith. He not only argues for it, but represents it.[16] In 1 Timothy and to a lesser extent in Titus, this is framed in terms of the household of God, whereas in 2 Timothy it is linked with the appeal to follow Paul on the way of suffering. In all three texts, the true faith and the proper manner of life as proclaimed and represented by Paul are set against the opponents who threaten the truth and undermine the community. It is not merely that the epistles function in the apostle's stead in his absence or as his extension, but the epistles themselves come to define true doctrine and correct behaviour. In that regard, the texts over time come to have a presence of their own and must be reckoned with in their own right. The epistles come to project both an apostolic presence and a textual presence. By itself this does not constitute the Pastoral Epistles as Scripture; but to the extent that these communities accept the apostolic authority of Paul as divinely given and submit to the authority of the texts as representing correct teaching, these epistles will come to be heard as sacred address.[17] Hence, the validity of these texts as Scripture depends in good measure on the authority invested in them by the communities to which they are addressed and in which they come to function.

---

[15] See the discussions by R.J. Karris, *The Pastoral Epistles* (NTM; Wilmington, DE: Michael Glazier, 1979), ix-xiv, and M.Y. MacDonald, *The Pauline Churches: A Socio-historical Study of Institutionalization in Pauline and Deutero-Pauline Writings* (SNTSMS 60; Cambridge: Cambridge University Press, 1988), 159-70.

[16] L.R. Donelson ('Studying Paul: 2 Timothy as Remembrance', *SBL Seminar Papers 1997*, 721) writes: 'Paul is not simply author. Paul inscribes himself in his own text. Or, in my opinion, an unknown author has Paul inscribe himself in his own text.'

[17] Cf. the discussion by Beker, *Heirs of Paul*, 36-39.

3. THE PASTORAL AND THE PAULINE EPISTLES

It is commonly thought that each of the Pastorals relates most closely to a different undisputed Pauline epistle: 1 Timothy–1 Corinthians; 2 Timothy–Philippians; and Titus–Galatians.[18] For the purposes of this argument, it is the relationship between Philippians and 2 Timothy—and to a lesser extent 1 Timothy and Titus—that is the starting point for understanding how the Pastoral Epistles relate to each other and to the undisputed Paulines. Achieving some clarity about these issues is important to this argument for two reasons: the sense of scriptural formation does not appear to develop in precisely the same way across all three Pastoral Epistles and the closest analogue between the Pastorals and the indisputable Pauline Epistles is crucial for considering the issue of Pauline imitation in the process of establishing apostolic and textual authority.

Stanley Stowers has argued for the connection between theology in Philippians and ancient friendship letters.[19] The Pastorals—2 Timothy in particular—exhibit some of the same epistolary characteristics as those identified by Stowers in Philippians: (1) a retrospective look (2 Tim 1:3-7–Phil 1:3-5), (2) autobiographical elements (2 Tim 3:10-11; 4:6-8–Phil 3:4-16), (3) opponents (1 Tim 1:8-10; 4:1-3; 6:11-19; 2 Tim 1:15; 2:22-26; 3:1-13; 4:1-16; Titus 1:10-16–Phil 3:2-11, 17-19), (4) a sense of partnership (2 Tim 2:1-26; 1 Tim 1:3-7, 18-20; Titus 1:5-9–Phil 1:12-30; 3:17-21; 4:10-20), (5) affection (2 Tim 1:3-7; Titus 1:4–Phil 1:3-11), (6) feeling of reciprocity (2 Tim 4:9-11–Phil 4:15-20), and (7) suffering and imprisonment (2 Tim 1:8, 12; 2:3, 9; 3:11; 4:5–Phil 1:7, 12-14, 22-23; 2:17; 3:8). In each of these respects, Paul is portrayed as united with the recipients of the letter—even in the face of certain opponents. The most conspicuous similarity between 2 Timothy and Philippians, however, is the common theme of suffering. In both epistles, Paul—the implied author—is in travail and the suffering of the apostle comes to the fore again and again in both texts. In 2 Timothy the references to Paul's suffering (1:12; 2:9;

---

[18] See Johnson, *Paul's Delegates*, 37 and 214.

[19] S.K. Stowers, 'Friends and Enemies in the Politics of Heaven: Reading Theology in Philippians', in J.M. Bassler (ed.), *Pauline Theology. I. Thessalonians, Philippians, Galatians, Philemon* (Minneapolis: Fortress Press, 1991), 105-21. As Stowers points out, scholars of ancient letter writing for a long time have made the connection between Philippians and letters of friendship, but in this essay he brings this to bear on his reading of the theology of Philippians.

3:11) are matched by a plea for Timothy to suffer as Paul has suffered (1:8; 2:3; 4:5). Only in 2:11 is it possible that the text suggests suffering with Christ, along the lines found in Rom 6:1-11. The structural paradigm of 2 Timothy runs like this: I have suffered, I am your example, now follow my example and suffer as I have suffered.[20]

Still other elements do not correspond so clearly: (1) 2 Timothy is ostensibly written to an individual rather than a community,[21] (2) the character of the opposition in 2 Timothy seems to be related more directly to doctrinal issues and the preservation of correct doctrine than in Philippians (2 Tim 2:18), (3) 2 Timothy alternates more conspicuously between instruction and paraenesis than is obviously the case in Philippians, (4) we do not find in Philippians the catalogue of vices that mark 2 Tim 3:1-5, and (5) the paraenetic quality of 2 Timothy is also more pronounced than in Philippians, as is the concern for adherence to correct belief and resistance to heresy. As important as friendship motifs are in 2 Timothy, it is not evident that the friendship letter model suggests a direct authorial link between 2 Timothy and Philippians, and certainly not between 1 Timothy and Titus and the letter to the Philippians.[22] Compared to 1 Timothy and Titus, the differences from Philippians are even more pronounced. The personal and affectionate tone so clear in Philippians is not as apparent in these epistles. 1 Timothy and Titus are highly instructive, often

---

[20] In both Phil 2:17 and 2 Tim 4:6, the term σπένδομαι is used, the only two places where it appears in the New Testament, and has sacrificial connotations relating to Paul's suffering.

[21] As Stowers ('Friends and Enemies', 108) points out, Seneca's friendship letters, too, were written to individuals rather than communities. As we have already noted, even though 2 Timothy is a very personal letter and clearly written as a private correspondence between Paul and Timothy, a larger audience is in view.

[22] 1 Timothy and Philippians present interesting theological images for the church and the faithful person's place in the world. In 1 Tim 3:15, the household of God is identified as the 'church of the living God', and in 1:4 the author appeals to Timothy to conform to the 'divine order in faith'. Paul writes in Phil 3:20 that 'our place of citizenship (πολίτευμα) is in heaven', and in 1:27 he urges the Philippians to 'live as citizens (πολιτεύεσθε) in a way that is worthy of the gospel'. In each of these examples, a cultural or social image is projected onto the church and the people in the church. At their root, 1 Timothy and Philippians represent quite different images. In the narrative of 1 Timothy, the structural images are the household and the social order based on the pattern of the Greco-Roman household, whereas in Philippians, the place of one's citizenship is projected into heaven.

focusing on the mandates of church order and the qualities of those who are to lead the community. Both in terms of genre and tone, 1 Timothy and Titus are distinct from Philippians.

As this discussion suggests, the case of 2 Timothy and Philippians is clearly a linchpin in the relationship between the Pastorals and the undisputed Paulines, and therefore the place of the Pastorals in the emerging notion of Pauline Scripture. If 1 Timothy and Titus did not come from the same author as Philippians and if the substantial differences between 2 Timothy and the other two Pastorals suggest different authors, the evidence indicates at least two, and possibly three, authors being responsible for the four epistles. Either Philippians and 2 Timothy were both written by Paul, and 1 Timothy and Titus were written by someone else;[23] or Philippians was written by Paul, 1 Timothy and Titus were written by someone in the Pauline tradition, and 2 Timothy was written by yet a third author who patterned his epistle loosely after features from Philippians and perhaps even 1 Timothy. While there are some—though modest—narrative and structural features linking Galatians, 1 Corinthians, and the Pastorals,[24] it is the relationship between Philippians and 2 Timothy that is critical in any argument connecting the Pastorals to Paul.[25] The

---

[23] J. Murphy-O'Connor (*Paul: A Critical Life* [Oxford: Oxford University Press, 1997], 356-59) concludes that 2 Timothy is written by Paul.

[24] Towner summarizes four themes or benchmarks for assessing continuity and discontinuity between the Pastoral Epistles and Paul as: local community; salvation-historical, eschatological context of ecclesiology; relation of the church to the gospel; and place and nature of church office/ministry/leadership.

[25] It should be observed that the points of structural theological similarity between 1 Timothy/Titus—especially 1 Timothy—and Galatians are real but very limited. What drives the narrative in Galatians theologically is substantially different from what drives the narratives in 1 Timothy and Titus. The points of narrative contact are more likely to be incidental, drawing on some deep structural similarities regarding the law in the churches in the Gentile lands of the first century, than they are evidence of an authorial connection between the two sets of texts. If 1 Timothy and Titus were consciously patterned after aspects of Galatians, the resultant overlap between them is in the end not very extensive. In the case of 1 Corinthians, there is no counterpart to the concern for qualities and qualifications of leadership so conspicuous in the narrative worlds of 1 Timothy and Titus. Groups of people are sometimes identified in 1 Corinthians but not in terms of the qualities necessary for leadership or particular roles in the community. In that regard, 1 Corinthians comes out of a different narrative world, and certainly draws on different metaphors to understand and describe the church. The 'household of God' metaphor is structurally different than the 'body of Christ'

upshot of this is that where 2 Timothy is structurally most like 1 Timothy and Titus, it is least like Philippians; and at the points where 2 Timothy is least like them, it is most like Philippians.[26]

With this in mind, it is clear that Pauline imitation in 2 Timothy turns to a significant degree on the issue of suffering and following Paul's example.[27] Not only is correct doctrine to be held fast but the proper manner of life, especially following Paul's example of suffering, is to be observed. In this way, the text of the epistle personifies the link representing and conveying the apostle, his theology, and suffering to the recipients of 2 Timothy in the hope that they will follow his example and be united with him in this act of suffering. If, as seems distinctly possible, the author of 2 Timothy is not Paul— or the writer of 1 Timothy or Titus for that matter—he has linked the example of Paul to a hoped for pattern of life (e.g., suffering) and correct belief that presumes an uneasy relationship between the recipients of the letter and their wider social world. If Paul has already died by the time 2 Timothy is written, the epistle keeps the example of the apostle alive in terms of its paradigmatic and exhortative value;[28] and the author of the epistle serves to bring that image of Paul and his audience into juxtaposition. In the case of the exhortations to true faith, it is not entirely clear whether the teachings derive from the apostle or whether Paul is in fact used to validate the teachings of the author of 2 Timothy. Of course, these are not mutually exclusive.

In the case of 1 Timothy and Titus, the function of the letters, in addition to preserving the true faith of the recipients, is to conform life

---

metaphor. Where the Pastorals and 1 Corinthians do overlap structurally and conceptually, they do so at a very general level. The narrative and theological affinity between them is neither marked nor extensive.

[26] The goal of this immediate discussion is not to argue for or against Pauline authorship as such but to illustrate that the presupposition of common authorship for the three Pastoral Epistles is not necessarily well-founded and that thus the formation of Scripture, or even canon, may not be identical in all three epistles. See the claim by M. Prior, *Paul the Letter-Writer and the Second Letter to Timothy* (JSNTSup 23; Sheffield: Sheffield Academic Press, 1989), 169.

[27] Dibelius and Conzelmann (*The Pastoral Epistles*, 98) emphasize that the exhortation to suffer is based on the bond between teacher and disciple. This clearly forms the immediate circumstance for the plea to suffer.

[28] Beker, *Heirs of Paul*, 37. Fiore (*Personal Example*, 36-37) argues that the function of example is not simply for better comprehension but for action. The example is a demonstration of what is being taught. See also Donelson, *Pseudepigraphy and Ethical Argument*, 93, 105-106.

in the communities to the pattern of the household, which is now identified as the household of God. The social order of this household is patterned after the qualities and qualifications necessary in the Greco-Roman household. The apparent accommodationist tendency of these epistles uses Paul to sanction a model for the church. Here Paul is less the compelling example than he is the authoritative teacher instructing the church in the way to live and organize itself in the face of both internal and external requirements.[29] As in the case of 2 Timothy, the epistles of 1 Timothy and Titus resound with the voice of Paul but do so in different ways and for different purposes. In a real sense, all three epistles become the voice of Paul for their respective audiences;[30] and to the extent his apostleship is thought to be from God, that voice and the text that projects it are also thought to be from God, to be Scripture, and as such transcend Paul.[31] The following diagram illustrates these relationships:

God/Christ —>	Paul —>	Voice of Paul —>	Pastoral Texts
	Slave of God	Example	Transmitter
	Apostle of Christ	Instruction	Amplifier
		Demonstration	Voice of Paul
			Voice of God

---

[29] Johnson (*Delegates*, 122 and 212) says that in 2 Timothy Paul's behaviour is exemplary whereas in 1 Timothy it is God's mercy. In the case of Titus, he says that the epistle takes the form of a *mandata principis* letter where Titus is to show himself as a model of good deeds.

[30] Donelson (*Pseudepigrapha and Ethical Argument*, 151) asserts: 'In order for the cosmological-ethical connections believed in by our author to gain a hearing in his church and thus acquire power and influence, this theology must be anchored in reliable roots. The ability of these teachings to persuade and thus to save reside in the believability of the fiction of Pauline origins.'

[31] In a concise summary, Brevard Childs (*The New Testament as Canon: An Introduction* [Philadelphia: Fortress Press, 1984], 381) sets forth the proposals regarding the function of these epistles made by those who hold these epistles to be pseudepigraphic: written 50 years after Paul by a follower who tries to apply Paul's teaching to a new situation in the church; a personalizing of the tradition; development of a commissioning office that would project Pauline authority into the next generation of the church; and the projection of an apostolic presence into the period after the death of Paul. The problem, as Childs points out, is that clear exegetical support for these claims is difficult to find.

4. Scripture and the Beginnings of a Pauline Canon

As important as it is for the presentation of this argument to make distinctions between 1 Timothy and Titus and 2 Timothy and to position the Pastoral Epistles broadly in relation to the undisputed Paulines, it is not the question of Pauline authenticity or pseudepigraphy that finally gets to the heart of the matter. Brevard Childs first sharpened this in canonical terms when he wrote:

> First of all, among those scholars who have recently attempted to interpret the Pastorals as an example of pseudepigraphical literature the model of strictly historical referentiality of meaning continues to remain dominant. The literary genre is continually interpreted in reference to its allegedly 'real' historical situation, namely, one some fifty years after the death of Paul. The effect of this move is that the literary genre is actually viewed as something 'pseudo', whose true meaning only emerges when the genuine historical setting is reconstructed. A concomitant effect of this hermeneutical model is that the description of the Pastorals as pseudepigraphical usually functions to establish from the outset the referentiality of the letters to be derived from the creative imagination of the author. As a result, a rich variety of possible relationships, both simple and complex, between the literature and its referent is lost because the genre description simply decides the issue as if by reflex... The kerygmatic witness of the text is, thereby, rendered mute, and its interpretation is made dependent on other external forces which are set in a causal relationship.[32]

To this we might add that a preoccupation with Pauline authenticity can, in some cases, also exhibit the same issue, an overriding concern with historical correspondences that obscures the complex internal relationships of the Pastoral Epistles as literary texts that claim the authority of Paul and indirectly the authority of God. Whether written by Paul or someone else, the Pastoral Epistles exhibit a web of internal relationships that reflect, however altered, a christology rooted in Paul and the early church,[33] preformed traditions,[34] quotations and echoes of the Scriptures of Israel,[35] and episodes from the life of

---

[32] Childs, *New Testament as Canon*, 382-83.
[33] See, e.g., the 'in Christ' language in 1 Tim 1:14; 3:13; 2 Tim 1:1, 9, 13; 2:1, 10; 3:12, 15.
[34] As candidates for pre-formed traditions, see 1 Tim 2:5-6; 3:16; 2 Tim 2:11-13; Titus 2:14; 3:5-7.
[35] See apparent echoes and quotations in 1 Tim 2:2, 8, 13-14; 5:5, 18-19; 6:7; 2 Tim 2:19; 3:8; 4:17; Titus 2:11, 14.

Paul.³⁶ This does not mean that the author(s) of the Pastoral Epistles have not reshaped the traditions at their disposal and creatively addressed their own audiences, but it indicates that the literary worlds of these texts display a kerygmatic and theological frame of reference that reaches back into the tradition and brings to the fore a remembrance of Paul and a reminder of the traditions that are being passed on.³⁷ In doing so, 1 and 2 Timothy and Titus are linked to an authoritative tradition, and it is that linkage that draws the Pastoral Epistles into the substantive beginnings of the Pauline canon and begins to leave its imprint on that canon.³⁸

The notion of remembrance and passing on the tradition is most poignant in 2 Timothy. In some cases, the remembrance refers to Paul or Timothy and their past (1:3, 5; 3:15), but still others refer to the passing on of the tradition from Paul to Timothy (1:6, 13; 2:2; 3:10, 14; cf. 1:12, 14). This chain of tradition is not limited to the past and the present but is also carried by Timothy from the present into the future (2:2, 15; 4:1-2), as he is called upon to instruct others. Perhaps only in 1:6 (Timothy) and 1:11 (Paul) is there anything approaching an office implied in 2 Timothy. The epistle clearly portrays, however,

---

36   See, e.g., 1 Tim 1:3, 20; 3:14; 4:13; 2 Tim 1:3-7, 15-18; 3:10-11; 4:6-22; Titus 1:5; 3:12-15.

37   E.E. Ellis, 'Traditions in the Pastoral Epistles', in C.A. Evans and W.F. Stinespring (eds.), *Early Jewish and Christian Exegesis: Studies in Memory of William Hugh Brownlee* (Atlanta: Scholars Press, 1987), 237-53, has addressed this, as has P. Trummer, *Die Paulustradition der Pastoralbriefe* (BBET 8; Frankfurt: Peter Lang, 1978).

38   In some measure, this issue turns on the dating of the Pastorals. If the Pastorals were written pseudepigraphically shortly after Paul's death, the early collection of the community letters would have had less time to develop a substantive shape and form than if they were written many decades following his death. Undoubtedly, the early selection and ordering of the community letters would have involved a process of shaping and framing. We might think that the result of this process was more malleable in the early period than it would become later. I think it is most plausible that the Pastorals were written before the end of the first century and probably within 20–25 years of Paul's death. If 2 Timothy was written by Paul, it, of course, would be an exception to this. To be sure, with this dating range it is likely there would have already been a process of compiling and ordering Paul's letters before the Pastorals were written. I presume, however, that whatever collection there was by this time it was still fairly fluid and subject to considerable refinement and reinterpretation. See also the proposal by B.P. Wolfe, 'Scripture in the Pastoral Epistles: Premarcion Marcionism', *PRSt* 16 (1989), 13-16.

a continuum of tradition from the past to the future that is to be remembered and preserved. This imagery culminates in 2 Tim 1:12 and 14, where the deposit (παραθήκην) is portrayed as being guarded. The translation problems associated with this term, especially in 1:12, are well known,[39] but at least in 1:14 Timothy is charged to guard the 'good deposit' through the holy spirit. Regardless of whether this deposit is understood in 2 Timothy in static or dynamic terms,[40] it is clearly situated in this chain of tradition and presumably has some kerygmatic content. On the historical level, Donelson is probably right that there never was a discrete deposit of doctrinal and moral teachings handed down as suggested by this imagery, but that may also be beside the point when it comes to the narrative world of the text.[41] The concept and perception of an authoritative body of teachings and moral standards is already being shaped within the literary text and within the larger narrative world we refer to as the Pauline tradition. Even if this is a fiction, it is a fiction with important and real consequences for the remembrance of Paul in the church. We will need to examine this more closely below;[42] but it is worth noting that according to Childs, the content of the gospel of Paul has not changed in the Pastoral Epistles but the manner in which the content is guarded. The teachings of Paul have become the medium through which truth and error are now to be confronted.[43]

1 Timothy also makes reference to guarding the παραθήκη in 6:20, but beyond that there are some clear differences when 1 and 2 Timothy are compared. In 1 Timothy, the tradition is conveyed primarily to Timothy through the plea to instruct the people in the sound teaching (e.g. 1:3, 18; 3:14; 4:6, 11, 13, 16; 5:21). Read on its own terms, this suggests that the tradition to be guarded in 1 Timothy is more clearly the correct doctrine to be taught than may be the case in 2 Timothy with its emphasis on preserving and handing on the

---

[39] See the discussions by Bassler, *1 Timothy, 2 Timothy, Titus*, 133-34, and Johnson, *Delegates*, 55. We also note the distinction between παράδοσις, which appears in the undisputed Paulines but not in the Pastorals, and παραθήκη, which appears only in 1 and 2 Timothy.

[40] Compare Childs, *New Testament as Canon*, 389, and Johnson, *Delegates*, 55.

[41] Donelson, *Pseudepigrapha and Ethical Argument*, 164.

[42] See below, section 4.

[43] Childs, *New Testament as Canon*, 389-90.

tradition,[44] indicated especially by the personal tone of the letter and the imagery of remembrance. As we have seen,[45] however, this does not mean that 2 Timothy has no concept of sound teaching. The view exhibited by 1 Timothy is also reflected in Titus 2:1: 'But as for you, teach what is consistent with the sound teaching.' In Titus 1:3 the entrusting of the kerygma to Paul is expressly said to be by the command of God the saviour, which highlights the divine origin of the proclamation and its consequent authority as passed from Paul to Titus and on to the other members of the church. What seems to separate 1 Timothy and Titus from 2 Timothy even more conspicuously is the concept of offices, qualifications for holding office, and the implicit handing on of the sound teaching of the church through these offices and the people who hold them (see 1 Tim 3:1-8; 4:14; 5:17, 22; Titus 1:5-9; cf. 1 Tim 1:12; 2:7), something only hinted in 2 Tim 1:6. Hence, in 1 Timothy and Titus the idea of an authoritative Pauline concept of sound teaching, perhaps even a canonical tradition, is developing alongside an emergent ecclesial structure that also has authority. In 1 Timothy and Titus, an incipient canonical process and a community structure are both in view and appear to work in tandem in the transmission and preservation of the Pauline tradition as it is projected into the church's anticipated future.[46] In that way, sound teaching can be preserved, error identified and hopefully corrected.

Even within these narrative frames of reference, it would be inaccurate to portray the Pastorals, 2 Timothy in particular, as benignly passing on a fixed, received Pauline deposit of authoritative teaching. The issue of Christology in the Pastorals is a good illustration of this dynamic. As we have seen,[47] the expression ἐν Χριστῷ in 1 and 2 Timothy is clearly reminiscent of Pauline language and Christology and appears to root the christology of the Pastorals, at least on an internal referential and emergent canonical level, in the Pauline tradition. However, the Christology of the Pastorals is also dramatically different from the undisputed Paulines and much of the rest of the New Testament. This is the case in primarily two ways: the designation 'saviour' for both God and Christ, a designation for Christ found only in Phil 3:20 in the undisputed Pauline Epistles, and the language of 'epiphany' to describe the coming of Christ, once again

---

[44] Cf. Johnson, *Delegates*, 55.
[45] See above, section 3.
[46] Donelson, *Pseudepigraphy and Ethical Argument*, 163, 166.
[47] See above, n. 33.

terminology not found in the undisputed Paulines. To be sure, Christology anchors the Pastorals in the kerygma of the early church, but the way it is expressed and developed in the three Pastoral Epistles is peculiar.

Considering first the saviour terminology, it is noteworthy that, in 1 Timothy, God alone is referred to as 'saviour', whereas in Titus the designation alternates between God and Christ. The single appearance of the term in 2 Tim 1:10 is also used in connection with Christ. In 1 Tim 1:1 and 2:3 God is simply referred to as 'our saviour' and in 4:10 God is identified as a living God who is saviour of all people. The verbal form of the word in 1 Tim 2:4 has God as the subject, whereas in 1:15 Christ is clearly the subject of the infinitive verb: '...Christ Jesus came into the world to save sinners...' In Titus 1:3, 2:10, and 3:4, similar to 1 Tim 1:1 and 2:3, God is designated 'our saviour', whereas in 1:4, 2:13, and 3:6 Christ carries this appellation. In Titus 3:5 the subject of the verb 'to save', referring back to 3:4, also has God as the subject. In 2 Tim 1:9 and 4:18, the verb 'to save' is used; and in the first case God is the subject whereas in the second the 'Lord', apparently referring to God, functions in that capacity. With regard to the identification of the saviour, the Pastoral Epistles con-sistently apply that designation to God or Christ, unlike the remainder of the New Testament Pauline tradition where the nominal form of the term rarely appears.[48] But within the three Pastoral Epistles, there are also some noticeable differences in usage. Titus is the epistle most ready to apply 'saviour' to Christ, whereas 1 Timothy does so only once in relation to the verb 'to save' and the activity of saving. 2 Timothy, on the other hand, is noteworthy for its relatively infrequent use of this terminology. The important point is that Paul's theological and christological language is thoroughly transformed into saviour terminology, especially in 1 Timothy and Titus, but to a lesser extent in 2 Timothy as well. A fixed, received christological tradition is not merely being handed on. Whatever the 'good deposit' is, it is not entirely disconnected from the christological traditions represented by Paul, but by no means is it a static replication of them either.

---

[48] The only other New Testament document outside the Pastorals where 'saviour' occurs with some regularity is 2 Peter (5 times) and in that epistle the term is used consistently of Christ. In that series of occurrences the only ambiguous reference is 3:2, but even here it is most assuredly a reference to Christ as well.

While most of the New Testament writings, Paul's included, use παρουσία to refer to the return of Christ, the Pastorals use ἐπιφάνεια to designate the appearances of Christ, both past and future.[49] This feature of the Pastorals has long been recognized,[50] and as Jouette Bassler indicates these epiphanies do not designate a process that moves from lowliness to exaltation but rather a revelation of something previously hidden. She writes:

> The two epiphanies do not define a process—for example, from lowliness to exaltation. Instead, each reveals a previously hidden divine reality... At least when applied to Jesus' first coming, the epiphany language does not refer primarily to a revelation or manifestation of Christ but to the revelation, through the Christ event, of a reality about God. This does not mean that we should not speak of an epiphany Christology, but that when used of the Pastorals, we must understand it to refer primarily to Christ as the vehicle, and not the content, of the epiphany.[51]

If this epiphany framework not only expresses the christology of the Pastorals but in some way restructures whatever received Pauline traditions the author(s)—assuming the letters are not from Paul—may have had,[52] this illustrates once again the dynamic and creative quality of this deposit that is to be guarded. From an authorial perspective, we perhaps could conclude that the imitation of Paul in the Pastorals is simply not very good, but we might also conclude that the writers are much more creative and transformative of the prior tradition than appears at first reading. This also indicates that the issue must be considered on two different levels: the imagery of the deposit to be guarded in the narrative of the Pastoral texts, which can suggest a rather static image, and the reality of what happens to the Pauline tradition in the Pastorals as the larger narrative world of Pauline Scripture begins to come into view in the early church, which is considerably more innovative.

Lest we incline to the view that the Pastorals are simply works of creative fiction with no reflection of Paul's theology or his controversies, we need to note some further Pauline images that surface in the narrative frameworks of these three epistles—that is, in

---

[49] 1 Timothy 6:14; 2 Tim 1:10; 4:1, 8; Titus 2:13; cf. Titus 2:11; 3:4. This term also occurs in 2 Thess 2:8.

[50] See Bassler, 'A Plethora of Epiphanies', 310-25, and Oberlinner, 'Die Epiphaneia des Heilswillens', 192-213.

[51] Bassler, 'A Plethora of Epiphanies', 313.

[52] Oberlinner, 'Die Epiphaneia des Heilswillens', 192-313.

addition to those connections between 2 Timothy and Philippians already identified. As we have seen in Titus 1:10-16, the Jewish character of the opposition in this epistle is identified in general terms. These problem people come especially from the 'circumcision', though apparently not exclusively so. They teach that which is improper to teach for shameful gain. The text goes on in 1:14 to say that those grounded in the true testimony should pay no attention to the Jewish myths and commandments of the people who reject the truth. In this regard, the narrative structures of Galatians and Titus have one thing in common. There is a problem with the Jewish law in both. But whereas two entire chapters are devoted exclusively in Galatians to the issue of faith and works of law, only three verses at most address the issue of the commandments in Titus. The place of the Gentiles in the covenant, so central in the Galatians debate, is nowhere to be found in Titus. 'Faith in Christ' is not juxtaposed to 'works of law' in the narrative world of Titus, even though Titus makes it clear in 3:5 that salvation is the result of divine mercy and not works of righteousness. The Pauline image at that point is unmistakable.[53]

1 Timothy deals with an opposition that is identified with myths, genealogies, and speculations (1:4). More specifically, the author writes against teachers who teach about things of which they have little understanding (1:7). As in Titus, the law is the point at issue. In response, the writer says the law is good if it is used legitimately, that is, if one understands that the law is set forth for the lawless and not the innocent (1:8-10). Galatians 3:19, read on its own terms in the context of Galatians, appears to suggest a view of the law that is similar: 'Why therefore the law? It was given because of transgressions...'[54] In both texts, the function of the law is to deal with lawlessness and transgressions. In the narrative of 1 Timothy this is, of course, related to the ascetic problem of forbidding marriage and not eating certain foods. The opponents are presumably trying to impose these requirements on those in the community who are faithful. That is a misunderstanding and misuse of the law, according to the author. In 1 Timothy, this is not a theoretical problem, and it does not pertain to the place of the Gentiles and the promises of God in salvation history. There is to be sure an emphasis on training oneself

---

[53] Cf. Rom 4:1-24; 9:30–10:4; Eph 2:8-11.
[54] See the discussion regarding the interpretation of Gal 3:19 by D.J. Lull, '"The Law Was Our Pedagogue": A Study in Galatians 3:19-25', *JBL* 105 (1986), 482-86.

in godliness in 1 Timothy (4:7), but there is no correlation between the law and a παιδαγωγός. While there is a structural connection in the way the law is understood in 1 Timothy and in Galatians—in both the law is given for transgressions and lawlessness—it should be noted that the law in Galatians is given *because of* or *on account of transgressions* (τῶν παραβάσεων χάριν) , whereas in 1 Timothy it is laid down for the *lawless and disobedient*. In the first instance the focus is on the transgressions and in the second it is on the transgressors. Once again, we hear the echo of Paul's words resounding through the words of 1 Timothy and Titus, yet at the same time they reverberate in quite new ways in the Pastorals.

It is not necessary to exhaust these parallel images to establish the point that in 1 and 2 Timothy and Titus concepts of sound teaching and the good deposit are coming to define how Paul and his teachings are to be remembered, preserved, and passed on. This is not simply a description of how the Pastorals conserved or transformed the Pauline traditions at their disposal. Neither is it a commentary on the Pastoral Epistles as some type of creative fiction made possible by pseudepigrapha as a type of literature. It is an observation about how an understanding of Pauline doctrine as a deposit is becoming a factor in the larger narrative world of Paul's teaching and its legacy. Of course, if there is ever to be a collection of Pauline Scriptures and in time a Pauline canon, there must be a remembrance of Paul and his teaching that is preserved. The claim that this legacy also has theological and christological authority only underscores its importance and urgency. But the point is that in the Pastorals we are witnessing the early formation of a larger narrative world that we might call the Pauline Scriptures or the Pauline canon. To that narrative world, each of the epistles eventually included in that Pauline legacy will contribute, but perhaps even more importantly each of the epistles will be read ultimately in light of that larger narrative world. The Paul of the Pastorals and the Paul of the community letters will start to be read in light of each other. When that happens, a Pauline collection of writings will start to function as a canon. The same principle came into play when the other letters attributed to Paul came to be read together instead of separately. It is at that point that the notion of a body of sound teaching or a Pauline deposit also has the potential to affect how the larger Pauline tradition is read. The letters may be read in church communities primarily for their doctrines and moral principles—in other words for the deposit of sound teaching—rather than for their contingent applications of the gospel in the context of the apostle's missionary work.

5. FOR TEACHING, REPROOF, CORRECTION, AND TRAINING: A CONCLUSION

The author of 2 Timothy writes in 3:14-16:

> But for you, remain in what you have learned and believed, knowing from whom you learned it, and that from childhood you have known the sacred writings (γράμματα) that are able to make you wise for salvation through faith in Christ Jesus. All scripture (γραφή) is God-breathed and profitable for teaching, for reproof, for correction, for training in righteousness.[55]

There is little doubt that what the author meant by sacred writings or God-breathed scripture are the scriptures of Israel. Even though we know that authoritative writings were beginning to emerge quite early in the church, it may well be anachronistic to think that the author had in mind a body of church produced writings that were now being referred to as God-breathed.[56] In any case, the text gives us rather direct clues about the utility of scripture for the author: to make wise for salvation—for teaching, reproof, correction, and training.[57] It may not be too much of a stretch to suggest that as an authoritative Pauline

---

[55] For a brief discusssion of the translation issue relating to 'all' Scripture being God-breathed or 'each' Scripture that is God-breathed, see Bassler, *1 Timothy 2 Timothy, Titus*, 167.

[56] Bassler, *1 Timothy 2 Timothy, Titus*, 166-67. Wolfe ('Scripture in the Pastoral Epistles', 13-15) argues that the language of 2 Tim 3:15-17 points to a broader authoritative tradition than simply the Old Testament. We cannot know for sure whether or not the Pauline community letters were thought of as Scripture by the time 2 Timothy was written (cf. 2 Pet 3:15-16), but it is tantalizing to consider this possibility. In any case, they were considered to have authority, and the writer(s) of the Pastorals intended to frame an understanding of Paul's teaching and legacy. In that sense, I am sure the writer(s) thought of themselves as framing and extending an authoritative Pauline tradition, but I doubt they thought of themselves as writing Scripture in any strict definition of the term. This may have some similarity to the way certain Jewish and perhaps even New Testament writers saw themselves as extending Hebrew biblical tradition in light of new circumstances and revelation. In light of the two-source hypothesis, it may also have some similarity to the way Matthew and Luke reframed, reinterpreted, and extended the Jesus tradition of Mark.

[57] Cf. 1 Tim 4:13.

narrative and canonical world began to come into view, it was precisely these types of assertions about the usefulness and the divine authority of the texts that started to have an effect on how the Pauline texts and the good desposit were thought to function—at least among those inclined to include the Pastorals in the Pauline canon.[58] To establish this claim would take us far beyond the scope of this essay, but the great—and much later—theological debates over this text from 2 Timothy and the inspiration of Scripture would seem to indicate that they were precisely conflicts over these kinds of claims about the sacred texts, how these claims were to be understood as pertaining to the whole of the Bible and its theological world (not just Paul), and how Scripture was thought to function. In other words, these were conflicts over how the Bible was thought to operate as canon. Hence, one may think that on this level these debates were simply a larger version of what had already happened in a limited and special way within the Pauline writings collection, in light of the Pastorals, over what it meant to preserve the good deposit of the apostle's sound teaching.

In light of 1 Timothy with its concern for passing on and preserving Paul's legacy not only through instruction but also through the people who occupy church positions, if not offices, we seem to be witnessing the laying of a structural foundation between Scripture and community (church). This would erupt full-blown into conflict centuries later in the great Reformation debates over the relative authority of the Scriptures and the tradition of the church, as preserved by the institution of the church—a situation where some came to think the two were in conflict. It would be simplistic to think that a Pauline canon could function without an interpretive community, in this case the church or churches, but as we know communities were also guided by these sacred texts and traditions that were thought to be authoritative, profitable for teaching, for reproof, for correction, and for training. In various ways, church communities early on were drawn into the narrative worlds produced by Paul and the literary texts that bore his name, and thus a process necessary for the formation of a Pauline canon was already put in place.

---

[58] For a brief discussion of the attestation to the Pastoral Epistles in the early church and by implication the complexity of the formation of the Pauline canon, see Knight, *The Pastoral Epistles*, 13-14. Cf. also 2 Pet 3:15-16.

THE FUNCTION OF THE PASTORAL LETTERS WITHIN THE PAULINE CANON OF THE NEW TESTAMENT: A CANONICAL APPROACH

ROBERT W. WALL

Seattle Pacific University
Seattle, WA, USA

1. INTRODUCTION

One of the principal interests of the canonical approach to biblical interpretation is the canonical process that resulted in a discrete literary product, the Christian Bible. Whether the particular interest in this literary history is hermeneutical[1] or theological,[2] whether its taxonomy is understood in terms of forming a community's identity or transmitting a textual (and fixed) word about God, the methodological presumption in every case is that certain writings were picked up and preserved by their faithful readers/auditors and ultimately canonized by the early catholic church because as bits and pieces of an entire canonical collection each was found useful in forming a Christian theological understanding of life and faith.[3]

Most modern constructions of the canonical process, however, fail to consider adequately the effective Christian formation of the faith community as a principal factor in the selection of individual writings

---

[1] J.A. Sanders, 'The Integrity of Biblical Pluralism', in J.P. Rosenblatt and J.C. Sitterson, Jr. (eds.), *'Not In Heaven': Coherence and Complexity in Biblical Narrative* (Bloomington: Indiana University Press, 1991), 154-69.

[2] B.S. Childs, *Introduction to the Old Testament as Scripture* (Philadelphia: Fortress Press, 1979), 46-106.

[3] This is the point I have attempted to score in a series of essays. See most recently, for example, R.W. Wall, 'Canonical Context and Canonical Conversations', in J.B. Green and M. Turner (eds.), *Between Two Horizons: Spanning Biblical Studies and Systematic Theology* (Grand Rapids: Eerdmans, 2000), 165-82.

and their placement in the emergent biblical canon. If we claim that the Bible is the church's book and that the church intended from the very beginning of the canonical process that these precious texts be read in agreement with the church's ecumenical confession of faith, then the act of biblical interpretation must be regulated by both the church's theological grammar[4] and by the more practical aims of Christian theological formation. The critical consideration of the earliest history of these sacred writings, then, must be interested in how canonical writings perform religiously when initiating believers into their life with God. It is my thesis that these interests cue their current readers to the orienting concerns of those same writings when read today as Scripture.

To illustrate this interpretive strategy, the present study will argue that the Pastoral letters (1–2 Timothy, Titus), which circulated as a discrete collection of Pauline letters, were added to an emergent ten (or nine)-letter Pauline collection, perhaps already in circulation by the end of the second century, to supply normative patterns of 'ecclesiastical discipline' to a Pauline conception of a missionary church.[5] It is my further contention that the orienting theological concerns of this distinctive 'pastoral' subject matter contribute to and complete Scripture's Pauline witness—without which the Pauline contribution to a fully Christian theological understanding of God's Gospel would be seriously compromised. Simply put, then, the late arrival of the Pastoral letters to complete the Pauline collection is constitutive of a more robust Pauline witness to the Christian faith.

The subtitle of this essay envisages its rather circumscribed purpose, which is finally more theological (and hermeneutical) than historical. While interested in the variety of attempts by historians to reconstruct the formation of the Pauline canon, including the trajectory of the Pastoral Letters as a discrete feature of its formation, my intent is not to offer yet another reconstruction of that history but to

---

[4] On the idea that Scripture's interpretation is regulated by the church's Rule of Faith, see R.W. Wall, 'Reading the Bible from within Our Traditions: The "Rule of Faith" in Theological Hermeneutics', in Green and Turner (eds.), *Between Two Horizons*, 88-107.

[5] For a canonical approach to Pauline ecclesiology, see R.W. Wall and E.E. Lemcio, *New Testament as Canon* (JSNTSup 76; Sheffield: Sheffield Academic Press, 1992), 184-207.

mine it for relevant clues that might supply current interpreters with an orienting concern for the study of the Pastoral Letters.[6]

2. The Formation of the Pauline Canon: A Brief Overview

According to H. Gamble's assessment, the 'early history of Paul's letters and the process by which they were collected are very obscure'.[7] We know, for instance, that the ancient church circulated various versions of the Pauline letter canon, differently formed and arranged according to theological, stichometric and chronological principles. Yet most modern efforts to reconstruct the formation of the Pauline corpus are concentrated by four decisive moments during its pre-canonical history, which I will follow in this 'brief overview'. I also take it that this history envisages a reception of individual sacred writings by their effective use in religious education (cf. 2 Tim 3:16b), finally shaping them into a canonical collection that preserved the memory and gospel of Paul the Apostle for subsequent generations of believers.

(1) Most reconstructions of the early history of the Pauline canon fail to take due note of the Pauline biography found especially in 2 Timothy, which many now think functions as Paul's (or a Pauline) 'last will and testament'. Surely this testamental Paul, whenever composed or by whom, suggests strongly that a 'canonical' collection of his writings is a logical if also likely next step. The memories of his apostolic persona and mission along with the summaries (or 'faithful sayings') of his message leave no doubt as to Paul's God-given authority and his lasting importance to the church—especially when stipulated in contrast to his various rivals. In fact, one argument against the Pauline authorship of the Pastorals, I think finally without much merit, is the rather immodest picture of Paul that is drawn by this biography of him: the author deliberately describes Paul as Christian saint and martyr whose unrivaled authority within the

---

[6] For this same reason, the present study will not deal with the historical-critical problem of the Pauline authorship of the Pastorals, which I—in conversation with Stanley Porter—have considered elsewhere; R.W. Wall, 'Pauline Authorship and the Pastoral Epistles: A Response to S.E. Porter', *BBR* 5 (1995), 125-28.

[7] H.Y. Gamble, *The New Testament Canon* (GBS; Philadelphia: Fortress Press, 1985), 36.

church insinuates the truth claims of his gospel as the norm for all who believe, and prescribes the memories of his piety as the norm of a truly Christian life and witness.

Even in most of his so-called 'authentic' letters, Paul routinely suggests that he intends to make a future apostolic 'house-call', presumably to check and see whether his epistolary instructions have been followed. As R. Funk argues in his now famous essay on Paul's 'apostolic parousia', the rhetorical function of a tacit warning of an imminent official visit is to intensify the importance of the letter itself, which supplies an inferior although effective substitute for Paul's persona and the edifying charisms he conveys within the faith community.[8] Sharply put, the letter represents the 'spirit' of the prophetic Paul, which communicates the word of the Lord in his personal absence. If so, then Paul himself offers support for the canonical perception that the New Testament collection of Pauline letters is an effective medium for continuing the true 'spirit' of Paul's witness to God's gospel within the post-Pauline church.

(2) My point is that even before the emergence of Pauline letter collections sometime early in the second century, there is the presumption—apparently proffered by the Apostle himself—of the immediate value of his writings to replace the irreplaceable Paul. We should not be surprised, then, of the first actual reference to a collection of Pauline writings, even called 'scripture', found in 2 Pet 3:16. Here the Pauline collection serves the church as a Christian appendix to the Jewish Scriptures.[9] Naturally, if we only knew the precise dating and *Sitz im Leben* of this letter, which remain contested and are in any case indeterminate, we could place this early collection in space and time. Suffice it to say that a collection of Pauline letters was in circulation before the idea of a New Testament was put forth by Irenaeus and an authorized New Testament finally produced.

Recently, D. Trobisch speculates that an earlier edition of this proto-Pauline collection was actually fashioned and used by Paul himself according to the contemporary convention of important teachers and rhetors (e.g., Seneca, Cicero). This prospect is even more

---

[8] R.W. Funk, 'The Apostolic Parousia: Form and Significance', in W.R. Farmer, C.F.D. Moule, and R.R. Niebuhr (eds.), *Christian History and Interpretation: Essays in Honor of J. Knox* (Cambridge: Cambridge University Press, 1967), 249-68.

[9] F.F. Bruce, 'Some Thoughts on the Beginning of the New Testament Canon', *BJRL* 65.2 (1983), 38-39.

likely if we place Paul, the missionary-teacher, in an urban (and thus well educated) church, and recognize that his letters are informed by the rhetor's practices and formed by rhetorical conventions. Trobisch suggests Paul's 'authorized recension' included only Romans, 1 and 2 Corinthians, and Galatians.[10] Subsequent to his death, his most influential colleagues (Timothy or Onesimus?) added a 'posthumous collection' to Paul's volume, which they perhaps edited and expanded as encyclicals to meet the needs of a wider audience, and published them together as his 'collected letters' with Ephesians serving as the collection's theological introduction (following the well-known thesis of E.J. Goodspeed followed notably by J. Knox). Trobisch includes all thirteen (!) letters in this posthumous collection, because I gather its practical aim is to make available to subsequent generations Paul's best thinking in response to a wide range of theological and ecclesiastical issues. While I agree for theological reasons that all thirteen Pauline letters are required to cultivate a fully Pauline understanding of Scripture's witness to the gospel (see below), Trobisch's historical basis for doing so strikes me as lacking.

Trobisch's essential hypothesis finds partial support in J. Barton's thesis that the frequency of quotation is tacit evidence of a letter's importance within the church and even its canonicity. When considering this citational evidence from the early second century, then, the very letters Trobisch includes in Paul's own collection are the very ones cited much more frequently than his other letters combined.[11] Even if conservative dates are accepted for early second-century writings, however, Barton fails to account for the curious silence of Justin Martyr, who never quotes from a known Pauline letter. Moreover, the more robust portrait of an authoritative Paul found in Acts (even though as prophet, not as literati!) does not come on board until the end of the second century when two versions of Acts were put back into circulation. Yet, at the very least, the studies of Trobisch and Barton are highly suggestive as to how we might constitute the Pauline collection mentioned in 2 Peter 3.

(3) The first known collector of Paul's letters is Marcion (160 CE). Given the prior history of the Pauline corpus to this point, Marcion's Pauline collection was likely an edited collocation of one popular

---

10 D. Trobisch, *Paul's Letter Collection* (Minneapolis: Fortress Press, 1994), 55-96.

11 J. Barton, *Holy Writings, Sacred Text: The Canon in Early Christianity* (Louisville: Westminster Press, 1997), 14-24.

version already in wide circulation.[12] Marcion collected and used Paul, however, with clear theological intent, since his theology was predicated on Pauline theology.[13] Often in sharp contrast to emergent catholic Christianity, which did not pay undo attention to Paul, Marcion's innovation was to vest an extant Pauline collection with normative authority for Christian formation: that is, the Pauline corpus was no longer 'scripture' (as in 2 Peter) but 'canon'.[14] This move was to push the catholic church in the direction of a Christian Bible of its own, perhaps sooner than would have been the case otherwise.

Tertullian describes a Marcionite canon that included ten Pauline letters—the nine letters to the seven churches with the surprising addition of Philemon. Most critics of Marcion, both ancient (e.g., Tertullian) and modern (e.g., Harnack), infer from this list that he intentionally excluded the Pastorals as canonical for his faith community. If so, his reasons for doing so remain obscure to most scholars, myself included, unless he recognized his own career in the profile of the opponents whom the author roundly attacks in these letters![15] In any case, the Beatty manuscript ($\mathfrak{P}^{46}$) from the end of the second century follows Marcion's list, suggesting that indeed his ten-letter edition of Paul does not diverge at all from the list of authorized letters generally 'in the air' at the time even if not yet as a formal literary collection.

---

12 Gamble, *New Testament Canon*, 41.

13 I find James A. Sanders's comment highly suggestive that the rich theological diversity found within the final form of the New Testament may well point back to the early church's legitimate concern with Marcion's exclusivist and hegemonic use of Paul; *Canon and Community* (GBS; Philadelphia: Fortress Press, 1984), 37. I suspect Marcionism (or some species of Protestantism!) is what Christianity looks like when using the Pauline letters as its 'canon within the Canon'.

14 In distinguishing between a text's canonical and scriptural authority, I follow the lead of C. Wood, *The Formation of Christian Understanding* (Philadelphia: Westminster Press, 1981), 82-105. On the one hand, the community's 'scripture' transmits formative traditions, important in learning the faith; on the other hand, a biblical 'canon' more narrowly norms the community's beliefs and practices. During the canonical process, many sacred texts used as (and even called) 'scripture' by the church catholic (including many Christian and Jewish apocryphal texts) were not finally included in the biblical canon because they did perform well in assessing and delimiting an emergent catholic faith and witness. The stakes are much higher for the performance of canonical texts.

15 As John Knox famously speculates in his *Marcion and the New Testament* (Chicago: University of Chicago Press, 1942).

Almost certainly Marcion's use of this Pauline collection as canonical for the formation of a 'heretical' (or non-catholic) Christianity triggered several counter-measures by the church's principal theologians. Ironically, one of these counter-measures was to promote the purchase of Paul's gospel and piety for 'catholic' consumption! That Marcion, perceived a heretic, would stipulate a Christian Bible for his faith community provoked Tertullian, his fiercest opponent and learned defender of catholic faith, to respond and offer his own version of a Pauline collection, which included the Pastorals, with Marcion's alleged omissions restored and the book of Acts serving as its narrative and biographical introduction.

(4) Two interdependent ideas put forward by this early catholic polemic against Marcion's Pauline canon generate the impetus for combining two discrete Pauline corpora. Tertullian (*Marc* 5.21) seems to suggest at the very end of his discourse on Marcion's Pauline canon that the heretic knew of the three Pastorals and 'rejected' them (*quod ad Timotheum duas et unam ad Titum de ecclesiastico statu composites recusauerit*), presumably because they are brief and written to individuals. Yet, this is evident conjecture and a rhetorical convention of Tertullian's sustained polemic against Marcion the heretic: Marcion is heretical because his Bible is incomplete—an argument that marks the beginning of a self-critical canonical process. Surely Marcion would have pointed out the flaw in Tertullian's argument by noting that he includes Philemon in his canon, which is also a brief letter and written to an individual!

More to my point, J. Quinn appeals to this text in Tertullian to supply patristic evidence for a discrete collection of three Pastoral letters at the time of Marcion.[16] Accordingly, the subsequent Muratorian fragment[17] envisages distinctions already widely understood within the ancient church between the nine congregational letters (plus Philemon) and these three briefer letters written to individuals about church orders. Thus, the *Muratorianum* commends two discrete Pauline collections, adding that the authority of the

---

16   J.D. Quinn, '𝔓46—The Pauline Canon', *CBQ* 36 (1974), 381-84.

17   The list's date and provenance are notoriously contested, especially since Albert C. Sundberg's case for a fourth-century date and a provenance in the Eastern (not Roman) church; 'Canon Muratori: A Fourth-Century List', *HTR* 66 (1973), 1-41, and more recently defended by G.M. Hahneman, *The Muratorian Fragment and the Development of the Canon* (Oxford: Oxford University Press, 1992).

second three-letter collection is based on their effective performance 'for the ordering of ecclesiastical discipline'.

This phrase, which suggests the theological function of the Pastorals, and the final shape of this list, which combines the ten-letter and three-letter Pauline corpora, are remarkable innovations—especially when compared to other contemporary lists of extant Pauline letters, which do not include the Pastorals in any case. The *Muratorianum* assessment of the Pauline corpus is almost surely reflects anti-Marcion politics, not in a petty way but to correct the broader consensus within the emergent catholic church. In fact, it seems highly unlikely, as Tertullian proffers, that Marcion rejected this second collection for the same facile reasons that would have prompted him logically to exclude Philemon as well. Nor is there any evident reason for excluding them on theological grounds. In fact, as C. Nielson rightly argues, the Pastorals display many of the characteristics of the church from which Marcion emerged and theological beliefs with which he would have agreed.[18] It therefore seems more likely that Marcion did not exclude this second collection for due cause and more probably simply did not know these writings—and we can only wonder why. What we do know, however, is that when the dust finally settled on the Marcion controversy at the dawning of the third (and pivotal) century, the theologians of the early catholic church not only had not only given us the very idea of a Christian biblical canon but also an expanded Pauline corpus that included the Pastoral letters.

3. THE FUNCTION OF THE PASTORAL LETTERS WITHIN THE PAULINE COLLECTION: A CANONICAL APPROACH

In his neglected 1955 monograph, *The Formation of the Pauline Corpus of Letters*, C. Leslie Mitton already signals a shift of interest in Pauline letters as separate literary entities to a consideration of them as a whole collection.[19] While overly optimistic that a scholarly consensus had emerged in settling the various historical critical problems of individual Pauline writings, he rightly points out that consideration of the literary whole necessarily concentrates on a range of

---

[18] C.M. Nielson, 'Scripture in the Pastoral Epistles', *PRSt* 7 (1980), 4-23.
[19] C.L. Mitton, *The Formation of the Pauline Corpus of Letters* (London: Epworth Press, 1955).

different problems, mostly indeterminate and unsettled: Why were these individual letters preserved together into a corpus? When and where did this formative process take place, by whom, by what process, and according to what criteria did the Pauline canon reach its final thirteen-letter form? The nature of these questions presumes the historian's hard work is sifting through available evidence, most of it indirect, to reconstruct the canonical process within the ancient church.

In fact, most responses to these important questions have been historical or sociological, based upon an interpreter's fluency of the canonical *process* and its *Sitz im Leben* in the early catholic church. The canonical approach to the Pauline corpus concentrates rather on the canonical *product* of this process. While every detail of the process remains contested, there stands one incontrovertible literary fact: the canonical form of the New Testament contains a thirteen-letter Pauline canon. Setting aside the large question of the various sequences of individual letters, virtually all scholars now also agree that either a nine-letter (consisting of letters to 'the seven churches') or a ten-letter collection of the sort that Marcion evidently knew was in wide circulation in the early catholic church of the second century. In addition, most suppose a second three-letter collection of Pauline Pastorals was put into circulation sometime during the second century. When, no one knows, although Marcion evidently had not heard of it even though Tertullian (and the other important catholic apologists) certainly had and speaks of this second collection with reverence rather than as a novelty item. Essentially from Tertullian forward, the thirteen-letter Pauline collection was the norm, as evinced by the Muratorian list and most other third century Pauline lists.

Perhaps this dynamic unfolding of the Pauline corpus to its thirteen-letter form, although listed in a variety of ways, can be explained by an internal 'aesthetic principle' rather than merely by some external apparatus, whether a particular heresy (e.g., Marcionism) or social process (e.g., catholicizing Christianity). By 'aesthetic principle' I refer to the church's immediate appreciation of the literary completeness and theological coherence of a particular construction or form of sacred writings. While certain individual letters (e.g., Romans, Galatians) were valued more than others—as indicated by frequency (or infrequency) of citation in early Christian writings—the canonical process 'fixed' a whole literary product as the ongoing norm for Christian theological formation rather than individual canonical compositions that were then thrown together in an arbitrary way. That is, the early catholic church canonized a thirteen-letter Pauline corpus and for theological reasons: *only in consideration of this thirteen-letter whole, and not a fraction thereof, is a complete understanding of the Pauline regula fidei possible for Christian nurture.* With respect to the inclusion of the collection of three Pastorals to the Pauline corpus, then, let me restate this principle in a more circumscribed manner: the earlier ten-letter Pauline corpus, which was then 'canonized' by Marcion, fails to supply a sufficiently rich deposit of Pauline writings by which the church is able to mine a fully Pauline understanding of the Christian faith.

Given the interests of a canonical perspective toward constructing a Pauline theological conception, the relevant question put forth is this: what would Scripture's testimony lead us to believe about Paul and his understanding of the gospel if the canonical form of the Pauline corpus did not include the three Pastorals? Or restated positively, what do the Pauline Pastorals contribute to a fully Pauline account of the church's *regula fidei* as delimited by Scripture? In putting the question this way, I need not supply yet another historical or sociological construction of the formation of the whole Pauline corpus; rather, my approach is to consider the final literary form of the corpus as comprising a theological whole, with each part complementing every other part of this integral whole. I presume on this basis that the Pastorals make a contribution to any critical analysis of Scripture's Pauline witness. Of course, this presumption is not without an historical reference point: at that moment when the canonizing, catholicizing community combined its two discrete Pauline corpora, ten-letter and three-letter, whatever the historical circumstance, it recognized that the Pauline witness was made complete at that moment and would no longer circulate among the congregations in any fraction of its earlier versions. The Pauline lists from an early period of Scripture's canonization would seem on balance to support this conclusion.[20]

---

[20] Of course, some early Pauline lists include Hebrews along with the thirteen letters—a fourteen-letter Pauline canon—and in still other cases the language of a relevant list is either vague or indeterminate. However, I take it that the present thirteen-letter Pauline corpus was fixed from the early fourth century. See 'Appendix IV: Early Lists of the Books of the New Testament', in B.M. Metzger, *The Canon of the New Testament* (Oxford: Clarendon Press, 1987), 305-15.

What are the implications of this conclusion for constructing a biblical account of Pauline (rather than Paul's) theology? Sharply put with the particular interest of the present essay in view, the interpreter must steadfastly avoid the current practice of setting aside the three-letter collection of Pauline Pastorals as 'inauthentic' and accept their teaching as complementary for a holistic Pauline theology that is, in fact, authorized by the church's Scriptures.[21] Let me illustrate in 'broad brush strokes' this interpretive principle by considering two important Pastoral theological thematics—indeed, two that help fund the modern critical sensibility that these letters should be set aside when constructing Paul's biblical theology: the church as 'God's household' and the 'good works' of the truly Christian life.[22]

The Church in the Pastoral Letters. The Muratorian Fragment prompts an important cue for understanding the contribution the Pastorals make to a Pauline theology of the church by claiming that these letters are 'for the ordering of ecclesiastical discipline'. Certainly since von Campenhausen's famous study, the Pastorals teaching

---

[21] One might argue that the 'implied author' of the Pastorals is the canonical (although not necessarily the historical) Paul; and on this basis, these are sacred texts approached by faithful interpreters as 'authored' by divine appointment. In any case, the interpreter makes a category mistake by linking historical constructions of a text's author with the text's canonical authority. Even the connection between inspired author and sacred text during the canonical process was never vested with historical-critical analysis and served theological purposes—so that the 'inspired author' represented an apostolic tradition authorized to carry the word of God by the church of Christ.

[22] This list of Pastoral thematics could be extended to include Christology, since most agree that the notion of 'Christ as Savior', found exclusively in the Pastorals, is an idiom for a conceptually different and more 'mature' idea of Christ's work than is found in Paul's 'authentic' letters; see now H. Stettler, *Die Christologie der Pastoralbriefe* (WUNT 2.105, Tubingen: Mohr Siebeck, 1998), esp. 328-44. In my opinion, most differences or lack of well-known Pauline themes in the Pastorals, noted by scholars (e.g., eschatology, role of the Spirit, providence of God, freedom from the law) are really matters more of occasion (i.e., personal letters to inexperienced missionary colleagues), literary style (i.e., theology restated as creed or 'Pauline tradition'), and cultural ethos (i.e., church as 'social institution') than of theological substance. In any case, I view these differences found in the Pastorals to be complementary and in continuity with the 'real' Paul. From the perspective of the New Testament, the teaching of the Pastorals (and every other part of the Pauline corpus) comes in some fashion from the 'canonical Paul' and makes an authorized contribution of the faithful reader's understanding of the Pauline gospel.

about 'ecclesiastical discipline' is viewed in socio-historical terms as the pronounced concern for church structure and male authority—a reflection of the institutionalization of earliest Christianity that had replaced the dynamic charisms of apostolic (i.e., Paul's) leadership within a cult-like religious movement with the intractable hierarchy that now orders life and liturgy within a 'domesticated' social organism, the Christian church.[23] This analysis seems to draw support in part from the evident shift in the Pastorals from the charismatic community of 1 Corinthians, where the church is a community of 'kindred spirits' who live and worship together as the 'body of Christ' under the aegis of the Spirit, who gives various 'spiritual gifts' to believers to empower their congregational ministries and who gives them various 'spiritual fruit' to empower their corporate solidarity.

But this modern social analysis of the Pastorals' idea of the church within the Pauline corpus is routinely overdrawn. As Johnson rightly notes, we do not find in the Pastorals what we should expect if von Campenhausen (and many others who follow his lead) is right: an elaborate hierarchy more similar to later ecclesiastical models of 'official' Christianity, details of a leader's roles and responsibilities, and a theological defense for such church orders. We find nothing in these letters that suggests the creation of a new organizational structure. Rather what we find is a congregation fashioned after a household (see Gal 6:1-10!), much more like the synagogal structure of diaspora Judaism[24] or even the Greco-Roman *collegia*—both social models, of course, very familiar to Paul.[25] 1 Timothy and Titus, the two Pastorals most interested in who leads the Christian congregation, are more interested in the moral character and spiritual maturity of those who lead the congregation than in rigid requirements or job descriptions. In fact, the titles designated for these leadership posts are hardly unique to the Pastorals but are found elsewhere in the Pauline

---

[23] H. von Campenhausen, *Ecclesiastical Authority and Spiritual Power* (Peabody, MA: Hendrickson, 1997), 106-23.

[24] Philip Towner's conjecture that the catchphrases 'people of God' or 'church of God' used in the Pastorals echo Old Testament teaching that asserts Israel belongs to God, central to the social identity of the diaspora synagogue, seems relevant here; see his *The Goal of Our Instruction* (JSNTSup 34; Sheffield: JSOT Press, 1989). That is, the distinctive idiom for the church in the Pastorals reflects a synagogal social identity, and by implication also its social structure.

[25] L.T. Johnson, *Letters to Paul's Delegates* (NTC; Valley Forge, PA: Trinity Press International, 1996), 14-16.

corpus (Rom 16:1; Phil 1:1) along with still other designations for congregational leaders—including 'ambassadors' (πρεσβεία) which extends to all believers (2 Cor 5:20)!

My intent in questioning the current critical conclusion about the Pastoral notion of an institutionalized 'church' is to shift the connotation of 'church discipline' from a concern for its social structure to its religious *function* as the 'household of God' (1 Tim 3:15). In cashing out this metaphor for the church, I take it that the Pastorals are primarily concerned with the protocol and importance of Christian formation: the congregation functions as a household comprised of believers where Christian tradition is passed on to the next generation and where Christian instruction is practiced in a disciplined, orderly manner.[26] In saying this, I take it that Paul's essential understanding of a missionary church, which must steadfastly guard its vocation against all sorts of intramural opposition to maintain theological purity, continues on in the Pastorals. Thus, even instructions given in supervision of liturgical prayers, found in 1 Tim 2:1-15, are justified by this missiological intent: the Christian congregation prays for secular rulers (2:1-2) and maintains current social decorum (2:8-15) because God desires to save all persons (2:3-4). But even here, as everywhere else in the Pastorals, this redemptive calculus is extended to Paul's appointment as 'teacher' (2:7b) for the expressed purpose of clarifying the theological foundations on which the congregation worships in this manner (2:5-7a). Clearly, here there is no dichotomy between missionary preaching (2:7a) and congregational teaching. What begins in an evangelistic crusade continues on in the formation of a truly Christian congregation.

As is well known, διδασκαλία/διδάσκαλός/διδάσκω is a featured element of the Pastorals 'special vocabulary', used far more in this literary subcollection than anywhere else in the New Testament: the predominant characteristic of the Pastorals idea of church is of the Pauline teacher (διδασκαλός) teaching (διδάσκω) Pauline (or 'sound') doctrine (διδασκαλία).[27] In fact, the creedal formulae of

---

26 See F. Young, *The Theology of the Pastoral Epistles* (NTT; Cambridge: Cambridge University Press, 1994), 79-85.

27 Consideration of the entire semantic subdomain for teaching (see Louw & Nida 33:224-50) would extend and deepen this impression enormously: there is a keener emphasis in the Pastorals on the activities and substance of Christian teaching, along with the moral character of the 'apt teacher', than anywhere else in Scripture.

Pauline theology scattered throughout these letters, often as 'faithful sayings', supply the curriculum for a faculty (exemplified by the letters' 'implied' audience) of the Pauline school—not unlike the sermons of Matthew's Jesus that effectively gather his relevant sayings under various thematics to facilitate the church's vocation to teach Jesus to the nations (so Matt 28:19-20). No matter who authored these writings, I take it that the intended readers are Paul's successors, whose vocation is to teach true (i.e., Pauline) doctrine to the post-Pauline church as the effective means of sustaining and extending Paul's Gentile mission/message, which continues under the threat of the same opponents he encountered (cf. Titus 1:9-11 and Gal 2:11-12; also Rom 16:17-20).[28] Naturally, since the Christian congregation has already been planted, although still in patently non-Christian places (like Crete; Titus 1:12), its life and faith are more fixed realities under God and within this pagan world, and the disciplines for sustaining and growing Christian faith are much different than those experiences of the sinner being initiated into Christian faith. Yet the church's missionary vocation remains the same as Paul's as the heirs of his legacy and mission. In this sense, teaching doctrine is a missionary endeavor, whose ultimate aim is to organize Christian congregations in a manner that effectively bears witness to the gospel.

This stress on the teachers and teaching ministry of the missionary church includes a set of important ingredients. I have already mentioned the curriculum these teachers are given to instruct—the 'new' Torah of the Pauline church: no collection of New Testament writings is so replete with theological summaries—often integrated with Pauline biography to warrant its canonical authority for Christian formation—as this one (e.g., 1 Tim 1:15-17; 2:3-6; 3:16; 4:10; 6:14-16; 2 Tim 1:9-10; 2:8-13; Titus 2:11-14; 3:4-7). What must be said here, against some recent scholarly opinion, is that the theological substance of this curriculum is consistent with the theological substance of Paul's 'authentic' letters,[29] even seeking to extend its formative significance for a post-Pauline ecclesial setting (real or imagined) by

---

[28] For an excellent summary of this point, see I.H. Marshall, *The Pastoral Epistles* (ICC; Edinburgh: T. & T. Clark, 1999), 518-21.

[29] I take it this is what Jouette M. Bassler means when she calls the Pastorals' theological argot 'mundane'; *1 Timothy, 2 Timothy, Titus* (ANTC; Nashville: Abingdon Press, 1996), 31-34.

vesting the core claims of Paul's gospel with a different language and additional layers of meaning.[30]

The pedagogical rules given have to do with the character of both the 'apt teacher' (e.g., 2 Tim 2:14-26) and the household qua school (e.g., Titus 2:1-10). In my opinion, the paraenetic materials (including the various catalogues of virtues and vices) given in rough interplay with the theological summaries define the sort of person or the kind of congregation where effective teaching can take place. For this reason, what characterizes the congregation's leaders, who 'give instruction in sound doctrine' (Titus 1:9), also characterizes the congregation's rank-and-file, who 'mentor' one another 'so that the word of God may not be discredited' (Titus 2:4-5). The vocation of the missionary church as 'household of God' is to be 'pillar and bulwark of the truth' within the world (1 Tim 3:15). Toward this end the entire congregation is engaged in the spiritual discipline of Christian instruction, not only to guard its truth from intramural rivals (e.g., 2 Tim 2:14-21) but also to disclose it to sinners who seek a Savior.

While cultivating the character of an 'apt teacher' is the entire congregation's responsibility, there is also the sense that Paul's immediate successors are enabled to teach others by the Spirit's 'special' gift (so 1 Tim 4:14; 2 Tim 1:6). Even von Campenhausen must admit that the authority of the 'teaching office' in the Pastorals is established more in the terms of Paul's own prophetic authority than in those terms associated with an 'office' established by a religious institution.[31] That is, the gifted teacher—including those who are Paul's immediate successors—is not 'authorized' by some congregational review of their character or academic credential; rather, the gifted teacher is set apart by apostolic appointment (2 Tim 1:6) and prophetic utterance (1 Tim 4:14). In this regard, it is a category mistake to understand the teacher as the holder of an ecclesiastical office; rather, the teacher is more like the prophet of God, who carries God's word

---

30   This is the essential point Brevard S. Childs makes in his programmatic discussion of the Pastorals' 'canonical shape' in *The New Testament as Canon* (Philadelphia: Fortress Press, 1984), 387-95. Although my thesis does not require it, Norbert Brox makes a strong, although hardly definitive, historical case for their pseudonymity and post-Pauline provenance in his *Die Pastoralbriefe* (RNT, Regensburg: Pustet, 1963).

31   *Ecclesiastical Authority*, 116; although von Campenhausen remains true to his larger polemic and thinks this move back towards a genuinely Pauline idea is fictional.

to instruct God's people under the Spirit's anointing—the Spirit of 'power and love and self-control' rather than of 'timidity' (2 Tim 1:7; cf. 1 Cor 2:13).

With this brief discussion in mind, we must entertain again the leading question of this essay: what is the purchase of the Pastorals within the Pauline canon of the New Testament? Whatever else we might say in response to this question, the Pastorals teaching about the church simply does not move a Pauline ecclesiology in an opposite or innovative direction: 'the ecclesiology of the Pastoral Epistles (is) akin to that of Paul'.[32] What the Pastorals do, in my opinion, is to clarify the church's missionary vocation, worked out in other Pauline letters, for a post-Pauline setting. There the successors of Paul's message and mission must establish a protocol and working principles/rules, much like those found in a 'household', that will effectively transmit Paul's theological and personal legacy to the next generation of his spiritual progeny (2 Tim 2:2). Only then will the church be able to extend his witness to God's gospel to the ends of the earth.

The Character of the Christian according to the Pastoral Letters. A second area of the Pastorals theological conception that has provoked critical attention is how they regard right behavior. Especially since the publication of Dibelius's commentary on the Pastorals,[33] primary consideration in this regard is of both the form and sources of their paraenesis. More recently, A. Malherbe has located the Pauline paraenesis in the intellectual culture of the wider Greco-Roman world,[34] which makes better sense of the keen emphasis on moral character in the Pastorals. The various catalogues of virtues found here identify Christian faith with the competent person, who is moderate, modest, self-controlled, and a good citizen, whose conscience protects him against imprudent conduct. In essence, the interplay between moral character of theological confession found in the Pastorals, already mentioned to make a different point, underscores this fundamental structure of Pauline thought: that 'there is an indissoluble connection between beliefs and behavior', between Pauline orthodoxy and social

---

[32] Marshall, *Pastoral Epistles*, 521.

[33] M. Dibelius, *Die Pastoralbriefe* (4th edition as revised by H. Conzelmann; HKNT 13; Tübingen: J.C.B. Mohr, 1955).

[34] Among several important studies on this topic, see especially his *Paul and the Popular Philosophers* (Philadelphia: Fortress Press, 1989).

orthopraxis.³⁵ Conversely, where this connection appears broken apart, where moral chaos is found, there is evidence found of opposition to the core claims of Paul's gospel. Thus, for every virtue list there is a contrasting vice list, together delineating the real difference between embodied truth and falsehood—this is also consistent with both Jewish theology and Greco-Roman moral philosophy. There is also clear continuity between the evangelical purpose of Paul's mission and this 'indissoluble connection' between 'sound doctrine' and virtuous character (so 1 Tim 1:8-11).

Given this fundamental continuity, then, are there distinctive emphases found in the Pastorals that round off the Pauline profile of the believer's lifestyle? I have already suggested that the differences one finds between the Pauline paraenesis generally and the Pastorals paraenesis particularly is best explained by the keen interest in teaching discussed above. Sharply restated, Pastorals paraenesis defines moral character in terms of that species of faithful disciple who can teach 'sound doctrine' to others who make up a 'household of God' dedicated to Christian instruction. Yet two features of this profile of the 'apt teacher' stand out and supply a moral standard for all faithful disciples: namely, their 'godliness' (εὐσέβεια; 1 Tim 2:2; 3:16; 4:7, 8; 6:3, 5, 6, 11; 2 Tim 3:5; Titus 1:1) and 'good work(s)' (ἔργον ἀγαθόν/καλόν; 1 Tim 2:10; 3:1; 5:10, 25; 6:18; 2 Tim 2:21; 3:17; Titus 2:7, 14; 3:1, 8, 14), catchwords critical to the Pastorals 'special' language. Rather than providing full-bodied word studies, which many others have already done, I want to make a couple of related points relevant to my thesis. First, the implicit consistency between the believer's internal (spiritual) character (εὐσέβεια) and the character of the believer's external (public) life (ἔργα ἀγαθά) subverts any attempt to internalize and privatize Christian formation—again, no doubt, in service of the community's missionary vocation. Godly believers produce good works as the concrete demonstration of the gospel's truth, and this 'indissoluble connection' within Pauline Christianity between beliefs and behavior.

Secondly, the idea of 'good works' in the Pastorals, so pivotal to how they portray the Christian life, defines those moral habits that result from the work of God's grace. 'Good works' characterize the life that accords with God's will and is therefore pleasing to God (2 Tim 3:17). In fact, the paraenetic contrast between evil and good

---

35   Bassler, *1 Timothy, 2 Timothy, Titus*, 34.

works, which typically frames the Pauline polemic against false teachers (who perform evil works), also illustrates the public effect of God's salvation-creating grace in the true believer's life (cf. Rom 12:1). This idea, then, is not only theologically considered but also the necessary evidence of the gospel truth that Paul and his successors preach. No matter the apparent agreements between the idea and character of these 'good works' with contemporary secular philosophy, it is deeply grounded and reflective of what stands at the epicenter of Paul's thought world: the sinner who believes the gospel is initiated into a new life with God, whose grace transforms the believer from doing evil to doing good.

This stress on 'good works' in the Pastorals as the effective, moral yield of receiving God's grace brings out in bold relief a point that is made elsewhere in the Pauline canon, most effectively in Rom 12:1, 2 Cor 9:8, and Eph 2:8-10. The net result is to correct what I think is a dangerous tendency of the (especially) Protestant misreading of Paul, which demonizes good works as somehow subversive of the sinner's dependency on Christ's death for salvation. Further, the Pastorals stress on the formation of a 'godly' character as the distinguishing mark of the faithful believer, who is then morally competent to perform 'good works', corrects another tendency of a (especially) Protestant misreading of Paul: namely, the emphasis on teaching a saving orthodoxy to the exclusion of any instruction in a practical divinity that embodies confessed truth in the hard work of Christian charity and virtue. In this regard, too, the emphasis of the Pastorals brings a necessary balance to the whole of Scripture's Pauline teaching.

PAUL'S LETTER TO THE LAODICEANS

M.-É. BOISMARD

École Biblique
Jerusalem, Israel

Paul wrote at the end of his letter to the Colossians: 'And once this letter has been read among you, cause it to be read also in the church of Laodicea; and the one from Laodicea, read it also' (4:16); the exchange of the letters was all the easier since the towns of Colossae and Laodicea were close. So, according to this text, Paul wrote a letter to the faithful of Laodicea at the same time as he wrote to those of Colossae. It seems, however, that all trace of this letter has been lost. A Latin text, which claims to reproduce it, is certainly inauthentic. A question immediately arises: why would the editor of the Pauline letters, in the 80s, omit this letter which he surely knew? In order to get around this difficulty, certain authors (Harnack, Dibelius, Quispel) have proposed identifying this letter with that to the Ephesians, which, according to the best manuscripts, did not bear the name of those for whom it was intended. But this hypothesis runs into so many difficulties that it appears now to have been abandoned.[1] The question remains unanswered: why would the editor of the Pauline letters have omitted the letter to the Laodiceans?

Taking up once more an hypothesis already formulated by A. Lindemann,[2] I think that the editor did not forget it, but combined it with the letter to the Colossians; consequently, it still exists, but in the form of *membra disjecta*, in a letter (Colossians) which we still

---

[1] My opinion is that, in its present form, the Epistle to the Ephesians contains an authentic letter from Paul to the faithful of Ephesus, but that it was later filled out with elements borrowed from the letter to the Colossians. See my book *L'énigme de la lettre aux Éphésiens* (EBib 39; Paris: Gabalda, 1999).

[2] *Der Kolosserbrief* (ZBK; Zürich: Theologische Verlag, 1983), 76-77.

possess.[3] It was all the easier to do this since, as we shall see, the two letters were in part parallel and dealt with similar themes. The compiler thus fulfilled at the same time the wish expressed by Paul in Col 4:16: both letters were to be read by the same readers; that would be easier if they were combined to form a single letter.

Such a way of doing things may appear odd to us. But it would correspond to what we know anyway of the methods of the editor of the Pauline letters. A number of commentators think that 1 Corinthians, in its present form, is the result of the fusion of two or three different letters. Similarly with 2 Corinthians and Philippians. Also Romans 9–11 and especially Romans 16 may have been added to the original letter. In the light of the way in which the editor of the Pauline letters went about things, the hypothesis that I am going to put forward does not seem, a priori, impossible.

1. A LETTER COMPOSED OF DOUBLETS

Anyone who reads the letter to the Colossians in its present form, will notice that it contains a fairly considerable number of doublets—too many in fact to be easily explained. I reproduce them here in a very literal translation.

A first doublet, 1:3-6 and 1:9-10:

1:3 We give thanks to God, the Father of our Lord Jesus Christ,	
	1:9 That is why we also, *since the day when we heard,*
always praying for you, 4 *having heard of* your faith...	do not cease praying for you
	and asking that you may be filled with the knowledge of his will...
[cf. 2:6-7, *infra*]	10...to walk in a way worthy of the Lord and which pleases him,
5...of the Gospel 6 which is present among you as also in all the world it is	in every good work

---

[3] I have developed this hypothesis in my book *La lettre de saint Paul aux Laodicéens* (CahRB 42; Paris: Gabalda, 1999).

bearing fruit and growing as also in you, *since the day you heard* and you knew the grace of God...	bearing fruit and growing through the knowledge of God.

In vv. 3b-4a, Paul writes that he prays *always* for his readers, having heard of their faith. Allowing for an inversion, the same idea is expressed in v. 9: Paul, having heard of (the good conduct of those to whom he is writing), *does not cease* praying for them. The same terms express the same idea. On the other hand, the words 'since the day when we heard' occur again in v. 6c, where, however, they express a different situation: in v. 6, the ones who have learnt are those to whom Paul is writing, and not Paul himself as in v. 9.

Similarly, the same Greek sequence recurs in vv. 6 and 10: ἐν παντὶ...καρποφορούμενον καὶ αὐξανόμενον and ἐν παντὶ... καρποφοροῦντες καὶ αὐξανόμενοι. In both verses, these two similar sequences are followed by the theme of *knowledge* of God, or of his grace. But the idea expressed is totally different. In v. 6 it is a question of the Gospel, whereas v. 10 speaks of those to whom the letter is written. Even the theme of 'knowledge' does not have the same import: in v. 6 it is knowledge of the grace of God, that is his plan for the salvation of the world; v. 10 concerns knowledge of his will, according to v. 9.

Verses 3-6 constitute a classic beginning of a Pauline letter (cf. Phlm 4-5 and especially 1 Thess 1:2-3). Verses 9-10 could also be the beginning of a letter, but the editor has simplified it by attaching it to v. 8, from the original letter to the Colossians, which mentioned the love of the faithful of Colossae. A comparison can also be made with Phil 1:3-11. Paul first mentions that he always prays for the faithful of Philippi (v. 4), then a little further on he specifies the object of his prayer: that they may abound in love 'in the knowledge' of God's will, so that they may be 'filled with a fruit (καρπόν) of justice' (vv. 9-11). That is the theme of Col 1:9b-10: Paul prays that his readers 'may be filled with the knowledge of his will' so as to be able to 'bear fruit' (καρποφοροῦντες).

A second doublet, 1:5b-6a and 1:23:

1:5...thanks to the hope which abides for you in the heavens,	1:23...without turning away from the hope
of which you formerly heard in the word of truth, *of the Gospel* 6 which is present among you as also in the whole world. 24...which is the Church 25 of which I myself have become the minister...	*of the Gospel* of which you heard which has been proclaimed in every creature under heaven, of which I, Paul, have become the minister.

Expressed largely with the same words, the two principal themes are identical: the hope (of a heavenly destiny) brought by the gospel of which Paul's readers have heard, this gospel which is spread everywhere.

The two final clauses differ in that one has an ecclesiastical and the other a missionary perspective. But it is surprising to find such a similar expression and with an identical structure repeated two verses later.

A third doublet, 1:10-12 and 2:6-7:

2:6 So then, as you received Christ Jesus, the Lord, walk in him	1:10...to walk in a way worthy of the Lord
7 rooted and built up in him and strengthened by the faith such as you have been taught it, overflowing with thanksgiving...	11...powerfully empowered according to the force of his glory 12...giving thanks to the Father...

What is interesting here is the sequence of three themes: to walk (περιπατεῖν) according to the Lord, to be strengthened in order to do it, to give thanks to God. Following 2:12, faith in God's power is the principle of our new life in Christ; vv. 11 and 7a express the same idea.

Fourth, fifth and sixth doublets, 1:27-28 and 2:2; 3:16; 1:22:

In ch. 1, vv. 24-29 forms a unit framed by the twofold mention of Paul's trials in vv. 24 and 29. This passage provides a certain number of parallels in the rest of the letter, but only as *membra disjecta*. We have already seen that the relative clause in v. 25 'of which I myself have become the minister' had its parallel in 1:23 (second doublet). Let us now turn to vv. 27-28:

1:27...to whom God willed *to make known* what is the richness of his glory	2:2...to all the richness of the fulness of understanding, to the *knowledge*
of this mystery among the Gentiles, which is Christ in you,	of the mystery of God, Christ, 3 in whom are all the treasures of *wisdom and knowledge*, hidden.
the hope of the glory, 28 whom we proclaim to you, admonishing every man and teaching *in all wisdom* so that we may present every man perfect in Christ.	3:16...*in all wisdom* teaching and admonishing one another... 1:22...so as to present you holy and spotless and irreproachable before him.

The parallel between 1:27 and 2:2 is obvious. Both verses are about knowing the richness of the mystery of God, which is Christ. The theme of wisdom, expressed in 2:3, appears also in 1:28. The perspective in 1:27 is missionary: Paul has the task of proclaiming the richness of the mystery; this perspective is less clear in 2:2-3, but these verses are the continuation of a text in which Paul mentions the struggle which he has had to undergo (2:1).

Let me note that, although constituted by Christ, the notion of 'mystery' is not identical. In 1:22, it consists in the fact that Christ is proclaimed even to the Gentiles; in 2:2, Christ himself is the mystery, because, thanks to his death on the cross, we obtain our reconciliation with God (cf. 1:21).

The parallel between 1:28a and 3:16 is also clear. But once again there is a difference of perspective. In 1:28a, it is missionary: Paul teaches and admonishes; in 3:16, it is communitarian: the faithful themselves teach and admonish one another.

I have only two remarks to make about 1:28b and 1:22: the verb 'present' (παρίστημι) occurs nowhere else in Colossians.

Furthermore, we have seen that the second doublet, 1:23, had its parallel in 1:5-6; so both v. 22 and v. 23 find a parallel elsewhere in Colossians.

A further detail. Paul ends the passage 1:27-28 by mentioning that he has worn himself out 'in struggling' (ἀγωνιζόμενος) in order to ensure his preaching; at the beginning of the passage 2:2-3 he recalls 'what a struggle' (ἀγῶνα) he has had to undergo.

A seventh doublet, 3:17 and 3:23:

3:17 And all that you do in word and in action may all [be] in the name of the Lord Jesus, giving thanks to God the Father through him.	3:23 Whatever you do, with all your soul accomplish it as for the Lord, and not for human beings.

The context of 3:17 has a liturgical tone since it comes just after the mention of 'psalms, hymns and spiritual canticles' which the faithful are to 'sing' in their hearts (v. 16). That of 3:23 is quite different: Paul sets out there the duties of slaves towards their masters (vv. 22-24).

An eighth doublet, 3:5, 12 and 3:8, 10:

3:5 so put to death your earthly members: fornication, impurity...	3:8 but now, lay aside also all that: anger, rage, malice, defamation, bad language... 9...having taken off the old with his actions
12 So put on...sentiments of mercy, goodness, humility, gentleness, patience...	10 and having put on the new...

Both passages express opposition between what is to be avoided and what is to be done. In 3:5, 12, it is expressed by the two verbs 'put to death' and 'put on'; in 3:8-9 by the three verbs 'put away', 'having taken off' and 'having put on'. In 3:5, Paul insists on sexual faults; in 3:8 on everything that could give offense to the neighbour. But this difference is made up for by 3:12, where Paul enumerates the virtues that should govern our relations with the neighbour.

A ninth doublet, 1:19-20 and 2:9; 1:22:

I describe this doublet separately because 1:19-20 belongs to the famous hymn that Paul quotes in 1:15-20.

1:19 Because in him He is pleased to cause to dwell all the fulness	2:9 Because in him dwells all the fulness of the Godhead, corporally.
20 and though him to reconcile all things to him, having made peace by the blood of his cross, both those that are on earth, and those that are in the heavens.	1:22...but now he has reconciled in his body of flesh, through death...

The theme of the 'fulness' ($\pi\lambda\acute{\eta}\rho\omega\mu\alpha$) which dwells in Christ is quite typical; it also happens to have given a lot of trouble to exegetes. We recall that 1:22 was already in parallel with 1:28 in the sixth doublet. I admit that this last doublet is less convincing than the others. Paul may have returned with a further precision ('the fulness of the Godhead') to the finale of the hymn that he quoted in 1:15-20.

Even without this last doublet, we have listed eight which are unarguable. Can we really think that Paul would have repeated himself in this way throughout his letter? One or two doublets at most could be explained: Paul may have felt the need to make his ideas more precise by coming back to a theme already expressed. But it is out of the question that he would have done so eight times. The only hypothesis that seems logical is that two parallel letters have been combined by the editor of the Pauline letters[4]. One of these letters was that to the Colossians; the other can only be that to the Laodiceans since, as we know from Col 4:16, both letters were written at the same moment and addressed to neighbouring communities which therefore had similar needs and problems.

---

[4] Something like this seems to have occurred in the case of Chrysostom's homilies on John's Gospel. Towards the end of the fifth century, the editor of Chrysostom's homilies inserted, as *membra disjecta*, a commentary on the same Gospel by Diodorus of Tarsus, Chrysostom's teacher at Antioch. This was all the easier as, in order to compose his homilies, Chrysostom made large use of his old teacher's commentaries, which explains the numerous doublets in the homilies in their present form. See M.-É. Boismard, *Un évangile pré-johannique* (3 vols. in 6 parts; EBib 17, 18, 24, 25, 28, 29; Paris: Gabalda, 1993–96).

2. THE LETTER TO THE LAODICEANS

In drawing up the inventory of the doublets contained in the present letter to the Colossians, I have placed in the right-hand column the texts originating in the letter to the Laodiceans. I now give my proposed reconstruction of this letter, filling out a little the doublets that I have listed. The letter constituted a real commentary on the baptismal liturgy which still remained in use in the fourth century and which is known to us from the *Mystagogical Catecheses* of Cyril of Jerusalem and the *De Mysteriis* of Ambrose of Milan. In reference to this baptismal liturgy, we can divide the letter into three parts.

First part:

> 1:9 That is why we also, since the day when we heard, do not cease praying for you and asking that you may be filled with the knowledge of his will in all wisdom and spiritual understanding, 10 so as to walk in a way worthy of the Lord, and which pleases him in everything, bearing fruit in every good work and growing through the knowledge of God, 11 powerfully empowered according to the force of his glory, in all constancy and endurance,

> with joy 1:12 giving thanks to the Father who has made you capable of sharing in the inheritance of the saints in light, 13 to him who has snatched us from the power of darkness and transferred us into the kingdom of the son [object] of his love, 14 in whom we have deliverance, the forgiveness of sins.

> 1:21 And you, being formerly foreigners and enemies in thought, [living] in evil works, 22 now he has reconciled you in his body of flesh, through death, in order to present you holy and spotless and irreproachable, before him, 23 if at least you persevere, founded through faith and firm, and without letting yourselves turn away from the hope of the gospel of which you have heard, which has been proclaimed in every creature that [is] under heaven, of which I, Paul, have become the minister.

In the baptismal liturgy, the neophytes first faced the west, the region of darkness under the power of Satan who incited human beings to accomplish 'evil works'; then they pronounced the formula 'I renounce Satan and his works'. Next they turned towards the east, the region of light, plunged into the baptismal font and came out pronouncing a formula by which they recognized Christ as the king of the new kingdom.⁵ This 'turning round' (ἐπιστρέφειν) from the west towards the east symbolized their interior conversion (ἐπιστρέφειν).

This baptismal rite is evoked in vv. 12-14. We have been 'snatched from the power of darkness'; this is the 'deliverance' to which the end of v. 14 refers. Thus delivered from the power of Satan, we have been made capable 'of sharing in the inheritance of the saints in light'. We have passed from the kingdom of Satan to that of Christ (v. 13), from darkness to light. In the Acts of the Apostles (26:18), Luke puts on Paul's lips a similar theme, but more explicit. Paul affirms that he has been sent to the Gentiles 'to open their eyes, so that they may turn (ἐπιστρέψαι) from darkness to light and from the power of Satan towards God, so that they may receive the forgiveness of sins and a place among the sanctified, thanks to the faith in me'.

The central part (vv. 12-14) is flanked by two complementary parts which describe the state of human beings *after* their baptism (vv. 9-11), and *before* they receive it (vv. 21-23). Before being baptized, they have solemnly proclaimed 'I renounce Satan and his works'. And in fact, Satan made them accomplish those 'evil works' spoken of in v. 21. Now that they are baptized, they can bear fruit 'in every good work' (v. 10; cf. Acts 26:20).

Still according to the baptismal liturgy, after having professed their faith in Christ, the newly baptized receive the Spirit by laying on of hands. The patristic commentaries explain that this Spirit is meant to give the newly baptized the force to resist Satan and to remain faithful to their promises. In this perspective, Paul can write in 1:11 that if we bear fruit now 'in every good work', it is because we are 'powerfully empowered according to the force of his glory [that of God = the Spirit] in all constancy and endurance'.

Verse 22 contains a very discrete allusion to the baptismal rite proper: '...now he has reconciled you in his body of flesh, through death'. By plunging into the baptismal font, the neophytes are united to the liberating death of Christ, as Paul will explain later (2:12).

Second part:

> 2:1 For I want you to know what a struggle I have for you [ ] and for all those who have not seen my face according to the flesh, 2 so that their

---

⁵ Here is a difference between the way baptism was practised at the beginning of Christianity and in the following centuries. The profession of faith in Christ, king of the new kingdom, was replaced by a profession of faith in the Trinity.

heart may be strengthened, closely united in love, [that they may come] to all the richness of the fulness of understanding, to the knowledge of the mystery of God, Christ, 3 in whom are all the treasures of wisdom and knowledge, hidden.

2:8 See that no-one robs you by means of philosophy and a vain seduction according to human tradition, according to the elements of the world, and not according to Christ, 9 because in him dwells all the fulness of the Godhead, corporally, 10 and you have been filled in him, who is the head of every Principality and Power, 11 in whom you have been circumcised by a circumcision not made by a human hand, in the stripping of the body of flesh, in the circumcision of Christ, 12 buried with him in baptism, in whom also you are risen with [him] thanks to faith in the energy of God who has raised him from the dead.

2:20 If you have died with Christ to the elements of the world, why make laws as if you were in the world: 21 'Do not take, do not taste, do not touch'? 22 —all that for things destined to be corrupted by use—according to human prescriptions and doctrines, 23 which may well have a semblance of wisdom, by their affectation of religiosity and humility and contempt of the body. In fact, they have no value for the contempt of the flesh.

In 1:22, Paul had made a discrete allusion to the baptismal rite proper, which unites us to the saving death of Christ. He is now going to develop it, but with a markedly polemical note.

The principal theme is announced in 2:2: the mystery of God is Christ. In what sense? Paul explains in v. 12: '...buried with him [Christ] in baptism, in whom also you are risen with [him] thanks to faith in the energy of God who has raised him from the dead'. Baptism is here mentioned explicitly. Paul takes up again the idea worked out in Rom 6:3-5. Plunging into the water (symbol of the powers of evil) then coming out again unites us symbolically to the mystery of the death and resurrection of Christ, if at least we believe in the power of God (his Spirit) who has raised up Christ and so can raise us up spiritually. This theme needs to be filled out by what Paul had to say in 1:22: Christ has reconciled us with God 'in his body of flesh, through death'. According to the biblical notion, the 'flesh' (which is not to be taken here in the physical sense) is everything that can lead us into evil; and Satan uses the opportunity presented by our 'flesh' to make us accomplish 'evil works'. By dying on the cross, Christ has as it were crucified the flesh, and made it powerless.

As in the first part, the central theme expressed in v. 12 is framed by two parallel passages in which Paul engages in a polemic against the 'Judaeo-Christians'. These thought that Christians should keep all the Jewish observances; that is the false philosophy that Paul attacks in v. 8. More precisely, he rejects the necessity of circumcision (v. 11). This consisted in removing a small part of a man's flesh. But thanks to Christ, through baptism, we receive the spiritual circumcision which alone is necessary: 'in the stripping of the body of flesh, in the circumcision of Christ'. Christ has killed the flesh by dying on the cross; by uniting ourselves to him through baptism (v. 12), we strip our 'body of flesh'.[6] The 'Judaeo-Christians' also thought that the observances of the Law allowed us to tame our flesh. Paul refutes this idea in vv. 20-23: all these observances 'may well have a semblance of wisdom'; but in fact, 'they have no value for the contempt of the flesh' (v. 23).

Third part:

> 3:8 But now, lay aside also all that: anger, rage, malice, defamation, bad language [coming] from your mouth; 9 do not lie to one another, having taken off the old man with his actions 10 and having put on the new, the one who is renewed in view of knowledge, in the image of his creator, 11 where there is no longer Greek or Jew, circumcision or uncircumcision, barbarian, Scythian, slave, or free, but [the one who is] all in all: Christ.
>
> 3:15 And may the peace of Christ reign in your hearts, for which also you have been called in a single body. And live in thanksgiving. 16 May the word of Christ dwell in you in all its richness; instruct one another and admonish one another in all wisdom; through psalms, hymns, spiritual canticles, in gratitude, sing to God in your hearts.

Before receiving baptism, the neophytes 'laid aside' all their clothes and were clothed in white once the ceremony was over. All this had a symbolic value. The clothes which they took off represented 'the old man' with his train of vices. The white robe which they put on afterwards symbolized the new life that they were meant to lead. Paul refers to this twofold rite: 'having taken off... having put on'. Notice that the first verb 'lay aside' echoes the technical term of the baptismal rite: one 'laid aside' one's clothes.

---

[6] Verses 9-10, on the πλήρωμα, are rather out of place in this context. They may have been added by the editor of the letter under the inspiration of 1:19-20, which he read in the letter to the Colossians.

The liturgical action is recalled in v. 16: the psalms, hymns and spiritual canticles that were sung during the baptismal ceremony and the eucharist which followed immediately.

Conclusion:

> 3:23 Whatever you do, with all your soul accomplish it as for the Lord and not for human beings, 24 knowing that you receive from the Lord the reward of the inheritance. Serve the Lord Jesus. 25 For whoever commits injustice will receive the wages of injustice; and there is no respect of persons.

> 4:7 What concerns me, Tychichus will make known to you, the well-beloved brother and faithful minister and my companion in the service of the Lord, 8 whom I have sent to you for that very reason: that you may know my situation, and that he may console your heart, 9 with Onesimus the faithful and beloved brother, who is among you; they will make known to you all that happens here.

By way of inclusion, the letter's conclusion refers back to its beginning by taking up again the theme of the 'inheritance'. If we are faithful to the promises of our baptism, we will receive the inheritance announced in 1:12, a share in the kingdom of Christ.

3. A Letter of Paul Himself

I think that there is no serious reason to deny the Pauline authenticity of the letter to the Laodiceans, such as I have tried to reconstruct it. The themes and the vocabulary are Pauline and present numerous parallels with other letters of Paul, especially those to the Galatians and the Romans. Like the letters to the Philippians and Philemon, Paul wrote it while he was in prison. But the date cannot be very late. Paul attacks the 'Judaeo-Christians' who wanted to keep not only circumcision (2:8, 11) but all the Jewish observances, especially the food-laws (2:20-23). These are the problems that are dealt with in the letters to the Galatians and the Romans; that to the Laodiceans cannot be much later. For that reason I propose the captivity at Caesarea, rather than that at Rome. Finally, the concrete details concerning Paul's life and struggles (2:1), as also the reference to sending Tychichus and Onesimus (4:7-9), would be incomprehensible if Paul himself had not written this letter (while he was still alive!). He may have used the services of a secretary, to whom he dictated the letter, as he did on other occasions.

THE HELLENISTIC LETTER-FORMULA AND THE PAULINE LETTER-SCHEME

DETLEV DORMEYER

University of Dortmund
Dortmund, Germany

1. THE FORM OF LETTERS IN ANTIQUITY

Letter literature is more closely related to speech than narrative literature. The letter substitutes for the physical presence of the writer, as it has been expressed in the popular paradox *apon–paron* (absent–present): 'For though absent in body I am present in spirit' (1 Cor 5:3).[1] Cicero writes to his friend Curio: 'That there are many kinds of letters you are well aware; there is one kind, however, about which there can be no mistake, for indeed letter writing was invented just in order that we might inform those at a distance if there were anything which it was important for them or for ourselves that they should know' (Cicero, *Fam* 2.4.1).

The first reflection on letter writing was made by a certain 'Demetrius' (erroneously identified in the manuscript tradition as Demetrius of Phalerum) who made an insertion about letters (Demetrius 223–235)[2] in a handbook on style entitled *De elocutione* (Gk. *Peri Hermeneias*, Eng. *About Style*). The exact date of the treatise is in dispute (with suggestions ranging from the third century BCE to the first century CE), but the treatise or its sources appear to go back to the second century, and at the latest to the first century BCE. According to Demetrius the absent writer uses the letter to make a fictitious speech. He says that Artemon, the editor of Aristotle's *Letters*,

---

[1] Koskenniemi 1956: 38-42; Thraede 1970: 97-99.
[2] Text with translation in Malherbe 1977: 19-23; Demetrius, *On Style* (ed. and trans. W.R. Roberts; LCL; Cambridge, MA: Harvard University Press, rev. edn, 1932).

indicated that 'a letter ought to be written in the same manner as a dialogue, a letter being regarded by him as one of the two sides of a dialogue' (Demetrius 223). Demetrius disagrees with this position. Because of its fictionality the letter is not merely the second half of an oral rhetorical dialogue, but rather it already belongs to the realm of independent written literature: 'There is perhaps some truth in what he says, but not the whole truth. The letter should be a little more studied than the dialogue, since the latter reproduces an extemporary utterance, while the former is committed to writing and is (in a way) sent as a gift' (Demetrius 224).

Cicero defines the letter similarly:

> I have no doubt my daily letter must bore you, especially as I have no fresh news, nor can I find any excuse for a letter. If I should employ special messengers to convey my chatter to you without reason, I should be a fool but I cannot refrain from entrusting letters to folk who are bound for Rome, especially when they are members of my household. Believe me, too, when I seem to talk with you, I have some little relief from sorrow, and, when, I read a letter from you, far greater relief. (Cicero, *Att* 8.14.1)

He varies his reflection about the autonomy of the writing-act:

> I have nothing to write. There is no news that I have heard, and all your letters I answered yesterday. But as a sick heart not only robs me of sleep, but will not allow me even to keep awake without the greatest pain, I have begun to write to you something or other without a definite subject, that I may have a sort of talk with you the only thing that gives me relief. (Cicero, *Att* 9.10.1)

The daily letters of Cicero do not transport 'fresh news' (*nova de re aliqua*), but serve to console and maintain a personal relationship. Because the writer has no 'definite subject' (*nullo argumento proposito*) he composes a literary form of talk (*ut quasi tecum loquor*). Does the letter as fictitious speech underlie the Aristotelian division of speech genres?

Two trends are apparent in the current exegesis of New Testament letters. One trend favours a direct classification of each letter into one of the speech genres of Aristotle;[3] the other prefers to distance the

---

[3] Betz 1988: 69-71.

'letter' genre somewhat from speech genres.[4] The question can be answered adequately only in the context of the whole of the letter literature of antiquity.

As fictitious written literature, letters are fundamentally different from oral speech. Moreover, the Aristotelian division classifies each genre of oral speech depending on its *Sitz im Leben*: trials are *genus iudicale*, council meetings are *genus deliberativum*, ceremonial addresses are *genus laudativum* or *demonstrativum* (Aristotle, *Rhet* 1.3.1 1358ab). But the *Sitz im Leben* of a letter is not precisely one of these clearly sociologically-defined situations, for it is not possible to substitute a letter for the central oral speeches in these situations. No trial, no council meeting, no public honouring can manage without a rhetorically shaped oral speech even today.[5] The fiction of a rhetorical *Sitz im Leben* like a trial creates a specific literary framework for a letter but not a real trial situation.[6]

Letters have an influence on other, more complex situations in writing: they can include legal questions, advice and honouring all at once. One aspect might dominate. But the fictitious form of the letter does not take on the features of an oral speech genre. As with narrative literature, Aristotle's genres only represent a basis upon which the new genre, letter, is constructed.[7] The 'letter' genre often mixes the *genera dicendi* and creates multiple subgenres.[8] That is why Deissmann suggested it would be worthwhile to distinguish between letter and epistle: a letter is private and written to an individual congregation or an individual person, whereas epistles are tractates with fictitious addressees.[9] However, an objection could still be raised to the effect that private writing is also fictitiously shaped, and, depending on the actual situation, can deliberately be designed that way (1 Thess 5:27). By the same token, epistles can have specific congregations as addressees (Eph 1:1-2).[10]

Therefore, with Cicero, it makes more sense to contrast the *literary letter* from other possible genres, for example, from purely *private*

---

[4] Berger 1984: 1326-28; Classen 1991: 7-9.
[5] Eisenhut 1982: 4-6.
[6] *Contra* Betz 1988: 69-70.
[7] Dormeyer 1989: 153.
[8] Deissmann 1923: 160; with research report Strecker 1992: 89-95.
[9] Deissmann 1923: 157-72, 193-208.
[10] Wendland 1912: 344-46; G. Schneider *RAC* 2 (1954): 574-75; Vielhauer 1975: 58-62.

letters or from *official* letters from authorities (the *epistula principum* and the *rescriptum*) or from recommendation-letters.[11] In a remark about the distances between sender and receiver in a letter to Curio, Cicero maintains a distinction between letter-types:

> A letter of this kind you will of course not expect from me; for as regards your own affairs you have your correspondents and messengers at home, while as regards mine there is absolutely no news to tell you. There remain two kinds of letters which have a great charm for me, the one intimate and humorous, the other austere and serious. Which of the two at least beseems me to employ, I do not quite see. Am I to jest with you by letter? On my oath, I don't think there is a citizen in existence who can laugh in these days. Or am I to write something more serious? What is there that can possibly be written by Cicero to Curio, in the serious style, except on public affairs? Ah! but in this regard my case is just this, that I dare not write what I feel, and I am not inclined to write what I don't feel. (Cicero, *Fam* 2.4.1)

Cicero delineates clearly three types of letters: the non-literary purely private letter, the literary letter and the public letter. The recommendation-letter must be added to this list, because recommendation is fundamental for social life.[12] Cicero uses also the recommendation-letter in the *Epistulae ad Familiares*, especially in book 13. Pseudo-Demetrius (so named because his manual *Typoi Epistolikoi* [Eng. *Epistolary Types*] was falsely attributed to Demetrius of Phalerum) proposes a formula for this type of letter:

> The commendatory type, which we write on behalf of one person to another, mixing in praise, at the same time also speaking of those who had previously been unacquainted as though they were (now) acquainted. In the following manner: 'So-and-so, who is conveying this letter to you, has been tested by us and is loved on account of his trustworthiness. You will do well if you deem him worthy of hospitality both for my sake and his, and indeed for your own. For you will not be sorry if you entrust to him, in any matter you wish, either words or deeds of a confidential nature. Indeed, you, too, will praise him to others when you see how useful he can be in everything.' (Ps.-Demetrius 2)

---

[11] Schneider *RAC* 2 (1954): 568-70; Aune 1987: 162-69; Berger 1984: 1326-28; Klauck 1998: 71-148.
[12] Klauck 1998: 75-80.

The many reasons for writing letters brought about the production of various standard manuals advising how to write literary and private letters according to good form. The manual by Pseudo-Demetrius, for example, introduces 21 subgenres.[13] But these subgenres merely offer 21 stylistic patterns for specific themes, and turn out to be only stylistic exercises on individual *topoi*.[14] Therefore, the title of Pseudo-Demetrius's work is τόποι ἐπιστολικοί (Eng. *Epistolary Types*). The last edition must have been in the third century CE. But some formulas go back to the second century BCE.

Pseudo-Demetrius begins with the literary friendship letter (Ps.-Demetrius 1). In antiquity, the *topos* 'cultivated friendship letter' was considered 'the epitome of epistolography'.[15] For the New Testament letters, therefore, the literary friendship letter type that was specifically cultivated by Cicero became dominant (Cicero, *Fam*).[16] Pseudo-Demetrius's definition of friendship letters could be seen as a pattern for the Pauline letters:

> The friendship letter 'type' [*typos*] is one which appears to be written by one friend to another. But they are not only written by friends. Quite often some people expect the powerful to write something friendly to less worthy or similarly ranked people, to generals, to war leaders, to administrators. There are also letters of the friendship type attested between people who did not know each other when they wrote. They did not behave this way because they were close friends or because they only knew how to write one way, but because they believed if they wrote in a friendly way they would not be refused and the addressee would tolerate and do what they wrote. This 'type' of letter is called a friendship letter as though it were written to a friend. Here is an example: 'When I am accidentally separated from you for a long time I only suffer physically. I can never forget you and our growing up together, inseparable as we were. I know that I can really put myself in your shoes, that you have the same opinion of me and that you would refuse me nothing. I know you will try your best to see to it that the lodgers (friends) lack nothing, that you will prepare for them something they have missed out on, and that you will write to us about what you want to do.' (Ps.-Demetrius 1)

---

[13] Malherbe 1977: 3-5.
[14] Malherbe 1977: 8-9.
[15] Koskenniemi 1956: 115-28; Thraede 1970: 3.
[16] Malherbe 1977: 6; Vielhauer 1975: 61-62; Bünker 1984: 47, 152-65; Schoon-Janssen 1991: 39-41; Klauck 1998; cautiously Thraede 1970: 95.

The first main part of 1 Thessalonians is composed unmistakably according to this format: full of friendly memories of the beginning of preaching the gospel together (1 Thess 1:2–3:10).[17] The other early Pauline letters clearly show similar friendly memories of the beginning of the preaching of the gospel, as well as requests for friendly service (1 Cor 1:10–4:21; 2 Cor 1:12–3:3; Gal 1:6-11; 3:1-5; Phil 1:18b–2:4; Phlm 8-20). In Romans, on the other hand, reminiscences on the friendly association through the preaching of their common belief in Christ are rare because Paul did not establish that congregation and had not yet met the congregation personally (Rom 1:8-17). The special friendship could only be established through the preaching of Paul's own gospel (Rom 1:15).

2. LITERARY AND RHETORICAL STRUCTURE

Systematic thought on literature began with Aristotle. It was no longer the poet who explained, like Homer, his understanding of poetry; rather it was the philosopher who put himself on the metalevel of theory over the poet. The philosopher analysed in metalanguage the function and nature of linguistic works of art; he did not stop at poetry, but examined, at the same time, elaborate speech. Aristotle placed 'poetics' next to 'rhetoric'. Plato and Augustine constructed a similar relation between rhetorical language and poetical expression. McKnight characterizes this connection as follows:

> In this poetic stage, subject and object are not clearly separated but are linked by a common power or energy, which may be brought into being by the articulating of words. The stage of language that was operative in the ancient and medieval church began with Plato and continued to the sixteenth century. In this stage words become essentially the outward expression of inner ideas or thoughts.[18]

In his *Poetics*, Aristotle limited himself to the analysis of genres in poetics. Book 1 deals with tragedy (chs. 6–22) and epic poems (chs. 23–26); book 2, which is missing, described comedy.[19] The prose genres like historiography, biography, letters and the other minor forms,

---

[17] Malherbe 1987: 72-74.
[18] McKnight 1988: 36.
[19] Fuhrmann 1973: 4.

all of which constitute the genres that are comparable to the New Testament, are not dealt with under the poetic genres; they are not strictly poetry. Horace, in his *Ars Poetica,* also left them out. The work *On the Sublime* (Pseudo-Longinus) touched on them briefly. Exceptionally, Lucian devoted a whole book, his *How to Write History,* to historiography; but this work was limited to practical suggestions and did not venture to offer a theory of literature.[20]

'Rhetoric', on the other hand, gave points of reference for an artistic shaping of literary prose genres.[21] In the narrow sense, rhetoric is the art (τεχνή, Latin *ars*) of public speaking at legal proceedings, and in the broader sense it is what is taught at school; so antiquity could describe itself as a 'rhetorical culture'.[22]

The Sophists in classical Greek times developed a reflective rhetoric from the rules experienced from public speeches. 'A catalytic effect' came over them, 'something like Latin lessons to the educated these days, where the decisive value equally does not depend on direct applicability'.[23] In the time of Hellenism and the principate, rhetoric spread from the area of speechmaking into all literature.[24] But, just as rhetoric did not directly define speechmaking, but rather organized the skills of speechmaking over a long process of training, literature too was not influenced by rhetoric as by a textbook.[25] It was more a question of literary prose coming closer to the rules of rhetoric, preserving, at the same time, its own characteristics.[26]

Since poetics and rhetoric beginning with Aristotle included different instructions on the individual elements, on *inventio, dispositio* and *elocutio* or in Greek *heuresis, taxis* and *lexis,* the literary forms were not laid down unambiguously. They gave individual instructions and were, simultaneously, analyses on the metalevel.[27] They justified the canon of classical works after the fact, legitimated the prevailing norms of literary taste and led current feuds with literary rivals. So there was a wide range of possible variations inside and outside the textbooks. Barthes rightly warned against 'assuming

---

[20] Hengel 1979: 19-20; Winkelmann *RAC* 15 (1991): 732.
[21] Fuhrmann 1990: 8.
[22] Eisenhut 1982: 93.
[23] Hommel 1970: 128.
[24] Lausberg 1960: par. 32-41; Hommel 1970: 138.
[25] Barthes 1988: 30-32.
[26] Eisenhut 1982: 93-94.
[27] Barthes 1988: 16-17.

one single canonic introduction' and analysing literature schematically according to it.[28]

Rhetoric proves itself to be a practical art through *memoria* and *actio*, 'whereas *inventio, dispositio* and *elocutio* are a poetic preparation for the practical delivery', so Lausberg emphasized with reference to Quintilian:[29]

> (12) For although the orator's task is to speak well, rhetoric is the science of speaking well. Or if we adopt another view, the task of the artist is to persuade, while the power of persuasion resides in the art. Consequently, while it is the duty of the orator to invent and arrange, *invention* and *arrangement* may be regarded as belonging to rhetoric. (13) At this point there has been much disagreement, as to whether these are parts or *duties of* rhetoric, or as Athenaeus believes, *elements* of rhetoric which the Greeks call *stoicheia*. But they cannot correctly be called *elements*. For in that case we should have to regard them merely as first principles, like the moisture, fire, matter or atoms of which the universe is said to be composed. Nor is it correct to call them duties, since they are not performed by others, but perform something themselves. We must therefore conclude that they are parts. (14) For since rhetoric is composed of them, it follows that, since a whole consists of parts, these must be parts of the whole which they compose. Those who have called them *duties* seem to me to have been further influenced by the fact that they wished to reserve the name of parts for another division of rhetoric: for they asserted that the parts of rhetoric were, *panegyric, deliberative* and *forensic* oratory. But if these are parts, they are parts rather of the material than of the art. (15) For each of them contains the whole of rhetoric, since each of them requires *invention, arrangement, expression, memory* and *delivery*. Consequently, some writers have thought it better to say that there are three *kinds* of oratory; those whom Cicero has followed seem to me to have taken the wisest course in terming them *kinds of causes*. (Quintilian, *Inst* 3.3.12-15)

Rhetoric is the science of good speechmaking with the pragmatic function of persuasion, *persuasio*.[30] As poetics emphasizes for the poet that he has with the *inventio* and the *dispositio* to produce the pragmatic function of purifying the passions of the listener with the help of compassion and fear (Aristotle, *Poetics* 6), rhetoric has the analogous function of making the speaker capable of rousing the *persuasio* of the listener with *inventio* and *dispositio*. Therefore

---

[28] Barthes 1988: 50; Eisenhut 1982: 82-84; Classen 1991: 1-34.
[29] Lausberg 1960: par. 34.
[30] Martin 1974: 2-4.

inventio and *dispositio* are parts of rhetoric and not functions (*opera*), which can be added or omitted. Due to the subject matter of the speech, since Cicero and Quintilian three genera of speeches have been differentiated: those of praise, those of advice and those given at legal proceedings. Aristotle's differentiation into epideictic, forensic and deliberative speech remained binding for the whole of antiquity (Aristotle, *Rhet* 1.3.1-3 1358ab).[31] Within these genres the speaker had to shape the *inventio, dispositio* and *lexis*. Through memoria (learning by heart) and *pronuntiatio* (delivery), the preparation of the speech became a practical art. Rhetoric and literature have the same but differently expressed pragmatic function: to edify and persuade the listener.

Therefore the ancient letter has a variable structure determined by literary, rhetorical and communicative rules. Within the rhetoric, *inventio, dispositio* and *lexis* construct a hierarchy with different levels. The inventio disclaims the highest level. The idea and the topoi of the argumentation are collected and sorted. On the second level the *dispositio* elaborates the inventio and develops the arrangement. According to Aristotle (*Rhet* 3.13-19 1414a-1420b) four parts became normative for the judicial speech:

1. *prooímion*, Lat. *exordium*
2. *diégesis*, Lat. *narratio*
3. *pístis*, Lat. *argumentatio*
4. *epílogos*, Lat. *peroratio*[32]

The *exordium* introduces the themes and motifs; the *narratio* tells the special case; the *argumentatio* discusses reasons and develops solutions; the *peroratio* admonishes the hearers to the right judgment.

In the laudatory and deliberate speech, the narration (Part 2) can be omitted (Aristotle, *Rhet* 3.16 1416b-17b).

The letter should have such rhetorical arrangement:

1. Prescript
2. *Exordium*
3. *Narratio* (necessary in the judicial speech)
4. *Argumentatio*
5. *Peroratio*
6. Postscript

---

[31] Martin 1974: 9-10.
[32] Dormeyer 1998: 208-13; Klauck 1998: 174-76.

The address (prescript) and the greetings (postscript) shape a new framework.

Because the letter is a fictional literary dialogue, the speech-genres are not strictly distinguished from each other but mixed. Within the letter they can be altered. Parts of dialogues or original letters can be collected and combined to form new letters. This results in formations of multiple literary types that do not follow classical speech-genres exactly. Pseudo-Demetrius accordingly included twenty-one 'Epistolary Types' in his short theory of letters. Now these letter-types are not imitations of public speeches, but differ from another in respect of literary norms and thematic motifs like friendship.

A rhetorical analysis cannot totally explain the letter-arrangement and needs the literary analysis of special letter-types. Deissmann had compared the letters of the New Testament with private letters.[33] Klauck followed him seeking the basic structure of all kinds of ancient letters.[34] He devised a three step pattern (introduction, body, closing) with usual subdivisions combined with usual motifs:

I. Preface (*Briefeingang*)
   A. Prescript (*Das Briefpräskript*)
      1. *superscriptio* (*Nominativ*)
      2. *adscriptio* (*Dativ*)
      3. *salutatio* (*Infinitiv*)
   B. Prooimion (*Das Briefproömium*)
      - health-wishes (*Wohlergehens*—e.g. *Gesundheitswunsch*)
      - words of thanks (*Danksagung*)
      - memory, prayer (*Gedenken, Fürbitte*)
      - joy (*Freudensäußerung*)
II. Body (*Das Briefkorpus*)
   A. Opening (*Korpuseröffnung*)
      - memory, joy etc. (*Gedenken, Freudensäußerung*)
      - information-formulae; petition-formulae (*Kundgabeformel; Ersuchensformel* etc.)
      - self-recommendation; recommendation (*Selbstempfehlung; Fremdempfehlung*)
   B. Middle
      - Information (*Information*)
      - Commandment, Admonition (*Appell, Anweisung*)
      - Admonition, Recommendation (*Mahnung, Empfehlung*)

---

[33] Deissmann 1923: 119-208.
[34] Klauck 1998: 29-55: he analyzed especially 2–3 John and the Egyptian private papyri-letters.

> - request (variably placed) (*Bitte* [*verschieden plaziert*])
> - diverse clichés (stereotyped ideas) (*diverse Klischees* [*stehende Wendungen*])
>
> C. End
> - possible request, admonition (*evtl. Bitte, Mahnung*)
> - plans of visiting and travelling (*Besucher- und Reisepläne*)
>
> III. Closing
> A. Epilogue (*Epilog*)
> - end-admonitions (*Schlußmahnungen*)
> - reflection of writing-act (*Reflexion auf den Schreibakt*)
> - wish of visiting (*Besuchswunsch*)
>
> B. Postscript (*Postskript*)
> - greetings (*Grüße*)
>   direct (1. Pers.)
>   order of greetings (2. Pers.)
>   transfer of greetings (3. Pers.)
> - wishes: 'Farewell', etc.
> - remark of personal signature (*Eigenständigkeitsvermerk*)
> - Date[35]

Analysis of ancient letters leads to the recognition of common basic rules of writing. Instruction in writing allowed standards to be maintained from Egyptian to Greco-Roman times and culture. The Old Testament participated on this process. The letters of the Old Testament had the basic letter arrangement of the Egyptian private papyri used in Greco-Roman times. In the Greco-Roman culture every educated writer was competent in the system of rhetorical speech and the autonomous system of letter-writing. Analysis should look to both systems and correlate them. Every letter is a construction of its own, combining basic rules of content-organization and rhetorical rules of speech—particulary of personal friendship-speech.

3. RHETORIC AND STYLE OF THE PAULINE LETTERS

Paul strove to attain a sophisticated rhetorical and literary level of Koine, but not the level of artistic prose, since he rejected the philosophical educational goals of the Greek paideia (1 Cor 1:18-31). Hence in 2 Corinthians (10–13), a fighting letter, he contrasts the 'weight and strength' of his letters with what the Corinthians thought was the 'contemptibility of his speech' (2 Cor 10:1, 9-11). One should

---

[35] Klauck 1998: 54.

not, however, take such Socratic self-stylization for granted.[36] Paul's intention was obviously to imbue his letters with the power to convince and to persuade through the use of rhetorical rules, but without taking on the role of a sophist or a philosopher. The rhetorical quality of the letters was not at issue in the quotation from the Corinthians just cited. Since Paul meant his letters to be read aloud at congregational meetings (1 Thess 5:27) he was forced to choose the public literary speech style. Contrary to the opinion of Deissmann, who classified the letters as being in the unliterary language of private papyrus letters,[37] it must be assumed that Paul had a Hellenistic education, consisting of more than the second stage of grammar school, which included the beginning of rhetorical studies.[38] Paul had no quarrel with the formal goals of education in antiquity, but with their contents. So in 2 Peter (3:15-16), quite rightly, a warning is given that people with no formal education (ἀμαθεῖς) might find Pauline letters difficult to understand and might twist the meaning. The reason is that Paul often employed the popular rhetorical modes of imagery, antithesis, diatribe, admonition, applied ethics, apology, self-recommendation, reproach and textual proof in his letters.[39]

Paul knew very well the rules of rhetorical speech, but like Cicero and the rhetorical handbooks he was interested in creating a personal friendly tone of friendship with his communities. A new form should develop the new Christian message. Therefore Paul accepted that some letters (1 Corinthians, 2 Corinthians, Romans) became longer than usual. The special situation of the community could need new complexity of content and rhetorical form.

4. THE FORM OF THE PAULINE LETTERS

Like the other letters of antiquity, the New Testament letters not only go beyond Aristotelian speech divisions and mix them as the other letters of antiquity also do, but they also do not strictly adhere to the standards of literary letters of antiquity. Since Pseudo-Demetrius allowed various types of literary letters (Group 1), the New Testament

---

[36] Betz 1972: 57-69.
[37] Deissmann 1923: 198-205.
[38] Becker 1989: 53-55; *contra* Dihle 1989: 219: a lack of rhetorical and philosophical education.
[39] Berger 1984: 1340-63.

letter writer saw no fundamental problem in creating new types by mixing the main types of literary letter and setting his own specific focuses. Thus it is again typical Christian style to lay out a literary letter according to the rules of literary Koine and artistic prose, and combine it with the stereotypical parts of a private letter, which would be laid out according to the rules of oral Koine. The content-arrangement of private letters influenced the new Christian writing. An original type was now created by the Christian writers: the Christian literary letter.[40] Pure private letters (Group 2) still are absent.

'Official correspondence' from the government, the third group of letters in antiquity, is also not present in the corpus of letters in the New Testament, because Paul and the other pseudepigraphical writers did not consider themselves to be hierarchically superior administrators. However, it is true that the letter containing the decisions made at the Council of Jerusalem (Acts 15:23-29), which is embedded in the New Testament history book Acts, does have the characteristics of an official edict: an *epistula principum*.[41]

The recommendation-letter, the fourth group of letters in antiquity, has an equivalent in Philemon. But the letter to Philemon contains more than recommendation. Philemon was adressed to a house-community. The letter was dealing with the fundamental problem of slavery. How should the Christian community handle this unjust differentiation within the Greco-Roman society? Recommendation became the outer form of this smallest Pauline letter. In the other Pauline letters, recommendation remains an important motif.

In the meantime, examinations of the rhetorical structure of most New Testament letters have become available. The genuine Pauline letters, the proto-Paulines, have been examined with special thoroughness. They all belong to the new Christian genre of literary letters that contain parts of oral speech like *pistis* formulae, homologies, prayers, songs, paraenesis patterns, dialogues, especially diatribes, and lists of woes.[42] Even the unusually long thanksgiving in the *exordium* owes its existence to oral Christian prayer language.[43] Specific terms and

---

[40] Wendland 1912: 344ff.; Vielhauer 1975: 62-63; Hübner 1992: 175-77; *contra* Dihle 1989: 217: non-literary continuation of sermon and spiritual welfare.
[41] Aune 1987: 128, 164-65.
[42] Strecker 1992: 82-84; Schnelle 1999: 48-58.
[43] Vielhauer 1975: 65-66.

metaphors from the Christian community characterize the *narratio*, *argumentatio* and *exhortatio*.[44]

The Proto-Paulines

According to the scholarly consensus Paul himself wrote at least seven letters: 1 Thessalonions, 1–2 Corinthians, Philippians, Galatians, Philemon and Romans.

The oldest letter is 1 Thessalonians (ca. 50 CE). Stylistically it is an advisory, deliberative friendship letter.[45] It deviates from the friendship letters of antiquity in that it has a long parenthetical concluding section (4:1–5:22).

The typical Pauline letter form is developed in this first letter:

Prescript	1:1
Exordium	1:2-10
(*Propositio*)	(1:8-10)
Argumentatio	2:1–3:13
Exhortatio	4:1–5:22
Postscript with *salutatio*	5:23-28

The prescript contains the usual three elements: the name of the sender (*superscriptio*), the name of the addressee (*adscriptio*) and the greeting (*salutatio*): 'Paul, Silvanus and Timothy to the congregation in Thessalonica in God the father and the Lord Jesus Christ, grace and peace to you!' (1 Thess 1:1). Deviating from the single element basic sentence of Western antiquity, which consisted of the sender (subject), greeting (verb), and addressee (object), here we find the two-element basic-sentence letter introduction of Eastern antiquity. The salutation is no longer linked to the greeting; it follows the separate double greeting corresponding to the usual Jewish double wish 'Greetings and good health' (2 Macc 1:10).[46] With the exception of the untypical letter of James and the two letters in Acts (Acts 15:23; 23:26), all the New Testament letters stick to the oriental form of greeting.[47]

Differing and contradictory suggestions for the subdivision of the main part 1:1–3:13 have been tendered: 1:1-5 *exordium* and 1:6–3:13

---

[44] Kitzberger 1986: 304-305.
[45] Schoon-Janssen 1991: 45ff.
[46] Vielhauer 1975: 65.
[47] Schnider and Stenger 1987: 3-5.

narratio;⁴⁸ 1:2–3:13 'Predominant Expressive Function',⁴⁹ that is, a long 'thanksgiving'.⁵⁰

Hughes refines this arrangement: *exordium* 1:1-10; *narratio* 2:1–3:10; *partitio* 3:11-13; *probatio* 4:1–5:5; *peroratio* 5:4-11; *exhortatio* 5:12-22; *conclusio* 5:23-28.⁵¹ Jewett and Hughes are interested to determine one part as narration. But the *narratio*, which usually follows the *exordium* and the *propositio*, does not always exist as a separate section. According to Aristotle the narrative is a necessary part of the judicial speech (Aristotle, *Rhet* 3.13 1414a). In the laudatory and deliberate speech the narration can be disconnected or selective or totally absent (Aristotle, *Rhet* 3.16 1416b-17b).

Olbricht considers Aristotle's approval of the shortening of the narration in his arrangement: prescript 1:1; *exordium* 1:2-3; *narratio* 1:4-10; *argumentatio* 2:1–5:11; epilogue 5:12-25; postscript 5:25-28.⁵² But the *argumentatio* must be subdivided in *argumentatio* and *exhortatio*. According to the majority view the postscript starts with 1 Thess 5:23. The preceeding epilogue (1 Thess 5:12-25) is a superfluous doubling of the postscript. The short narration has been set in the wrong place. Content-analysis clarifies that the *exordium* is not limited to the small section 1 Thess 1:2-3, but includes the motifs 'apostolic team-work in Thessalonica', 'imitation' as reaction of the community, 'setting an example' for other believers in other regions, 'reputation', 'passing over with supplement', 'memory of conversion', 'faith formula' (1 Thess 1:4-10).⁵³ This section belongs to the *exordium* and does not constitute a narration. The *exordium* has the function of indicating the main motifs of the speech or the letter or other literary works. Today this sort of function can be experienced effectively in overtures of operas, because the old operas are styled according to the ancient rhetoric. The overtures cite briefly the main motifs of the opera.

The motif of the dynamic preaching of the gospel (1 Thess 1:5) dominates the section 1 Thess 2:1–3:13. The mention of the imitation of Paul and the example-function of the community (1 Thess 1:6-7) prepares the anti-Jewish polemic of 1 Thess 2:13-16. Therefore this

---

[48] Jewett 1986: 72-74.
[49] Johanson 1987: 67-79.
[50] Strecker 1992: 78.
[51] Hughes 1990.
[52] Olbricht 1990.
[53] Klauck 1998: 271-72.

polemic should not be cut out as a deutero-Pauline addition. The notice of reputation and memory of conversion (1 Thess 1:2-3, 8-9a) point forward to the discussion in 1 Thess 3:1-5 of the consolation Paul experienced during and after his crisis in Athens. The faith formula (1 Thess 1:9b-10) focuses the apocalyptic theme that is explained in 1 Thess 4:13-18 and 5:1-11.

The direct transition from the orientalized prescript and *exordium* through prayer and memories to the *argumentatio* in 1 Thessalonians again corresponds to the usual letter form of antiquity. On the other hand, appending an *exhortatio* is uncommon. This is a typically Christian sort of addition. *Exhortationes* are usually dealt with in the *argumentatio*. Wuellner, therefore, sees in this first letter of Paul a time when *exhortatio* and *argumentatio* were still a single unit, but the later division of the unit into two was already emerging.[54] The division in the case of 1 Thessalonians into a main part and an *exhortatio* is generally accepted.

Paul does not stick strictly to the pattern of speech divisions of antiquity. According to the content-analysis, differing divisions of the first main part with the central theme of preaching the gospel are possible: prescript 1:1; *prooimion* 1:2-10; body 2:1–5:22 (opening 2:1-12; middle I 2:13–3:13; middle II 4:1–5:11; end 5:12-22); closing 5:23-28.[55] This content-division corresponds exactly to the proposal above following rhetorical rules. Rhetoric explains the outline of the letter and guides the reader-expectation. Content-analysis comments on the special arrangement of the motifs. Paul calls to memory the dynamic beginning of the gospel (1 Thess 1:2-10). He was its preacher and he remained its apostolic interpreter. So the main part is going to be about the relationship between Paul and his community. The opening brings the self-recommendation; middle I, the visitation-wishes and messenger-sending; middle II, the admonitions and advices for the daily life before the apocalypse; and the end, the admonitions concerning the present problems.

With the addition of the *exhortatio* as the second main part Paul became the creator of the new Christian letter form in which the *argumentatio* is followed by the Christian *paraenesis* in the form of an *exhortatio*.

---

[54] Wuellner 1990: 130-32.
[55] Klauck 1998: 267-82.

2 Thessalonians, which is deutero-Pauline, follows the rhetorical structure of 1 Thessalonians:[56]

Prescript	1:1-2
Exordium	1:3-12
Propositio	2:1-2
Probatio	2:3–3:5
Exhortatio	3:6-13
Postscript with Epilogue	3:14-18[57]

Instead of *propositio* Klauck substitutes *partitio*. But the *partitio* explains the *propositio* and does not replaces it.[58] Klauck took over Jewett's rhetorical outline: *exordium* with prescript: 1:1-12; *partitio* (?): 2:1-2; *probatio* 2:3–3:5; *exhortatio* 3:6-15; *peroratio* 3:16-18,[59] but he correctly criticizes the extension of the *exhortatio* to 3:14-15 and the setting of the *peroratio* 3:16-18 instead of the postscript with epilogue 3:14-18.[60]

The fact that 2 Thessalonians parallels the rhetorical arrangement of 1 Thessalonians should illuminate the readers. The letter wants to be recognized as authentic Pauline Scripture. The sections *propositio* (2 Thess 2:1-2) and postscript with epilogue (2 Thess 3:14-18) emphazise the personal writing-act of Paul. The writer supplements the apocalyptic theme and the exhortations. In contrast to the positive memory of 1 Thessalonians, the second letter exaggaretes warnings and dangers. The fact that Christians in the late first century were no longer as expectant of the end of the world determines the atmosphere.

1 and 2 Corinthians do not stick exactly to this new form. They are unique, extensive compositions. It can be shown, however, that 2 Corinthians is a composite of many letters originally written by Paul where each individual letter does correspond to the original Pauline pattern:[61]

1. 2 Cor 10–13 is 'the sorrowful letter' about conflicts with the congregation about apostolic authority
2. 2 Cor 1:1–6:14; 7:2-16 is a 'letter of reconciliation'

---

[56] Trilling 1980: 23-25; Hughes 1989: 80-82.
[57] Cf. Klauck 1998: 297-98.
[58] Lausberg 1984: 25.
[59] Jewett 1986: 82-85.
[60] Klauck 1998: 297-98.
[61] Lang 1986: 13-15.

3. 2 Cor 8 is a 'collection' letter
4. 2 Cor 9 is another 'collection' letter
5. 2 Cor 6:14–7:1 is a post-Pauline addition

The 'sorrowful letter' (chs. 10–13) is written in the tradition of a Socratic, ironic, judicial apology.[62] It imagines a court situation and employs the judicial style, but without giving up the deliberative 'friendship' relationship with the Corinthians. It is a deliberative letter spiced up with judicial language. The letter of reconciliation that came later (1:1–6:14; 7:2-16) is in the deliberative style of the friendship letter all the way through. The two short letters (chs. 8 and 9) asking for money (the 'collection' letters) are also written in the deliberative style and are attached to the letter of reconciliation by Paul himself.

The post-Pauline collector or Paul himself put the 'sorrowful letter' at the end in order to give the most weight to the apology in the newly created composition. However, with the redefinition of the emphasis he concealed the historical sequence of Paul's correspondence with the Corinthians.[63] The rhetorical outline of the unit formed by the letter of reconciliation and the letter of sorrow are difficult to determine. The content-analysis is more accessible:

Prescript	1:1-2
Prooimion	1:3-11
Body I	1:12–9:15
Body II	10:1–13:10
Closing	13:11-13[64]

The rhetorical arrangement corresponds:

Prescript	1:1-2
Exordium	1:3-11
Narratio	1:12–2:13
Propositio	2:14-17
Partitio	3:1-3
Probatio I	3:4–6:13; 7:2-16

---

[62] Betz 1972: 13-14.

[63] Klauck considers that parts of the older letter of tears (2 Cor 2:4) could be reserved in the sorrowful letter 2 Cor 10–13 so as to be immediately put together with the letter of reconciliation by Paul himself (Schnelle 1999: 104); but Klauck seems to prefer the mainstream-solution of a deutero-Pauline redaction of both letters (Klauck 1998: 234-35).

[64] Klauck 1998: 234-35; on the rhetorical outline, cf. Bieringer 1994: 121-28.

Exhortatio	8:1–9:15
Probatio II	10:1–13:10
Postscript with Epilogue	13:11-13

Two self-apologies dominate the *probationes*. The narration (2 Cor 1:12–2:13) shows the case which demands the self-apology. The *propositio* is so openly formulated, that not only the letter of reconciliation but also the sorrowful letter can be subordinated.

Christ's triumph and Paul's fragrance from death to death and from life to life (2 Cor 2:14-16) comprise the apologies of both letters. The *partitio* (2 Cor 3:1-3) explains the theme of recommendation in the acts of writing, preaching and christological faith.

The introduction of the letter of reconciliation (2 Cor 1:1–3:3) allows the supplement of analogous letters. But the collector had difficulty in finding an appropriate ending. The postscript 2 Cor 13:11-13 remains a fragment. Greetings ('finally, brethren, farewell') introduce final admonitions and instructions (v. 11) and constitute a short epilogue. Then begins the postscript with a second series of greetings: admonition to greet each other and transmission of greetings from all the saints of the fictitious community in which Paul is writing (v. 12). The phrase 'Greet one another with a holy kiss' is repeated from the postscript in 1 Corinthians (16:20). The last wish is overloaded with three members.[65] Remarks of personal signature or direct greetings are omitted. The postscript does not really summarize the letter. The epilogue is a dry standard-formula.

1 Corinthians also consists of many letter sections on current questions in the congregations, but these were deliberately put together into a large composition by Paul himself.[66] It exceeds the usual bounds of a literary letter of antiquity, but the repetitive letter structure of the individual sections corresponds to letter collections of antiquity.[67] Paul chooses the unusual composite form again for the last letter to the Romans. He deliberately goes against literary conventions and thereby transmits to the later collectors an example of how to edit together a collection of his own originally separate letters.

The content-analysis of Paul's redaction in 1 Corinthians results in the following scheme:

---

[65] Bultmann 1995: 253.
[66] Lang 1986: 6-7.
[67] Probst 1991: 369.

Prescript	1:1-3
Prooimion	1:4-9
Body	1:10–16:12
Closing	16:13-24[68]

The rhetorical outline corresponds:

Prescript	1:1-3
Exordium	1:4-9
Propositio	1:10
Narratio	1:11-17
Argumentatio	1:8–15:58
Exhortatio	16:1-18
Postscript	16:19-24[69]

The *exordium* collects the main motifs of this letter: grace, speech, spiritual gifts (1 Cor 12–14), knowledge (1 Cor 1:18–4:21), testimony (1 Cor 5–11), waiting for the day of Christ (1 Cor 15). The *propositio* leads to the narration and anew to the speaking of spiritual gifts (1 Cor 12–14). *Propositio* and *narratio* introduce the whole argumentation.

The *argumentatio* can be divided into several units with rhetorical speech-structure: 1:1–4:21; 5:1-13; 6:1-20; 7:1-40; 8:1–11:1; 11:2-34; 12:1–14:40; 15:1-58. These parts are rhetorically-formed answers to questions of the community and constitute a long catalogue of answers.[70]

The *exhortatio* summarizes the letter and creates a real end. Unity or agreement and concern for leaders (1 Cor 16:13-19) is the counterpart of splits (σχίσματα 1 Cor 1:10). The travel plans (1 Cor 16:5-12) go back to the narration in 1 Cor 1:11-17 and renew the friendship between Paul and the Corinthians. The postscript is very concrete and personal (1 Cor 16:19-24). The master gave the letter-collection the final polish.

---

[68] Klauck 1998: 232.

[69] Cf. Mitchell 1991: 192-290; the last parts, 1 Cor 16:1-24, are combined and named 'Epistolary Closing' (Mitchell 1991: 291-96). Mitchell leaves rhetorical analysis of the end as unnecessary.

[70] Probst 1991: 295-359; Bünker for 1 Cor 1:1–4:21; 15:1-58 (Bünker 1984: 51-73); the hypothesis of autonomy of several letters A (lost), B and more is problematic and superfluous (*contra* Bünker 1984: 52; Probst 1991: 361-68).

The letter to the Philippians is, like 1–2 Corinthians, a composition, but has the length of a usual ancient letter. For this reason the unity is controversial. Two parts can be distinguished:

1:1–3:1a; 4:2-7, 10-23 letter from prison
3:1b–4:1, 8-9 letter warning about false teachers.[71]

This letter from prison with its intense Christian mysticism has the typical structure of a deliberative-friendship letter:[72]

Prescript	1:1-2
Exordium	1:3-11
Narratio	1:12-18a
Argumentatio	1:18b–2:11
Exhortatio	2:12-30
Postscript	3:1a; 4:2-7, 10-23

Even the autobiographical-narrative and argumentative-warning letter has the structure of a deliberative-friendship letter:[73]

Exordium	3:2-3
Narratio	3:4-11
Argumentatio	3:12-21
Exhortatio	4:1-3, 8-9

Because the collector embedded the warning-letter into the friendship letter, a genuine rhetorical and literary unity was reestablished:

Prescript	1:1-2
Exordium	1:3-11
Narratio	1:12-18a
Probatio	1:18b–3:21
Peroratio	4:1-20
Postscript	4:21-23[74]

---

[71] Gnilka 1968: 10-11; *contra* Schenk 1984: 334-36 and Aune 1987: 210: 4:10-23 is a personal thank-you letter.
[72] Similar to Schenk 1984: 29-248.
[73] Dormeyer 1989: 152-53; Schenk differs in 1984: 277-80: judicial apology.
[74] Klauck 1998: 240-41; cf. Strecker 1992: 65; similar Bloomquist 1993: 118-38: 1:3-11 *exordium*; 1:12-14 *narratio*; 1:15-18a *partitio*; 1:18b–4:7

Watson first claimed the rhetorical unity of Philippians; but he made the *exordium* too long (Phil 1:3-26); he divides it rightly into two parts: 'thanksgiving and prayer (vv. 3-11) and personal narrative (vv. 12-26)'.[75] But the narrative must end with v. 18a and must be separated from the *exordium*, for vv. 18b-26 belong to the *probatio*. Watson however has the *probatio* begin with 2:1 and conclude with 3:21. For Watson, the brief passage 1:27-37 constitutes the narrative.[76] This construction is not convincing. But the proposal of Watson established the basis of the rhetorical reconstruction of the outline of Philippians without the late double narration: prescript 1:1-2; *exordium* I 1:3-11; *exordium* II (*narratio*) 1:12-26; *probatio* 2:1–3:21; *peroratio* 4:1-20; postscript 4:21-23.

The *exordium* emphasizes the motifs of friendship: memory, prayer, partnership in the gospel, completion of the good work, holding others in the heart, partaking of grace in imprisonment and defense, a bonding of love, knowledge and discernment, approval of the excellent things and righteousness (Phil 1:3-11). Hints about struggle with opponents are hidden, but can be recognized. Friendship and faith are always threatened by imprisonment, accusations, trials and possible splits. The *narratio* explains the relationship between imprisonment and splits within the community. Preparation is made for the warning-section Phil 3:2–4:3. The admonitions in Phil 2:12-30 lose their independence as *exhortatio*. Now they must be read as part of the long *probatio*. The rhetorical rules and the literary content allow the permanent alternating between argumentation and admonition. The *probatio* gets two climaxes: first the christological hymn in Phil 2:5-11, second the struggle with the opponents in Phil 3:2-21. The *peroratio* now formes a meaningful unity: Phil 4:1-20. For the division-hypothesis this segment was very unclear and controversial. Indeed Paul shaped a rhetorical and literary coherence by putting together two different parts. Probably the warning-letter was historically the first with the prison-letter following.

The letter to Philemon is the shortest independent letter of Paul. It shows even more clearly than the other short letters in 2 Corinthians the rhetorical elegance of a short literary letter that was written for

---

argumentatio; 4:8-20 *peroratio*; 4:21-23 postscript; but the *peroratio* should begin with 4:1.

[75] Watson 1988: 61.
[76] Watson 1988: 65-67.

publication, as Philemon functioned as leader of a house church (Phlm 1-2):

Prescript	vv. 1-3
Exordium	vv. 4-7
Argumentatio	vv. 8-16
Peroratio (Exhortatio)	vv. 17-22
Postscript	vv. 23-25[77]

Paul discusses the case of the runaway Onesimus, who is looking for protection, in a friendship-deliberative request letter to his master, as was usual in such cases in antiquity.

Pliny wrote a letter about the conflict of a freedman with his master Sabinianus. The freedman had fled to Pliny and obtained his recommendation to Sabinianus.

1 To Sabinianus.
2 Your freedman, whom you lately mentioned as
3 having displeased you, has been with me; he threw
4 himself at my feet and clung there with as much
5 submission as he could have done at yours. He
6 earnestly requested me with many tears, and even
7 with the eloquence of silent sorrow, to intercede for
8 him; in short, he convinced me by his whole be-
9 haviour, that he sincerely repents of his fault. And
10 I am persuaded he is thoroughly reformed, because
11 he seems entirely sensible of his delinquency.
12 I know you are angry with him, and I know too, it
13 is not without reason; but clemency can never exert
14 itself with more applause, than when there is the
15 justest cause for resentment.
16 You once had an
17 affection for this man, and, I hope, will have again:
18 in the meanwhile, let me only prevail with you to
19 pardon him. If he should incur your displeasure
20 hereafter, you will have so much the stronger plea
21 in excuse for your anger, as you shew yourself more
22 exorable to him now. Allow something to his youth,
23 to his tears, and to your own natural mildness of
24 temper: do not make him uneasy any longer, and I
25 will add too, do not make yourself so; for a man of

---

[77] Gnilka 1982: 7-10; Aune 1987: 206-208; Wolter 1993: 236-37; but Wolter's addition of v. 22 to the epilogue is not convincing.

26 your benevolence of heart cannot be angry without
27 feeling great uneasiness.
28 I am afraid, were I to join my entreaties with his,
29 I should seem rather to compel, than request you to
30 forgive him. Yet I will not scruple to do it; and so
31 much the more fully and freely as I have very
32 sharply and severely reproved him, positively threat-
33 ening never to interpose again in his behalf. But
34 though it was proper to say this to him, in order to
35 make him more fearful of offending, I do not say it
36 to you. I may, perhaps, again have occasion to
37 intreat you upon his account, and again obtain your
38 forgiveness; supposing, I mean, his error should be
39 such as may become me to intercede for, and you to
40 pardon.
41 Farewell. (Pliny, *Ep* 9.21)

The letter shows a similar rhetorical outline and content like Philemon:

Prescript	Line 1
Exordium	Line 2-11
Propositio	Line 12-15
Argumentatio with *Exhortatio*	Line 16-40
Postscript	Line 41

The *exordium* tells the plea for help and the impressions of Pliny. The *propositio* respects the feelings of Sabinianus and introduces the norm (clemency) which rules the *argumentatio*: *sed tunc praecipua mansuetudinis laus, cum irae causa iustissima est*. The *argumentatio* is always alternating between affirmations, admonitions and self-reflections. The relations within the triangle writer—adressee—freedman are discussed in a very personal and humorous way, as in Philemon.

More rigorously than Pliny, Paul appeals to the Christian house-church leader Philemon to forgive the slave and to give him to Paul as his assistant. The apostle leaves the decision with Philemon as to whether Onesimus should serve him with the legal status of a house-slave or of a freedman; but Paul hints that he would prefer Onesismus to be freed (vv. 13-20).[78]

---

[78] Dormeyer 1983: 223-24.

The case of the fugitive slave demands the recommendation-motif. The letter picks up elements of the recommendation-letter type (*argumentatio* Phlm 8-17). Paul also uses the self-recommendation in his other letters (2 Cor 3:1-3 etc.). With the position of apostle and community-founder Paul needs regular self-recommendation as friend and authority. Therefore all Pauline letters carry a touch of recommendation, but especially the letter to Philemon.

Galatians is a unity in which the form of the deliberative letter has been perfected.[79] According to Betz this letter shows most clearly the structure of a Pauline letter that has been orientated to the pattern of a letter in antiquity:[80]

Prescript	1:1-5
Exordium	1:6-11
Narratio	1:12–2:14
Propositio	2:15-21
Probatio (Argumentatio)	3:1–4:31
Exhortatio	5:1–6:10
Postscript	6:11-18

The *argumentatio* is in the style of a diatribe and discusses the repealing of the Old Testament laws. The *narratio,* in contrast to the narratives in other Pauline letters, contains the most detailed autobiographical section. Paul puts himself forward as an example of the accurate liberal understanding of the law.

Romans, Paul's last letter, leaves behind the friendship-deliberative letter genre. For the development of the gospel he orientates himself more strongly towards laudatory admonitory speech, but he also retains some deliberative elements, especially in the closing *exhortatio* (12:1–15:13).[81] The structure of the laudatory letter corresponds to the usual Pauline letter pattern:[82]

Prescript	1:1-7
Exordium	1:8-17
Argumentatio	1:18–11:36

---

[79] Hübner 1984: 249-50; Aune 1987: 206-208; *contra* Betz 1988: 55-72; Berger 1984: 128-30: judicial apology.

[80] Betz 1975; 1988: 57-68; Betz first introduced rhetorical analysis for the letters of the New Testament and proposed a convincing structure for Galatians.

[81] Wuellner 1976: 34-36; Aune 1987: 219; Botha 1991: 142-43.

[82] Zeller 1985: 8-9; Aune 1987: 219; Hübner 1992: 169.

Exhortatio	12:1–15:13
Postscript	15:14–16:23

Even more clearly than in Gal 3:1–4:31 the diatribe shapes the extended *argumentatio* section which is on the subject of courts and justice (1:18–11:36).[83] The prescript is also unusually long because Paul has to recommend himself to the Christians in Rome, whom he did not know personally.

Doubtless without intending it, in Romans Paul composed his theological legacy, since his plan to preach the gospel in Spain after his first visit to Rome (Rom 15:24) fell through due to his arrest in Jerusalem (Acts 21:27-40). He finally arrived in Rome as a prisoner (Acts 28:16-31) and suffered the death of a martyr there (Acts 20:23-25; *1 Clem* 5.2).

Deutero-Paulines

The deutero-Pauline letters to the Colossians and to the Ephesians exhibit the typical Pauline structure of a deliberative-friendship letter with an added *exhortatio*.

The authorship of Colossians is controversial. Consensus exists that this letter was written very late by Paul himself[84] or by his secretary[85] or by the Pauline school as early as 70 CE.[86]

In imitation of Galatians, the rhetorical structure shines clear with the specific Christian appendix of *exhortatio*:

Prescript	1:1-2
Exordium	1:3-23
(Propositio)	(1:21-23)
Narratio	1:24–2:5
Argumentatio	2:6-23
Exhortatio	3:1–4:6
Postscript	4:7-18[87]

The letter to the Ephesians depends upon Colossians. It varies the rhetorical outline by omitting the *argumentatio*:

---

[83] Bultmann 1984: 103.
[84] Kümmel 1973: 305-306, who cites the relevant literature.
[85] Timothy Col 1:1; Schweizer 1976: 20-28.
[86] Schenk 1987: 3335; Hoppe 1994: 1-4.
[87] Wolter 1993: 47-49, 98-99, 114-16, 214.

Prescript	1:1-2
Exordium	1:3-23
Narratio	2:1–3:21
Exhortatio	4:1–6:20
Postscript	6:21-24[88]

The deutero-Pauline pastoral letters go new ways with the letter genre. The rhetorical outline of 1 Timothy follows the Pauline scheme but departs from the type of friendship-letter:

Prescript	1:1-2
Exordium	1:3-20
Argumentatio	2:1–6:2
Exhortatio	6:3-19
Postscript	6:20-21[89]

The narration is omitted, and the *probatio* is a collection of instructions. Arrangement and style indicate the type 'official letter'. The *rescripta* of emperor Trajan to Pliny show this official style very well, for example the well-known answer to Pliny's question about the judicial intercourse with Christians (Pliny, *Ep* 10.96-97).[90]

2 Timothy goes back to the friendship-letter:

Prescript	1:1-2
Exordium	1:3-5
Argumentatio	1:6–3:17
Exhortatio	4:1-8
Postscript	4:9-22[91]

The long postscript expresses the tone of the last will. 2 Timothy should close the small collection of the three 'pastoral letters'.[92]

Titus develops a third form of pastoral letter:

---

[88] Gnilka 1971: 29-31; Gnilka emphasized that the typical Pauline distinction between teaching and admonition is preserved (Gnilka 1971: 29-30); Klauck describes the postscript as *peroratio* (Klauck 1998: 238-39).
[89] Roloff 1988: 48-50.
[90] Klauck 1998: 244 with a parallel content-structure.
[91] Klauck organizes similarly according to content-analysis: prescript 1:1-2; *prooimion* 1:3-5; mainpart 1:6–4:8; end 4:9-22 (Klauck 1998: 245-46).
[92] Oberlinner 1995: 1-5.

Prescript	1:1-4
Propositio	1:5
Argumentatio	1:6–3:7
Exhortatio	3:8-11
Postscript	3:12-15[93]

Narration is missed as in the other pastoral letters. The *exhortatio* is short as in those letters. But the omitting of the *exordium* indicates a failure. Maybe the contrast of long prescript and abrupt jump into the *propositio* of the argumentation makes the whole letter become an introduction to the small pastoral collection.[94]

All deutero-Pauline letters conserved the specific Pauline sequence from teaching to admonition. They varied the rhetorical and content arrangement. Like some proto-Pauline letters, they established singular forms. 2 Thessalonians imitated 1 Thessalonians, the first Christian and thoroughly classical friendship-letter. Colossians with the dependent Ephesians imitated 1 Thessalonians, Galatians and Philemon in a free way. Two pastoral letters introduced the official letter type and created singular forms adapted to the fictitious communication. The Pauline and deutero-Pauline letters played upon the expectations of their audience. In respect of the real and fictitious situations of communication they established singular forms. The literary and theological shaping of the vivid friendly relationship led to a rich reservoir of creative letters.

The anonymous letter to the Hebrews has a special role. It is an epideictic and deliberative sermon in letter form.[95] The author shows most clearly the knowledge of Greco-Roman rhetoric. The outline observes the rules of written speech:

Exordium	1:1-4
Narratio	1:5–2:18
(*Propositio*)	2:17-18
Argumentatio	3:1–10:18
Peroratio	10:19–13:21
Postscript	13:22-25[96]

---

[93] Cf. the theme-analysis of Brox 1969: 14-15.
[94] Klauck 1998: 246.
[95] Aune 1987: 212-13.
[96] Klauck 1998: 252-54; but according to Klauck the distinction between *narratio* and *argumentatio* is not exact; therefore the *narratio* varies between 2:18 and 4:13 with *argumentatio* 4:14–10:18.

Admonitions are regularly inserted, giving the speech deliberative moments; in the last part these admonitions dominate and create the *peroratio*. The written sermon therefore is made of deliberative parts as well as epideictic parts. The closing is an appendix converting the written sermon into a letter. The writing already had a Pauline colouring,[97] and this explains the addition of the Pauline-type greeting. This greeting makes the completed work fit for the Pauline-letter formula and strengthens the Pauline style. The Pauline letter-scheme can also be recognized from the view of the end (Heb 10:19–13:25). The prescript is omitted, but *narratio, argumentatio, peroratio* and postscript are included.

In contrast to the proto- and deutero-Pauline letters, the seven so-called catholic letters use various genres. The pseudepigraphical letters of 1 and 2 John are literary deliberative letters written to specific people and congregations. They do not use the rhetorical outline.[98] The pseudepigraphical 1 John and 1 Peter are again deliberative paraenetic sermons.[99] More clearly than in the case of 1 John, 1 Peter takes up the traditions of congregational worship. And moreover it retains the Pauline form of a Christian letter through the division into two parts of the *argumentatio* and *exhoratio*, and through the addition of a postscript and the inclusion of a prescript, whereas 1 John merely has a short paraenetic ending.[100] The pseudepigraphical 2 Peter and the letter of Jude, upon which 2 Peter depends, once more exhibit the Pauline letter form.

In the taking up of the oral apostolic traditions with their forms, themes and innovations and in the shaping of the letter forms of antiquity for his own purposes, Paul and the pseudepigraphical authors after him managed to develop their own theology, which became fundamental to nascent Christianity.

---

[97] Backhaus 1993.
[98] Klauck 1998: 41-55.
[99] Klauck 1991: 74ff.
[100] Strecker 1992: 67-71.

WORKS CITED

Aune, D.E.
1987 *The New Testament in its Literary Environment* (LEC 8; Philadelphia: Westminster Press).

Backhaus, K.
1993 'Der Hebräerbrief und die Paulus-Schule', *BZ* NS 37: 183-208.

Baeck, L.
1961 *Paulus, die Pharisäer und das Neue Testament* (Munich and Frankfurt: Nev Tamid).

Barthes, R.
1988 'Die alte Rhetorik', in R. Barthes, *Das semiologische Abenteuer* (Frankfurt: Suhrkamp): 15-102.

Becker, J.
1989 *Paulus: Der Apostel der Völker* (Tübingen: Mohr Siebeck).

Berger, K.
1984 'Hellenistische Gattungen im Neuen Testament', *ANRW* 2.25.2 (Berlin: W. de Gruyter): 1031-1432.

Betz, H.D.
1972 *Der Apostel Paulus und die sokratische Tradition* (Tübingen: Mohr).
1975 'The Literary Composition and Function of Paul's Letter to the Galatians', *NTS* 21: 353-79.
1985 *2 Corinthians 8 and 9* (Hermeneia; Philadelphia: Fortress Press).
1988 *Der Galaterbrief: Ein Kommentar zum Brief des Apostels Paulus an die Gemeinden in Galatien* (Munich: Kaiser).

Bieringer, R.
1994 'Der zweite Korintherbrief als ursprüngliche Einheit. Ein Forschungsüberblick', in R. Bieringer and J. Lambrecht (eds.), *Studies on 2 Corinthians* (BETL 112; Leuven: Peeters): 107-31.

Bloomquist, L.G.
1993 *The Function of Suffering in Philippians* (JSNTSup 78; Sheffield JSOT Press).

Botha, J.
1991 *Reading Romans 13: Aspects of the Ethics of Interpretation in a Controversial Text* (doctoral dissertation, University of Stellenbosch, South Africa).

Brox, N.
1969 *Die Pastoralbriefe* (RNT 7.2; Regensburg: Pustet, 4th edn).

Bünker, M.
1984 *Briefformular und rhetorische Disposition im 1. Korintherbrief* (Göttingen: Vandenhoeck & Ruprecht).

Bultmann, R.
1995 *Die Geschichte der synoptischen Tradition* (Göttingen: Vandenhoeck & Ruprecht, 10th edn; ET: *The History of the Synoptic Tradition* [Oxford: Basil Blackwell, 1972]).
1984 *Der Stil der paulinischen Predigt und die kynisch-stoische Diatribe* (Göttingen: Vandenhoeck & Ruprecht).

Classen, C.J.
1991 'Paulus und die antike Rhetorik', *ZNW* 82: 1-34.

Deissmann, A.
1923 *Licht vom Osten: Das neue Testament und die neuentdeckten Texte der hellenistisch-römischen Welt* (Tübingen: Mohr, 4th edn).
1925 *Paulus: Eine kultur- und religionsgeschichtliche Skizze* (Tübingen: Mohr, 2nd edn).

Dihle, A.
1989 *Die griechische und lateinische Literatur der Kaiserzeit: Von Augustus bis Justinian* (Munich: Beck).

Dormeyer, D.
1983 'Flucht, Bekehrung und Rückkehr des Sklaven Onesimos. Interaktionale Auslegung des Philemonbriefes', *Evangelischer Erzieher* 35: 214-28.
1989 'The Implicit and Explicit Readers and the Genre of Philippians 3:2–4:3, 8-9: Response to the Commentary of Wolfgang Schenk', *Semeia* 48: 147-59.
1998 *The New Testament among the Writings of Antiquity* (Sheffield: Sheffield Academic Press; ET of *Das Neue Testament im Rahmen der antiken Literaturgeschichte. Eine Einführung* [Darmstadt: Wissenschaftliche Buchgesellschaft, 1993]).

Eisenhut, W.
1982 *Einführung in die antike Rhetorik und ihre Geschichte* (Darmstadt: Wissenschaftliche Buchgesellschaft, 3rd edn).

Fuhrmann, M.
1973 *Einführung in die antike Dichtungstheorie* (Darmstadt: Wissenschaftliche Buchgesellschaft).
1990 *Die antike Rhetorik. Eine Einführung* (Munich and Zürich: Artemis).

Gnilka, J.
1968 *Der Philipperbrief* (HTKNT 10.3; Freiburg: Herder).
1971 *Der Epheserbrief* (HTKNT 10.2; Freiburg: Herder).
1982 *Der Philemonbrief* (HTKNT 10.4; Freiburg: Herder).

Hengel, M.
1979 *Zur urchristlichen Geschichtsschreibung* (Stuttgart: Mohr).

Hommel, H.
1970 'Rhetorik', *Lexikon der Antike: Literatur 4* (Munich: Deutscher Taschenbuchverlag): 127-43.

Hoppe, R.
1994 *Der Triumph des Kreuzes: Studien zum Verhältnis des Kolosserbriefes zur paulinischen Kreuzestheologie* (SBS 28; Stuttgart: Katholisches Bibelwerk).

Hübner, H.
1984 'Der Galaterbrief und das Verhältnis von antiker Rhetorik und Epistolographie', *TLZ* 109: 241-50.
1992 'Die Rhetorik und die Theologie: Der Römerbrief und die rhetorische Kompetenz des Paulus', in C.J. Classen and H.J. Müllenbrock (eds.), *Die Macht des Wortes*: *Aspekte gegenwärtiger Rhetorikforschung* (Ars Rhetorika 4; Marburg: Koch): 165-79.

Hughes, F.W.
1989 *Early Christian Rhetoric and 2 Thessalonians* (JSNTSup 30; Sheffield: JSOT Press).
1990 'The Rhetoric of 1 Thessalonians', in R.F. Collins (ed.), *The Thessalonian Correspondence* (BETL 87; Leuven: Peeters): 94-116.

Jewett, R.
1986 *The Thessalonian Correspondence: Pauline Rhetoric and Millenarian Piety* (Philadelphia: Fortress Press).

Johanson, B.C.
1987 *To all the Brethren*: *A Text-Linguistic and Rhetoric Approach to 1 Thessalonians* (ConBNT 16; Uppsala: Almqvist & Wiksell).

Kitzberger, I.
1986 *Bau der Gemeinde*: *Das paulinische Wortfeld oikodome/(ep)oikodomein* (FzB 53; Würzburg: Echter).

Klauck, H.J.
1991 *Die Johannesbriefe* (EdF 276; Darmstadt: Wissenschaftliche Buchgesellschaft).

1998 *Die antike Briefliteratur und das Neue Testament* (UTB 2022; Paderborn: Schöningh).

Koskenniemi, H.
1956 *Studien zur Idee und Phraseologie des griechischen Briefes bis 400 n. Chr.* (Helsinki: Academiae Scientarum Fennicae).

Kümmel, W.G.
1973 *Einleitung in das Neue Testament* (Heidelberg: Quelle & Meyer).

Lang, F.
1986 *Die Briefe an die Korinther* (NTD 7; Göttingen: Vandenhoeck & Ruprecht).

Lausberg, H.
1960 *Handbuch der literarischen Rhetorik: Eine Grundlegung der Literaturwissenschaft* (2 vols.; Munich: Huber).
1984 *Elemente der literarischen Rhetorik* (Munich: Huber, 8th edn).

McKnight, E.V.
1988 *Post-Modern Use of the Bible: The Emergence of Reader-Oriented Criticism* (Nashville: Abingdon Press).

Malherbe, A.J.
1977 'Ancient Epistolary Theory', *Ohio Journal of Religious Studies* 5: 3-77.
1987 *Paul and the Thessalonians: The Philosophical Tradition of Pastoral Care* (Philadelphia: Fortress Press).

Martin, J.
1974 *Antike Rhetorik: Technik und Methode* (Munich: Beck).

Mitchell, M.M.
1991 *Paul and the Rhetoric of Reconciliation: An Exegetical Investigation of the Language and Composition of 1 Corinthians* (HUT 28; Tübingen: Mohr Siebeck).

Oberlinner, L.
1995 *Die Pastoralbriefe. Kommentar zum zweiten Timotheusbrief* (HTKNT 11.2.2; Freiburg: Herder).

Olbricht, T.H.
1990 'An Aristotelian Rhetorical Analysis of 1 Thessalonians', in D. Balch *et al.* (eds.), *Greeks, Romans and Christians* (FS A.J. Malherbe) (Philadelphia: Fortress Press): 216-36.

Probst, H.
1991 *Paulus und der Brief: Die Rhetorik des antiken Briefes als Form der paulinischen Korintherkorrespondenz (1 Kor 8–10)* (WUNT 2.45; Tübingen: Mohr Siebeck).

Roloff, J.
1988 *Der erste Brief an Timotheus* (EKKNT 15; Zürich: Benziger; Neukirchen: Neukirchener Verlag).

Schenk, W.
1984 *Die Philipperbriefe des Paulus*: Kommentar (Stuttgart: Kohlhammer).
1987 'Der Kolosserbrief in der neueren Forschung (1945–1985)', *ANRW* 2.25.4 (Berlin: W. de Gruyter): 3327-3365.

Schnelle, U.
1999 *Einleitung in das Neue Testament* (Göttingen: Vandenhoeck & Ruprecht, 3rd edn).

Schnider, F., and W. Stenger
1987 *Studien zum neutestamentlichen Briefformular* (Leiden: Brill).

Schoon-Janssen, J.
1991 *Umstrittene 'Apologien' in den Paulusbriefen: Studien zur rhetorischen Situation des 1. Thessalonicherbriefes, des Galaterbriefes und des Philipperbriefes* (GTA 45; Göttingen: Vandenhoeck & Ruprecht).

Schweizer, E.
1976 *Der Brief an die Kolosser* (EKKNT; Zurich: Benziger; Neukirchen: Neukirchener Verlag).

Strecker, G.
1992 *Literaturgeschichte des Neuen Testaments* (Göttingen: Vandenhoeck & Ruprecht).

Thraede, K.
1970 *Grundzüge griechisch-römischer Brieftopik* (Zetemata 43; Munich: Beck).

Trilling, W.
1980 *Der zweite Brief an die Thessalonicher* (EKKNT 14; Zürich: Benziger; Neukirchen: Neukirchener Verlag).

Vielhauer, P.
1975 *Geschichte der urchristlichen Literatur* (New York: W. de Gruyter).

Watson, D.F.
1988 'A Rhetorical Analysis of Philippians and Its Implications for the Unity Question', *NovT* 30: 57-88.

Wendland, P.
1912 *Die urchristlichen Literaturformen* (Tübingen: Mohr, 2nd and 3rd edn).

Wolter, M.
1993 *Der Brief an die Kolosser. Der Brief an Philemon* (ÖTK 12; Gütersloh: Mohn; Würzburg: Echter).

Wuellner, W.
1976 'Paul's Rhetoric of Argumentation in Romans', *CBQ* 38: 330-51.
1990 'The Argumentative Structure of 1 Thessalonians as Paradoxial Encomium', in R.F. Collins (ed.), *The Thessalonien Correspondence* (BETL 87; Leuven: Peeters): 117-37.

Zeller, D.
1985 *Der Brief an die Römer* (RNT; Regensburg: Pustet).

WHEN AND HOW WAS THE PAULINE CANON COMPILED?
AN ASSESSMENT OF THEORIES

STANLEY E. PORTER

McMaster Divinity College
Hamilton, ON, Canada

1. INTRODUCTION

There are three periods in the development of the Pauline canon: the period during which the letters were actually written (whether by Paul or by later authors), the period during which the letters were gathered into a corpus, and, finally, the period of transmission during which the texts of these letters were firmly and finally established and used by the Church.[1] There is some, almost inevitable, overlap between these three periods. For example, for those who do not believe that Paul wrote all of the letters attributed to him (that is, probably the majority of New Testament scholars), the period during which the letters were actually written is an extended period that clearly overlaps with the period during which the letters were gathered, as will be discussed below. However, despite some of this apparent contiguity of the developmental periods, I find it perplexing to note just how little significant insight into this overlap there is in the scholarly discussion. As an example, it is not uncommon for those who are concerned with the authorship of the Pauline letters, even those who discuss the purportedly pseudepigraphic letters, such as Ephesians or the Pastoral Epistles, not to enter into serious discussion of the gathering together or collection of the Pauline corpus, even though theories regarding pseudepigraphic authorship are often directly related to how the

---

[1] This is similar to D. Trobisch, *Paul's Letter Collection: Tracing the Origins* (Minneapolis: Augsburg Fortress, 1994), 50, but without prejudging the role of Paul in the collection. Cf. now also his *The First Edition of the New Testament* (New York: Oxford University Press, 2000).

gathering togethether of the letters took place—for example, the pseudepigrapher is often thought to be dependent upon knowing some of the authentic Pauline letters. Similar comments can be made about those who are concerned to describe the transmission of the Pauline letters. Often discussion is about the transmission of a particular letter (or parts of a letter, when purportedly composite letters are discussed, such as 2 Corinthians or Philippians), or, more usually, the transmission of a particular textual variant unit (such as the doxology of Romans in 16:25-27)—almost as if a Pauline canon did not exist (apart from the necessary reference to manuscripts that sometimes have other Pauline letters in them, such as that designated 𝔓[46], etc.). Even for those relatively few scholars who are convinced of widespread interpolation into the Pauline letters (to say nothing of composite letters), previous discussion has usually been of individual books, rather than of the larger Pauline corpus.[2] Discussion of the process of gathering the letters is often kept completely apart from that of the role that the letters have played in the Christian Church.[3] However, even though integrated study of all three dimensions is clearly necessary, there have been relatively few such dedicated studies.

One of the reasons for the lack of such research is that important primary evidence for especially the earliest stages of the development of the Pauline canon is lacking. What is known[4] is that by the mid-

---

[2] See J.C. O'Neill, *The Recovery of Paul's Letter to the Galatians* (London: SPCK, 1972); *idem*, *Paul's Letter to the Romans* (Harmondsworth: Penguin, 1975); W.O. Walker, Jr., 'The Burden of Proof in Identifying Interpolations in the Pauline Letters', *NTS* 33 (1987), 610-18; *idem*, 'Is First Corinthians 13 a Non-Pauline Interpolation?', *CBQ* 60 (1998), 484-99; *idem*, 'Romans 1.18–2.29: A Non-Pauline Interpolation?', *NTS* 45 (1999), 533-53; and their essays in this volume.

[3] This is a common problem of so-called canonical critical methods. See S.E. Porter and K.D. Clarke, 'Canonical-Critical Perspective and the Relationship of Colossians and Ephesians', *Bib* 78 (1997), 57-86.

[4] This information can be found in virtually every introduction to the canon. Volumes worth examining include: B.F. Westcott, *A General Survey of the History of the Canon of the New Testament* (London: Macmillan, 7th edn, 1896 [1855]); C.R. Gregory, *Canon and Text of the New Testament* (Edinburgh: T. & T. Clark, 1907); A. Souter, *The Text and Canon of the New Testament* (rev. C.S.C. Williams; London: Duckworth, rev. edn, 1954 [1913]); H. von Campenhausen, *The Formation of the Christian Bible* (trans. J.A. Baker; Philadelphia: Fortress Press, 1972 [1968]); B.M. Metzger, *The Canon of the New Testament*

second century, at or by the time of the formation of Marcion's canon, there was some form of consolidated group of Pauline letters. The evidence is that Marcion knew of ten Pauline letters, most scholars thinking that he did not know the Pastoral Epistles because they had not yet been written (if so, an instance of overlap between the first two periods mentioned above). The fact that the Pastoral Epistles are not mentioned, however, does not necessarily mean that they had not been written—he may not have known of them or may have rejected them.[5] In any case, there is a canon of at least ten letters by this time, and these include what is called a letter to the Laodiceans, which may well be what is now called Ephesians.[6] By around AD 200, if the generally accepted dating of $\mathfrak{P}^{46}$ is correct, we have tangible documentation of a corpus that is in many ways very similar to Marcion's, with ten Pauline letters plus Hebrews. However, recently it has been plausibly argued that the way in which the scribe of $\mathfrak{P}^{46}$ has compressed his letters may indicate that he found space to copy the Pastoral Epistles into his codex (he may, of course, also have simply added extra pages).[7] During the second to fourth centuries, a number of Church writers attest to varying degrees of knowledge of the Pauline letters. If one dates the Muratorian canon to the second century, a list of thirteen letters is known by then.[8] In any event, by the fourth century

---

(Oxford: Clarendon Press, 1987); F.F. Bruce, *The Canon of Scripture* (Glasgow: Chapter House, 1988); and L.M. McDonald, *The Formation of the Christian Biblical Canon* (Peabody, MA: Hendrickson, 1995); among others.

[5] See G. Milligan, *The New Testament Documents: Their Origin and Early History* (London: Macmillan, 1913), 217.

[6] See M.D. Goulder, 'The Visionaries of Laodicea', *JSNT* 43 (1991), 16.

[7] J. Duff, '$\mathfrak{P}46$ and the Pastorals: A Misleading Consensus?', *NTS* 44 (1998), 578-90. It must be noted that there have been attempts to date $\mathfrak{P}^{46}$ to as early as the late first century: see Y.K. Kim, 'Palaeographical Dating of P^{46} to the Later First Century', *Bib* 69 (1988), 248-57. See the assessment by S.R. Pickering, 'The Dating of the Chester Beatty-Michigan Codex of the Pauline Epistles ($\mathfrak{P}^{46}$)', in T.W. Hillard, R.A. Kearsley, C.E.V. Nixon and A.M. Hobbs (eds.), *Ancient History in a Modern University* (2 vols.; New South Wales, Australia: Ancient History Documentary Research Centre Macquarie University; Grand Rapids: Eerdmans, 1998), 2.216-27.

[8] On dating, see G.M. Hahneman, *The Muratorian Fragment and the Development of the Canon* (OTM; Oxford: Clarendon Press, 1992), who follows A.C. Sundberg, Jr., 'Canon Muratori: A Fourth-Century List', *HTR* 66 (1973), 1-41, in arguing for a fourth-century date. This has been disputed by a number of people: see, e.g., E. Ferguson, 'Canon Muratori: Date and Provenance', *StudPat* 17 (1982), 677-83; *idem*, Review of Hahneman, *JTS* 44 (1993), 691-97; P. Henne,

(Muratorian canon or not), virtually all canonical lists know a Pauline canon of at least thirteen if not fourteen letters, the fourteenth being Hebrews (this will be discussed further below).

So much is fairly well agreed. The major issue is how it is that the Pauline group of letters got to such a position of consolidation. I do not intend to provide here a study of all three dimensions noted above, but wish instead to focus upon the second dimension, that of the gathering of the Pauline canon. In this essay, I wish first to critically assess a number of the better-known theories regarding the gathering of the Pauline canon, and then to examine in particular the recent theory by Trobisch, which, although it takes into account the first two dimensions in a highly enlightening way, concentrates upon the second.

2. THEORIES OF ORIGIN OF THE PAULINE CANON

A number of different theories regarding the origin, gathering together or collection of the Pauline letter corpus have been proposed in modern critical scholarship. Although these have been usefully surveyed and assessed before,[9] there is more to be said about them,

---

'La datation du canon de Muratori', *RB* 100 (1993), 54-75; C.E. Hill, 'The Debate over the Muratorian Fragment and the Development of the Canon', *WTJ* 57 (1995), 437-52. On issues related to the ordering principles of the Muratorian canon, see K. Stendahl, 'The Apocalypse of John and the Epistles of Paul in the Muratorian Fragment', in W. Klassen and G.F. Snyder (eds.), *Current Issues in New Testament Interpretation: Essays in Honor of Otto A. Piper* (London: SCM Press, 1952), 239-45, who raises the issue of particularity. See also N.A. Dahl, 'The Particularity of the Pauline Epistles as a Problem in the Ancient Church', in *Neotestamentica et Patristica: Eine Freundesgabe, Herrn Professor Dr. Oscar Cullmann zu seinem 60. Geburtstag überreicht* (NovTSup 6; Leiden: Brill, 1962), 261-71.

[9] Recent surveys that have especially helped me in my study include H.Y. Gamble, *The New Testament Canon: Its Making and Meaning* (GBS; Philadelphia: Fortress Press, 1985), 35-46; D. Trobisch, *Die Entstehung der Paulusbriefsammlung: Studien zu den Anfängen christlicher Publizistik* (NTOA 10; Freiburg: Universitätsverlag; Göttingen: Vandenhoeck & Ruprecht, 1989), 1-10; A.G. Patzia, *The Making of the New Testament: Origin, Collection, Text & Canon* (Downers Grove, IL: IVP, 1995), 80-87; and J. Murphy-O'Connor, *Paul the Letter-Writer: His World, his Options, his Skills* (Collegeville, MN: Liturgical, 1995), 114-30; cf. the brief summaries in V.P. Furnish, 'Pauline Studies', in E.J. Epp and G.W. MacRae (eds.), *The New Testament and its Modern Interpreters*

especially now that Trobisch's theory has been proposed and so ably defended. There are four major theories often discussed regarding the gathering of the Pauline canon, with some major and minor variations on each. I will look at each of these theories in turn but do so by keeping an eye on Trobisch's basic framework, even though I will not present his theory until the next section.

Gradual Collection or Zahn–Harnack Theory
The first theory regarding how the Pauline letter collection came about is what has come to be called the 'snowball' or 'gradual collection' theory.[10] In modern critical scholarship, the origins of this theory are attributed to Theodor Zahn and Adolf Harnack.[11] Zahn and Harnack disagreed on several details in their description, but essentially concurred that interest in the Pauline letters had existed from the time of their writing. Zahn examined the evidence in Marcion, the Apostolic Fathers (e.g. Clement, Polycarp and Ignatius), and later canonical lists, and concluded that the consistent references among these various writers, and reference to them in churches separated in distance (e.g. Rome, Smyrna, Antioch, and Corinth, where the actual process of collection may have taken place),[12] indicated that the

---

(Atlanta: Scholars Press, 1989), 321-50, esp. 326-28; and H.Y. Gamble, 'The Canon of the New Testament', in Epp and MacRae (eds.), *New Testament and its Modern Interpreters*, 201-43, esp. 205-208.

[10] The language is that of Gamble, *New Testament Canon*, 36, and Patzia, *Making of the New Testament*, 80. See C.F.D. Moule, *The Birth of the New Testament* (San Francisco: Harper & Row, 3rd edn, 1982), 263, for the original reference to 'snowball', and who is sympathetic to this position.

[11] See T. Zahn, *Geschichte des Neutestamentlichen Kanons* (2 vols.; Erlangen and Leipzig: Deichert, 1888–1892), 1.811-39; idem, *Grundriss der Geschichte des Neutestamentlichen Kanons: Eine Ergänzung zu der Einleitung in das Neue Testament* (Leipzig: Deichert, 1904), esp. 35-37; A. Harnack, *Die Briefsammlung des Apostels Paulus und die anderen vorkonstantinischen christlichen Briefsammlungen* (Leipzig: Hinrichs, 1926), 6-27. This encapsulation also draws upon the summaries in B.S. Childs, *The New Testament as Canon: An Introduction* (Valley Forge, PA: Trinity Press International, 1994 [1984]), 423; C.L. Mitton, *The Formation of the Pauline Corpus of Letters* (London: Epworth, 1955), 15.

[12] See also G. Zuntz, *The Text of the Epistles: A Disquisition upon the Corpus Paulinum* (Schweich Lectures 1946; London: British Academy, 1953), 278-79, who discusses Ephesus and Corinth as places where this process may have occurred, though he endorses Alexandria as the place of origin as a corpus (p. 279).

Pauline letters had early on been collected together. Zahn's explanation for this was that they had served a vital liturgical purpose in public worship. He thought that the corpus consisted of ten letters (excluding the Pastoral Epistles), and was completed after the writing of Acts but before the writing of *1 Clement*, so sometime around AD 80 to 85.[13] Harnack, drawing upon such passages as 2 Thess 2:2, 3:17, 1 Cor 7:17, 2 Cor 3:1, and 10:9, 10, all of which refer to the letter-writing process in some way (e.g. exalting Paul as a letter-writer, or warning against false letters, etc.),[14] saw this as evidence of an early collection of Paul's letters, but placed the conclusion to the process a little later (around AD 100) and included the Pastorals as well.[15] Both Zahn and Harnack recognized that a process of selection and limitation in the Pauline corpus had occurred. However, their major difference revolved around the canonical status attributed to this accumulating Pauline material. Zahn tended to bestow a canonical status on the letters because of their being read publicly and being used in worship in this way, and thought that Marcion was responding to this canon; Harnack thought that formal canonical status for the corpus, in which its status was equal to that of the Old Testament, did not occur until the second century as a response to Marcion, who had forced this process by his creating the first Pauline canon.[16]

Whereas Zahn and Harnack emphasized the limitation in number of the Pauline letters in the canon, Kirsopp Lake emphasized the number of letters available. He thus proposed a more gradual collection process, and saw the focus of importance being upon the different churches, each of which had its own collection of Pauline letters that differed from the others. Lake also extended the time that the process took, on the basis of the supposition of limited contemporary knowledge of the on-going process and the varied ordering of the Pauline letters among the Church Fathers and the canonical lists.[17] This

---

[13] Zahn, *Geschichte des Neutestamentlichen Kanons*, 1.835.
[14] Harnack, *Die Briefsammlung*, 7-8.
[15] Harnack, *Die Briefsammlung*, 6.
[16] Followed by W. Bauer, *Orthodoxy and Heresy in Earliest Christianity* (London: SCM Press, 1971 [1964]), 221-22. On the possible response to Marcion, see also Bruce, *Canon of Scripture*, 144, and von Campenhausen, *Formation of the Christian Bible*, 148.
[17] K. Lake, *The Earlier Epistles of St. Paul: Their Motive and Origin* (London: Rivingtons, 1911), 356-59. Cf. K. Lake and S. Lake, *An Introduction to the New Testament* (London: Christophers, 1938), 96-101.

position has been followed by a number of people, and may well be the predominant theory regarding the formation of the Pauline canon. One of the best known advocates has perhaps been B.H. Streeter, who traces four separate and distinct stages in the long-term growth of the Pauline corpus: (1) the nucleus of Romans, 1 Corinthians, Ephesians and perhaps Philippians (known by AD 96 in *1 Clement*), (2) the ten letters as evidenced by Marcion (ca. AD 140), (3) the thirteen letters before AD 200 (as attested by the Muratorian canon), and (4) the fourteen letters with Hebrews ca. AD 350.[18]

The length of time that this position has been seriously considered, and by such significant and influential New Testament scholars as noted above, attests to its abiding significance in New Testament studies. There are a number of arguments that can be raised against such a position, however. One is the apparent discrepancy between those who posit a short period of time for the collection, such as Zahn and Harnack, and those who posit a much longer period, such as Lake and Streeter—but each by appealing to the same body of evidence often in much the same way. Further, for those who accept the shorter period of time, the evidence marshalled by those who argue for the longer period of time might be thought damaging, especially as none of the lists of the second and third centuries seems to know all of the Pauline letters. For example, according to Lake, Marcion's, the Muratorian canon's, Tertullian's and Origen's lists are all different in length and in order.[19] In fact, however, the latter two only include eight letters, whereas the earlier two include ten (one of these being that to the Laodiceans for Marcion). One must wonder, however, whether the differing orders actually says anything about the collection process itself, although the failure to have a complete list indicates that all did not share the same group of letters. The further argument that lack of mention of a letter means lack of knowledge of it—an argument relied upon especially in the long-term view—must also be questioned,[20] even on Lake's grounds, since the process he records and Streeter follows is upset by the later, shorter lists of

---

[18] B.H. Streeter, *The Four Gospels: A Study of Origins* (London: Macmillan, 1930), 526-27; cf. also his *The Primitive Church: Studies with Special Reference to the Origins of the Christian Ministry* (London: Macmillan, 1929), 159-62.

[19] Lake, *Earlier Epistles*, 358-59.

[20] See D. Guthrie, *New Testament Introduction* (Downers Grove, IL: IVP, 3rd edn, 1970), 646.

Tertullian and Origen.[21] Streeter's proposal is also potentially thrown off if the Muratorian fragment, as many recent scholars posit (see above), is a fourth-century rather than a second-century document.

These several criticisms of the long-term view do not necessarily leave the short-term collection process intact, however. One objection might be raised in terms of the relation of the Pauline corpus to the writing of Acts. If Acts was written at a date from the AD 80s on, then it is surprising that the book does not make any overt or explicit reference to the Pauline letters, an assumption of much contemporary scholarship. If the letters had been collected, the author of Acts, being such a devoted follower of Paul, would have been expected to know and use them.[22] There is also the significant lack of evidence regarding how and whether such a compositional process occurred. For example, there is the difficulty of why it is, especially if Corinth was a centre of the gathering process, that there is so much confusion over the Corinthian letters. Even for those who argue that there are portions of all four of Paul's Corinthian letters to be found in canonical 1 and 2 Corinthians, two of the letters preserved would appear to be quite fragmentary.[23] There is the question of why these fragmentary letters were preserved in such a state, when the Corinthians were responsible in large part for the preservation process, something that they would appear to have taken quite seriously. The theory that Zahn and Harnack advocate has a selection process going on from the start, but it is unclear upon what basis such selection would have occurred

---

[21] Lake (*Earlier Epistles*, 357) admits that Tertullian probably knew Colossians and the Pastoral Epistles, even though he did not list them.

[22] E.g. W.G. Kümmel, *Introduction to the New Testament* (trans. H.C. Kee; Nashville, TN: Abingdon Press, 17th edn, 1975), 186; responded to by W.O. Walker, Jr., 'Acts and the Pauline Corpus Reconsidered', *JSNT* 24 (1985), 3-23; repr. in S.E. Porter and C.A. Evans (eds.), *The Pauline Writings* (BibSem 34; Sheffield: Sheffield Academic Press, 1995), 55-74; cf. also Streeter, *Four Gospels*, 555. It is fair to say that much recent work is finding more of the Pauline letters in Acts (see below).

[23] On the various letter hypotheses of the Corinthian letters, see, among others, J.C. Hurd, Jr., *The Origin of I Corinthians* (Macon, GA: Mercer University Press, new edn, 1983 [1965]); *idem*, 'Good News and the Integrity of 1 Corinthians', in L.A. Jervis and P. Richardson (eds.), *Gospel in Paul: Studies on Corinthians, Galatians and Romans for Richard N. Longenecker* (JSNTSup 108; Sheffield: JSOT Press, 1994), 38-62; M. Thrall, *A Critical and Exegetical Commentary on the Second Epistle to the Corinthians* (2 vols.; ICC; Edinburgh: T. & T. Clark, 1994, 2000), 1.3-49.

among the letters that Paul wrote (and even by whom). It is perhaps easy to say that those letters that were useful in the churches were the ones preserved, but this seems like an overly glib and probably circular explanation, especially when there are no other letters available for comparison.[24] There is lastly the serious question of whether the forming of the Marcionite canon was as instrumental, either as challenge (not very likely)[25] or response, to the formation of the Pauline canon as is often thought.[26] One cannot help but think that the gradual collection theory of the Pauline corpus—as popular as it has been—is one of expedience, designed to weave a narrative around the disparate evidence of the first four centuries, but without a firm foundation established as to how such a process actually occurred.

Lapsed Interest or Goodspeed–Knox Theory

The second major theory to consider is the one propounded by Edgar J. Goodspeed and John Knox, known as the Goodspeed or Goodspeed–Knox theory. In many ways a response to the theory/ies of Zahn and Harnack,[27] Goodspeed proposed that, rather than there being a process of gradual accumulation, the evidence instead indicated widespread neglect of Paul's letters. This has been called by Guthrie the theory of 'lapsed interest'.[28] Goodspeed consistently maintained his theory over a number of publications.[29] The theory that he proposed is far more complex than is often reported in summaries of it,

---

[24] See Guthrie, *New Testament Introduction*, 647.

[25] Lake and Lake, *Introduction*, 96, who note that it is 'rather improbable that [Marcion] made the Corpus, for the Church would hardly have accepted the work of a heretic'.

[26] Childs, *Canon*, 424. Cf. Trobisch, *First Edition*, 5, who notes that the influence of Marcion remains unresolved in scholarly discussion.

[27] In some ways, Goodspeed was anticipated by J. Weiss, *Earliest Christianity: A History of the Period A.D. 30–150* (2 vols.; completed by R. Knopf; trans. ed. F.C. Grant; New York: Harper & Row, 1937; repr. Gloucester, MA: Peter Smith, 1970), 2.682-83. This work was completed after Weiss's death in 1914, but this part appears to have been written by him.

[28] Guthrie, *New Testament Introduction*, 647.

[29] See, especially, E.J. Goodspeed, *New Solutions of New Testament Problems* (Chicago: University of Chicago Press, 1927), esp. 1-103; *The Meaning of Ephesians* (Chicago: University of Chicago Press, 1933); and *An Introduction to the New Testament* (Chicago: University of Chicago Press, 1937), esp. 210-21. The following is based mostly upon his *Introduction*, but with reference to the other two sources.

and bears more detailed presentation here. Goodspeed notes that Acts does not know of Paul's letters, but that the book of Revelation (chs. 1–3), and much of the literature following the composition of Acts, as well as every Christian corpus of letters to follow, seems to know of Paul's letters. Rather than there being a number of Pauline collections, Goodspeed argues that there was one collection after which the later collections are patterned. To be more specific, the book of Ephesians shows familiarity with all nine of the accepted Pauline letters[30] (not counting the Pastorals, which for Goodspeed constitute later letters reflecting Pauline knowledge). On the basis of these supposed data, Goodspeed reconstructs the formation of the Pauline canon in the following way. The writing of the book of Acts, which occurred around AD 90,[31] with its clear and forceful depiction of Paul, revived interest in Paul as the apostle to the Greeks. There was no way to neglect this book, and the only thing to be added to such an important volume was to collect Paul's letters together, something Paul himself had hinted at (see Col 4:16). However, Colossians is not mentioned in Acts, which leads Goodspeed to speculate that Colossians and Philemon, which he took to be the letter to the Laodiceans (how else, he thought, could one account for its being in the collection?),[32] was the nucleus of the corpus. This is further confirmed by the widespread use of Colossians by Ephesians. Ephesus, which by AD 90 had become the second most important Christian centre (second only to Antioch), was probably the focus of the gathering of the Pauline letters from surrounding cities, since Ephesus became the centre for later letter-writing activity, such as Revelation and the letters of Ignatius, as well as the Gospel and letters of John, works that clearly reflect Pauline influence. Ephesus also had Paul's letter of introduction of Phoebe (Romans 16). Ignatius later wrote that Paul mentions the Ephesians in every letter (*Eph* 12.2), which Goodspeed contends makes sense if the collection originated in Ephesus.[33] The Pauline corpus, therefore, originated and began to be circulated from Ephesus, with Ephesians,

---

[30] See Goodspeed, *Meaning of Ephesians*, 82-165.

[31] See Goodspeed, *New Solutions*, 94-103. Cf. J. Knox, 'Acts and the Pauline Letter Corpus', in L.E. Keck and J.L. Martyn (eds.), *Studies in Luke–Acts* (Philadelphia: Fortress Press, 1966), 279-87.

[32] Goodspeed, *Meaning of Ephesians*, 7.

[33] Others do not think that this phrasing makes so much sense in the light of textual difficulties. See B. Weiss, *A Manual of Introduction to the New Testament* (trans. A.J.K. Davidson; 2 vols.; London: Hodder & Stoughton, 1887), 1.43 n. 1.

an encyclical letter that drew widely upon the entire Pauline corpus, as the introduction.

This theory has been developed and expanded in some ways by later writers. For example, Knox, a pupil of Goodspeed, proposed that Onesimus was the letter collector, a means of justifying inclusion of the book of Philemon,[34] and thought that, on the basis of Marcion's canon and the Marcionite prologues, one could reconstruct a seven-letter Pauline canon (grouping the Corinthian letters, Thessalonian letters, and Colossians and Philemon together, along with Romans, Galatians, Philippians and Colossians), with Ephesians at its head (Marcion had transposed Galatians and Ephesians to emphasize the anti-Jewish elements of the canon).[35] Nevertheless, it is to Goodspeed's formulation that attention is usually drawn.

Despite much positive attention to the theory, especially in the United States where Goodspeed was rightly a highly regarded scholar (not surprisingly, the theory appears to have been largely neglected in British scholarship until Mitton,[36] and in German scholarship even longer), there was also much negative attention as well. The major arguments against Goodspeed's theory are telling.[37] For example, there is no text-critical evidence that Ephesians was ever at the head of a Pauline corpus (or at the end, where Zuntz thinks a covering letter also could have stood).[38] Marcion seems to have had Galatians at the

---

[34] J. Knox, *Philemon among the Letters of Paul* (London: Collins, rev. edn, 1959 [1935]), 10, referring to how his idea (found in the first edition of his work in 1935) was later accepted by Goodspeed in his *The Key to Ephesians* (Chicago: University of Chicago Press, 1956). Some scholars have thought that Tychicus was the author of Ephesians (e.g. W.L. Knox, *St. Paul and the Church of the Gentiles* [Cambridge: Cambridge University Press, 1939], 203; C.L. Mitton, *Ephesians* [NCB; Grand Rapids: Eerdmans, 1973], 230), but that does not necessarily mean he was the collector of the corpus (*contra* R.P. Martin, *New Testament Foundations*. II. *The Acts, the Letters, the Apocalypse* [Grand Rapids: Eerdmans, rev. edn, 1986], 278 n. 9).

[35] Knox, *Philemon*, 67-78. On the seven-letter corpus, see Hahneman, *Muratorian Fragment*, 117-18; H.Y. Gamble, *Books and Readers in the Early Church: A History of Early Christian Texts* (New Haven: Yale University Press, 1995), 59-61.

[36] C.L. Mitton, *The Epistle to the Ephesians: Its Authorship, Origin and Purpose* (Oxford: Clarendon Press, 1951), 45-54; expanded in his *Formation*. An early exception was Knox, *St. Paul and the Church of the Gentiles*, 184 and n. 4.

[37] See, e.g., E. Best, *A Critical and Exegetical Commentary on Ephesians* (ICC; Edinburgh: T. & T. Clark, 1998), 66.

[38] Zuntz, *Text of the Epistles*, 276.

head, $\mathfrak{P}^{46}$ has Romans, and the Muratorian canon refers to Corinthians. There is the further difficulty with the idea that Ephesians is an appropriate encyclical letter to introduce the Pauline canon, especially since so much of it reflects the language of Colossians, and does not reflect many of the major themes of the rest of the Pauline corpus. Zuntz argues that the lack of ascription in Ephesians indicates an early tradition but that the editor of the collection could not have prefaced the collection of Paul's letters with a blank left in the address, since this runs contrary to the very notion of an archetypal collection, which Goodspeed is trying to describe.[39] There are also a number of ques-tions raised by Goodspeed's historical reconstruction itself. Some still maintain that the Pastoral Epistles are authentically Pauline,[40] and if so, the relation of these letters to his reconstruction is not clear. Their pseudonymity must be granted for Goodspeed's theory to work. Goodspeed's view of the dating of the composition of Acts, while widely held by a preponderance of scholars, is not universally main-tained, with a number of scholars opting for a much later date (ca. AD 125) or a much earlier date (as early as ca. AD early 60s).[41] If either is correct, the Goodspeed chronology falls apart. There is the further problem of how one goes about showing that Paul's letters had indeed fallen into neglect, since the evidence that Goodspeed uses can be interpreted in different ways. The lack of mention of the letters in Acts does not necessarily speak to the question of whether they existed in a collection. In fact, as noted above, a number of scholars have recently argued that the letters were

---

[39] Zuntz, *Text of the Epistles*, 276-77. Goodspeed (*Meaning*, 18) does not take the opening of Ephesians as having the blank, but interprets it as part of the encyclical opening: 'to God's people who are steadfast in Christ Jesus'. See also his *New Solutions*, 11-12, 17. F. Blass and A. Debrunner, *A Greek Grammar of the New Testament and Other Early Christian Literature* (trans. R.W. Funk; Chicago: University of Chicago Press, 1961), 213, take this as 'impossible'. Its existence in the manuscripts might make one wonder if it is, indeed, impossible, or just unusual.

[40] The most recent major advancement of this theory is by G.W. Knight, *The Pastoral Epistles* (NIGTC; Grand Rapids: Eerdmans, 1992), 21-52.

[41] The major representatives of the late and early dates are J.C. O'Neill, *The Theology of Acts in its Historical Setting* (London: SPCK, 1970), 21; and A. Harnack, *Neue Untersuchungen zur Apostelgeschichte und zur Abfassungszeit der Synoptischen Evangelien* (BENT 4; Leipzig: Hinrichs, 1911), a revision from his earlier view, which conformed to the majority position.

indeed used by the author of Acts.⁴² There is also the difficulty of establishing a causal relation between the writing of Acts and the collecting of the letters. Lastly, other Pauline cities have been proposed as the major places for gathering of the Pauline letters. These include, besides Ephesus, Corinth (noted above as a favourite of some scholars) and Alexandria.⁴³ Since a number of cities can lay claim to evidence for the Pauline collection taking place there, it is also possible that there may have originally been a number of smaller Pauline corpuses, something that Goodspeed wishes clearly to dispute.⁴⁴

Composite Anti-Gnostic or Schmithals Theory
The third theory is that of the German scholar Walter Schmithals. Reflecting his German heritage, Schmithals is a firm believer in the Baur hypothesis about the origins of Christianity,⁴⁵ with the decided difference that the motivating event was not opposition between Pauline and Judaistic elements but opposition to Gnosticism.⁴⁶ His

---

42   Besides above, see now S. Walton, *Leadership and Lifestyle: The Portrait of Paul in the Miletus Speech and 1 Thessalonians* (SNTSMS 108; Cambridge: Cambridge University Press, 2000), who cautiously marshals a number of parallels between the Miletus speech and 1 Thessalonians that point to the author of Acts knowing and using this letter.

43   See Bruce, *Canon*, 130 n. 47; Patzia, *Making of the New Testament*, 81.

44   See Best, *Ephesians*, 66.

45   F.C. Baur developed his reconstruction in a number of important works. These include a series of articles, such as, 'Die Christuspartei in der korinthischen Gemeinde, der Gegensatz des petrinischen und paulinischen Christentums in der alten Kirche, der Apostel Petrus in Rom', *Tübinger Zeitschrift für Theologie* 4 (1831), 61-206 (repr. with other essays in *Historisch-kritische Untersuchungen zum Neuen Testament* [introduction by E. Käsemann; Stuttgart-Bad Cannstatt: F. Frommann, 1963], 1-146); and are reflected in two major works of relevance for New Testament studies: *Paulus, der Apostel Jesu Christi: Sein Leben und Wirken, seine Briefe und seine Lehre* (Stuttgart: Becher & Müller, 1845; ET *Paul, the Apostle of Jesus Christ, His Life and Work, his Epistles and his Doctrine* [2 vols.; trans. A. Menzies; ed. E. Zeller; London: Williams & Norgate, 2nd edn, 1873, 1875]); and *Das Christentum und die christliche Kirche der drei ersten Jahrhunderte* (Tübingen: Fues, 2nd edn, 1860 [1853]; repr. with introduction by U. Wickert; Stuttgart-Bad Cannstatt: F. Frommann, 1966; ET *The Church History of the First Three Centuries* [2 vols.; trans. A. Menzies; London: Williams & Norgate, 3rd edn, 1878, 1879]).

46   W. Schmithals, *Paul and the Gnostics* (trans. J.E. Steely; Nashville, TN: Abingdon Press, 1972 [1964]), 239-74, in a chapter first published as 'Zur

hypothesis is that the Pauline corpus was formed with a clear anti-gnostic intent. Schmithals's theory is also predicated upon his view of the composite nature of the Pauline letters. He finds the authentic letters of Paul in a group of letters written during the third missionary journey and within a very short space of only a couple of years. On the basis of various criteria, he determines that there are six Corinthian, one Galatian, three Philippian, two Roman and four Thessalonian letters. On the basis of other lists of Paul's letters (e.g. the Muratorian fragment, Tertullian, Marcion [on the basis of Tertullian, *Marc* 4.5; *Haer* 36], 𝔓⁴⁶, D 06 Codex Claromontanus, and Athanasius), he further determines that there was a seven-letter Pauline corpus in fixed order, with the Corinthian letters at the head, and with Romans at the close (the order was 1 and 2 Corinthians, Galatians, Philippians, 1 and 2 Thessalonians, Romans). Thus, Schmithals concludes that the original Pauline corpus consisted of a construct made out of the authentic fragments into a seven-letter canon, with 1 Cor 1:2b as the introduction and the doxology of Rom 16:25-27 as the conclusion (a passage long established, so Schmithals believes, as non-Pauline).[47]

There is no denying the creativity of Schmithals's theory and reconstruction. However, the fact that so much creativity is required leaves the scenario open to serious question. One must also accept several basic presuppositions. For example, many scholars, even if they recognize interpolations in the Pauline canon, or even composite theories for a given letter (e.g. 2 Corinthians or Philippians),[48] do not recognize the composite character of so many of the Pauline letters. There is the further difficulty, even if one accepts in principle the theory of composite letters, of whether one accepts Schmithals's fragments, especially since their determination and arrangement is so closely related to his hypothesis of anti-Gnosticism driving the creation of this letter collection. Without denying that Gnosticism (or proto- or pre-Gnosticism) was present at the time, one may well question whether it was so pervasive as to have coloured so many of the

---

Abfassung und ältesten Sammlung der paulinischen Hauptbriefe', *ZNW* 51 (1960), 225-45.

[47] For important discussion, see H. Gamble, Jr., *The Textual History of the Letter to the Romans* (SD 42; Grand Rapids: Eerdmans, 1977), esp. 129-32.

[48] For review of such theories regarding Philippians, see J.T. Reed, *A Discourse Analysis of Philippians: Method and Rhetoric in the Debate over Literary Integrity* (JSNTSup 136; Sheffield: Sheffield Academic Press, 1997), esp. 124-52.

original writings, as well as driven the later situation. Schmithals's ideas regarding the number seven also bear further scrutiny. His defence of the seven-letter canon, to which the other letters were added later, is based upon his estimation of an ancient belief in the sacredness of the number seven; however, he must do quite a bit of forcing to make this construction fit, including hypothesizing that the later canonical lists (that do not follow his order) are deviants from the original list, which had Corinthians at the head and Romans at the end. If the Muratorian fragment is a fourth-century list rather than a second-century one (see above), and if his other speculations are not correct, then the justification for the neatly packaged seven-letter group is severely weakened. There is also the problem that many would accept more than the seven letters as genuine. Even for those who do not accept a thirteen-letter canon, the evidence seems to be lacking for only a seven-letter canon.[49]

Personal Involvement or Moule and Guthrie Theories
In the light of the uncertainties of the previous proposals, especially as they often seem to create an inexorable process without a personal character to it, a number of scholars have proposed that a single significant individual was responsible for the gathering and creation of the Pauline corpus. A number of variations on this theory have been proposed. As already noted above in the discussion of the Zahn–Harnack theory, some have proposed that Marcion may have been the first to gather together a body of Pauline letters. Most scholars do acknowledge that Marcion's list is the earliest that we have, since the reference to a few of the Pauline letters in earlier writers, such as Clement, does not constitute a corpus.[50] However, the nature of Marcion's canon, and the later evidence of Tertullian, seem to indicate that Marcion was not the first to create such a corpus, but was probably responding (defensively?) to another such body of writings.[51] Another proposal—that of Knox, as noted above—is that

---

[49] Gamble, *New Testament Canon*, 39.
[50] Moule, *Birth of the New Testament*, 260.
[51] Lake, *Introduction*, 96; cf. Gamble, *New Testament Canon*, 41; idem, 'Canon', 207. This would follow the view of Zahn, noted above. Following the ideas of Harnack, J. Knox (*Marcion and the New Testament* [Chicago: University of Chicago Press, 1942], 39-76) proposed that Marcion was responding to an already gathered corpus, noting similarities between Marcion's list and that in the Muratorian canon. As Moule notes in response (*Birth of the New Testament*, 260-

Onesimus was instrumental in gathering the letters, but this theory is based upon a number of speculative hypotheses, and makes it probably the least plausible of any of the personal involvement theories.

Of the remaining theories, two merit further mention here. The first is that of C.F.D. Moule, who suggests that Luke may have been such a person to gather the Pauline letters together.[52] Having discussed and rejected theories related to Marcion and Onesimus, as well as questioning the so-called snowball or gradual development theory, Moule raises the question of whether Luke gathered the letters. Appreciating that Acts does not seem to know of the Pauline letters, he posits that Luke gathered the corpus after writing Acts and after Paul's death, when he revisited the major Pauline cities. Moule believes that the similarities in vocabulary, content and perspective of the Pastoral Epistles and Luke–Acts tend to support this hypothesis.[53] The second such theory is that of Donald Guthrie, who proposes that Timothy may have been the person involved in collecting Paul's letters. Guthrie begins by calling into question any theories that are based upon neglect of Paul, since at his death, Guthrie claims, all of the major churches had either direct or indirect Pauline foundations or strong personal connections to him.[54] To support such remembrance

---

61), however, Knox's theory is based upon the books being on two rolls each that were rewound backwards. Moule considers this an implausible hypothesis on both counts, since codexes may well have been used and the error in rolling easily detected and corrected. See also E.C. Blackman, *Marcion and his Influence* (London: SPCK, 1948), 23-41, esp. 38-41 on Knox; J.J. Clabeaux, *A Lost Edition of the Letters of Paul: A Reassessment of the Text of the Pauline Corpus Attested by Marcion* (CBQMS 21; Washington, DC: Catholic Biblical Association, 1989).

[52] Moule, *Birth of the New Testament*, 264-65.

[53] Moule (*Birth of the New Testament*, 265; 'The Problem of the Pastoral Epistles: A Reappraisal', *BJRL* 47 [1965], 430-52, with corrections and additions in *Birth of the New Testament*, 281-82) has also proposed that Luke was the author of the Pastoral Epistles. This would account for why the Pastorals were not present in the earliest references to the Pauline letters, and is reflected later by Marcion. Cf. S.G. Wilson, *Luke and the Pastoral Epistles* (London: SPCK, 1979). See also F.J. Badcock, *The Pauline Epistles and the Epistle to the Hebrews in their Historical Setting* (London: SPCK, 1937), 115-33, who proposes a follower of Paul but does not name him.

[54] Guthrie (*New Testament Introduction*, 653) must mean churches outside of Palestine, since relations near the end of Paul's life with the Jerusalem church were apparently strained at best. See S.E. Porter, *The Paul of Acts: Essays in*

of Paul, Guthrie notes such factors as the exchange of Pauline letters (Col 4:16), their public reading (1 Thess 5:27) and wider distribution (see 1 Corinthians), the circular character of some of the letters (e.g. Romans and Ephesians), and the respect shown for Paul's writings in the early Church writers, such as Clement (*1 Clem* 5.5-7). As to the lack of explicit mention of Paul's letters in Acts, Guthrie attributes this to its early composition. More problematic is the apparent loss of some of Paul's letters (e.g. parts of the Corinthian correspondence), but this he attributes to their lack of edificatory value. In the light of these factors, as well as a reconstruction of the closing days of Paul's life, especially as testified to by the Pastoral Epistles, Guthrie posits that Timothy would have been the collector of Paul's letters.

There is much of merit in such personal involvement theories, since any gathering process seems to demand the involvement of individuals, whether they are named or not, recognized or anonymous, singular or more than one. This factor undoubtedly accounts for why so many of the theories noted above have involved individuals as part of the scenario, even if emphasis is not placed upon them. The question here is whether there is evidence for Luke or Timothy to have made the collection. The Lukan hypothesis in some ways has more evidence upon which to base it, since there is some (what I would consider substantial) evidence for estimating Luke's literary actions. That is also its shortcoming, however, since the hypothesis that Luke was the author of the Pastorals has never been widely accepted in Pauline scholarship. This seems to be one of the major links, and without it other more difficult questions are raised in terms of the Pauline chronology. For example, the question of why Luke would write Acts but not mention the Pauline letters, yet be involved in their collection, is not so easily solved by positing the writing of Acts before the collection, since surely Luke must have known of the letters all along. It is unlikely that he only realized their value after writing Acts and after Paul had died. The hypothesis that Timothy orchestrated the collection does not fall victim to the same criticism as for Luke, but is not necessarily aided by this, since the already thin lines of literary connection with Paul are stretched even thinner. We have no evidence of Timothy's literary abilities, and the hypothesis seems to be based upon one particular Pauline chronology. Although

---

Literary Criticism, Rhetoric, and Theology (WUNT 115; Tübingen: Mohr Siebeck, 1999 [repr. *Paul in Acts* (Peabody, MA: Hendrickson, 2001)]), 172-86.

Guthrie is vigorous in his defence of the authenticity of the Pastoral Epistles,[55] and hence their placement at the end of Paul's life, after the close of Acts, most scholars do not accept this hypothesis.[56]

With the evidence of this chronology, and the relation to the Pastoral Epistles, seriously compromised, the reasons for positing Timothy as the collector—even if all that Guthrie says about Paul not being neglected after his death is true—are reduced significantly. In the light of these difficulties, and more in line with the findings of critical orthodoxy, a Pauline school hypothesis has been posited as a corrective.[57] This theory recognizes the importance of individuals in collecting the letters—such as Onesimus, Luke or Timothy, along with nameless other later Pauline followers and co-workers, possibly even including Polycarp—but attempts to overcome the chronological difficulties noted above. After Paul's death, a number of Paul's followers not only gathered, possibly edited, and passed on the Pauline tradition, including his letters, but also continued to apply Paul's theology to contemporary church situations, thereby generating the pseudepigraphic deutero-Pauline letters. This significant variation on the personal involvement hypothesis indeed answers some of the questions raised above, but it too raises its own difficulties. These include a number of major problems with the concept of pseudepigraphy, recently brought to the fore in scholarly discussion.[58] The

---

[55] See, e.g., D. Guthrie, *The Pastoral Epistles and the Mind of Paul* (London: Tyndale Press, 1956); *New Testament Introduction*, 584-622, 671-84; *The Pastoral Epistles* (TNTC; Grand Rapids: Eerdmans, 2nd edn, 1990), esp. 224-40.

[56] For a recent survey, which also addresses some of the ethical issues involved, see M. Davies, *The Pastoral Epistles* (NTG; Sheffield: Sheffield Academic Press, 1996), 105-18.

[57] Gamble, *New Testament Canon*, 39. Cf. H.-M. Schenke, 'Das Weiterwirken des Paulus und die Pflege seines Erbs durch die Paulusschule', *NTS* 21 (1975), 505-18.

[58] See Davies, *Pastoral Epistles*, 113-17; E.E. Ellis, 'Pseudonymity and Canonicity of New Testament Documents', in M.J. Wilkins and T. Paige (eds.), *Worship, Theology and Ministry in the Early Church: Essays in Honor of Ralph P. Martin* (JSNTSup 87; Sheffield: JSOT Press, 1992), 212-24; *idem, The Making of the New Testament Documents* (BIS 39; Leiden: Brill, 1999), esp. 322-24; S.E. Porter, 'Pauline Authorship and the Pastoral Epistles: Implications for Canon', *BBR* 5 (1995), 105-23; and D.A. Carson, 'Pseudonymity and Pseudepigraphy', in C.A. Evans and S.E. Porter (eds.), *Dictionary of New Testament Background* (Downers Grove, IL: IVP, 2000), 857-64. For a collection of earlier statements, see N. Brox (ed.), *Pseudepigraphie in der heidnischen und jüdisch-christlichen*

question of deception, and in this case how a devout follower of Paul could have perpetuated such deception,[59] even if for a noble cause,[60] seems in many ways a high price to pay for accounting for the supposedly deutero-Pauline letters.

In the light of the above discussion, it becomes evident why scholars are still undecided regarding the formation of the Pauline canon. For the most part, discussion over the last one hundred years has debated various forms of the major theories noted above, with the occasional new proposal thrown in.

3. Trobisch's Theory of the Origin of the Pauline Canon

In his survey of Pauline studies, Furnish says that 'There has been no one major study of these questions [of the collection, redaction, and circulation of the Pauline letters] over the last forty years'.[61] This situation has recently been changed by the publication of David Trobisch's analysis of the formation of the Pauline canon, concentrating upon the first four letters and Paul's possible personal involvement.[62] If the theory of an early personal involvement by a close associate of Paul has any merit, as many scholars seem to recognize, it seems that Paul himself could also have been involved in this process, and it is this idea that Trobisch develops. After establishing that the Pauline letters constitute one of the divisions of early biblical New Testament manuscripts,[63] Trobisch examines the principles of arrangement of the letters within the Pauline group.[64]

Antike (Wege der Forschung 484; Darmstadt: Wissenschaftliche Buchgesellschaft, 1977).

[59] The question must be raised of why pseudepigraphic authorship would have been necessary, if the recipients would have known that the letters were not written by Paul.

[60] See L.R. Donelson, *Pseudepigraphy and Ethical Argument in the Pastoral Epistles* (HUT 22; Tübingen: Mohr Siebeck, 1986), 18-22, who notes that the 'noble lie' is still a lie.

[61] Furnish, 'Pauline Studies', 327.

[62] Trobisch's major works in this regard are *Die Entstehung*; *Paul's Letter Collection*; and now *First Edition*. There is significant overlap among these volumes, all of which I draw upon in the summary that follows, though concentrating upon *Paul's Letter Collection*.

[63] Trobisch, *Paul's Letter Collection*, 5-17; cf. *First Edition*, 38-41.

[64] Trobisch, *Paul's Letter Collection*, 17-26; and *Die Entstehung*, 56-62.

Trobisch finds a principle of arrangement that is highly consistent in many of the early manuscripts, especially the early codexes such as Sinaiticus (ℵ 01), Alexandrinus (A 02), Vaticanus (B 03) and Ephraem (C 04) (essentially modern canonical order). 𝔓46, the oldest of the Pauline manuscripts (apart from those that are highly fragmentary), arranges the Pauline letters essentially according to length. The exception in 𝔓46 is the book of Hebrews, which appears before 1 and 2 Corinthians but is actually shorter than 1 and longer than 2 Corinthians. However, Trobisch thinks that the placement of Hebrews is explainable in terms of the scribe not wanting to separate 1 and 2 Corinthians.[65] In any case, Hebrews is the one book of the Pauline group that varies regarding ordering, which Trobisch takes to mean that it was added later to the thirteen-letter Pauline collection.[66] Trobisch further believes on the basis of the common form of title of the Pauline letters that they imply their having been gathered together under the name of Paul.[67] He also posits that the overall arrangement of the letters is based upon the addressees, with the letters to the church congregations preceding the letters to the individuals (and being ordered by length within these two major groups),[68] with letters to the same place or person (1 and 2 Corinthians; 1 and 2 Thessalonians; 1 and 2 Timothy) kept together.[69]

Having noted a number of significant literary features of the Pauline letters as well,[70] Trobisch then claims to have established that Romans to Galatians is a single literary unit, and that 'It is highly probable that this old collection was edited and prepared for publication by Paul himself'.[71] This, he contends, was the first stage in a three-stage process that led to the canonical Pauline collection (the second stage is expansion of the corpus, and the third comprehensive editions).[72] Inadvertently, Trobisch claims to provide support for Goodspeed's hypothesis (see above), in that the thirteen-letter corpus is an

---

[65] Trobisch, *Paul's Letter Collection*, 17.
[66] Trobisch, *Paul's Letter Collection*, 20; but cf. his opinion in *Die Entstehung*, 60. This point was already made by Zuntz, *Text of the Epistles*, 15-16.
[67] Trobisch, *Paul's Letter Collection*, 24.
[68] See Trobisch, *Paul's Letter Collection*, 52-54.
[69] Trobisch, *Paul's Letter Collection*, 25.
[70] Trobisch, *Paul's Letter Collection*, 25-47.
[71] Trobisch, *Paul's Letter Collection*, 54.
[72] Trobisch, *Paul's Letter Collection*, 54.

expansion upon the original four letters. Accepting Goodspeed's analysis of Ephesians as reflecting the other Pauline letters, Trobisch sees Ephesians (now in its rightful place according to the tradition) as the introductory letter for the appendix to the Pauline corpus.[73] Trobisch then concentrates on analysis of the four authentic Pauline letters, studying them in terms of ancient editorial practice.[74] He believes that Paul edited these letters so as to unite them together in terms of the thought and amount of personal detail included (e.g. personal greetings are only important in terms of travel plans; one of their common ideas is the collection).[75] As a result, Trobisch claims to show that Romans 16 is a cover letter for a copy of Romans (due to its style of personal greetings),[76] the Corinthian letters are a composite of seven Pauline letters,[77] and Galatians is a legal-type document[78]—all written as Paul's defence to the Jerusalem church over the collection and his related activities.

In the light of Trobisch's work on the manuscript evidence, especially the ordering of the individual books and the implications of this ordering, J. Murphy-O'Connor has developed this scheme further.[79] Murphy-O'Connor adopts a similar three-stage collecting process, in which collection A consists of Romans, 1 and 2 Corinthians and Galatians, which originated at Corinth, collection B consists of those letters from neighbouring churches in Asia Minor and Greece, to which collection C, the personal letters, was added. Murphy-O'Connor uses the violations of the consistent decrease in length (e.g. from Galatians to Ephesians, and 2 Thessalonians to 1 Timothy), reinforced by the varying placement of Hebrews, as indicators of the section breaks. He also minimizes problems over the different canonical orderings that Trobisch draws attention to on the basis that other possible determiners of length besides number of characters, such as stichoi and Euthalian numbers, indicate very similar lengths between the books of Galatians and Ephesians and Colossians and

---

[73] Trobisch, *Paul's Letter Collection*, 101 n. 22.
[74] See Trobisch, *Paul's Letter Collection*, 55-96; cf. *Die Entstehung*, 100-104, 128-32.
[75] See Trobisch, *Paul's Letter Collection*, 62-70.
[76] Trobisch, *Paul's Letter Collection*, 71-72, 88.
[77] Trobisch, *Paul's Letter Collection*, 73-86, 89-91.
[78] Trobisch, *Paul's Letter Collection*, 86-87.
[79] Murphy-O'Connor, *Paul*, 120-30.

Philippians.⁸⁰ The result is a very consistent pattern of division of the Pauline corpus that in many ways strengthens Trobisch's analysis. However, Murphy-O'Connor does not require Paul as the instigator to promote his theory. Instead, he sees possibly Timothy and more likely Onesimus as involved in this process.⁸¹

Trobisch is not the first to propose that Paul may have been instrumental in gathering his own letters together.⁸² For example, working at about the same time, E. Randolph Richards argued that Paul used a secretary (much like Cicero had his secretary, Tiro). Hence, as indicated by 2 Tim 4:13, Paul had copies made of his letters, and these letters constituted the origin of the Pauline letter collection, possibly then assembled by Paul's secretary, Luke.⁸³ Trobisch's formulation of the theory of direct Pauline involvement is obviously a challenging and provocative version of the hypothesis, however, especially because it combines a number of what might at first seem to be contradictory or at least unusual ideas—such as the notion that Paul may have been instrumental in initiating the collection of his own letters, while at the same time limiting the authentic Pauline corpus to Baur's four letters. Whereas a number of scholars might very well welcome the idea that Paul was involved in his letter-collecting, these same scholars might not wish to limit the number to four.⁸⁴ The opposite might also be the case, that is, that some might wish to limit the number of authentic letters to four, but in the light of Trobisch's pattern of subsequent development—which in many ways

---

⁸⁰ See Murphy-O'Connor, *Paul*, 121, 123. A still standard work on stichometry is J.R. Harris, *Stichometry* (London: Clay, 1893).

⁸¹ Murphy-O'Connor, *Paul*, 130.

⁸² According to Guthrie (*New Testament Introduction*, 657), it was proposed by R.L. Archer, 'The Epistolary Form in the New Testament', *ExpTim* 63 (1951-52), 296-98, that, using Seneca as his model, Paul kept copies of his letters (p. 297).

⁸³ E.R. Richards, *The Secretary in the Letters of Paul* (WUNT 2.42; Tübingen: Mohr Siebeck, 1991), esp. 164-65, 187-88; followed by E.E. Ellis, 'Pastoral Letters', in G.F. Hawthorne, R.P. Martin, and D.P. Reid (eds.), *Dictionary of Paul and his Letters* (Downers Grove, IL: IVP, 1993), 660; idem, *Making of the New Testament Documents*, 86, 132, 297.

⁸⁴ This seems to include Ellis, *Making of the New Testament Documents*, *passim*, who apparently wants to maintain a thirteen-letter corpus, with Paul as its originator.

mirrors the gradual development theory—not find a need to involve Paul in the initial gathering process.[85]

In any event, much of Trobisch's thesis is nevertheless open to at least some question. One of the major question marks must be placed against the very notion that Paul was the one who instigated the collection of his letters. Trobisch introduces this idea in a subtle way. Having noted the three purported stages of development of letter collections, and working backwards, Trobisch suddenly concludes by claiming that it is 'highly probable' that Paul was responsible for stage one, the authorized recensions.[86] The basis for this is posited rather than proved, but, as Murphy-O'Connor's similar proposal has shown, Paul's direct involvement is not necessary to a theory of staged development such as Trobisch proposes based upon the ancient canonical lists.[87] There is little to no direct evidence to promote this idea of Pauline involvement except the analogy of Cicero and Tiro. However, as Trobisch notes, Cicero (*Att* 16.5.5) makes an explicit claim regarding the gathering of his letters.[88] The only similar statement in Paul that might give the idea that Paul had something of this sort in mind is in 2 Tim 4:13 (although it is subject to other interpretations as well), a book that Trobisch contends is not authentically Pauline, and can therefore hardly be used as evidence by him.[89] What we might have here is a later pseudepigrapher including such a statement in order to create Paul as collector of his letters, rather than Paul himself making such a claim. A further difficulty in comparing the letter collection of Cicero and what Trobisch contends that we have in the first four of Paul's letters concerns the nature of their respective letters. Cicero's known collection, and the one that Trobisch refers to explicitly in his work (*Fam* Bk 13), consists of a number of letters of recommendation,

---

[85] This would seem to hark back to the Baur hypothesis, with the beginning stage being the four letters.

[86] Trobisch, *Paul's Letter Collection*, 54. Note that it is not just 'probable', but 'highly probable'.

[87] It must also be noted that Richards's theory that Paul made copies of his letters does not necessitate Paul as the direct instigator of the collection of his letters, as Richards himself clearly notes in his advocacy of a secretary hypothesis.

[88] Trobisch, *Paul's Letter Collection*, 55; and *Die Entstehung*, 100. See also Cicero, *Att* 16.7.1, for an indirect reference.

[89] This passage can be used, however, by those who argue for authenticity of the Pastoral Epistles, such as Richards (*Secretary*, 164-65) and Ellis (*Making of the New Testament Documents*, 86, 297, but who also cites 1 Cor 5:19ff.).

not the purportedly composite letters of 1 and 2 Corinthians, for example, that Trobisch and Murphy-O'Connor argue for.[90] The analogy is at best approximate according to their description of the corpora involved.

There is a further difficulty in Trobisch's analysis concerning the distinction between public and private letters.[91] Trobisch apparently needs to prove that Paul's letters are public letters in order to use the categories of analysis that he does (including wishing to show that such letters were kept in copies), so much so that he overstates his case. He contends that a private letter is one that needed to be sent to fulfil its purpose, and that it is never a copy but the original. Not only are both of these specific characteristics questionable,[92] but the entire construct of public versus private letter has been subject to criticism. As Stowers says, the distinction

> does not hold well for either Greco-Roman society in general or for letter writing. Politics, or example, was based on the institutions of friendship

---

[90] Trobisch, *Paul's Letter Collection*, 56 on Cicero, *Fam* Bk 13, and 73-86 on the Corinthian letters; Murphy-O'Connor, *Paul*, 127. Murphy-O'Connor (*Paul*, 118) contends that Richards's theory of a secretary using Paul's copies cannot account for those letters that are composites. Murphy-O'Connor clearly assumes that theories of composite letters are proven.

[91] Trobisch, *Paul's Letter Collection*, 48-50; idem, *Die Entstehung*, 84-88. The distinction goes back to G.A. Deissmann (*Bible Studies* [trans. A. Grieve; Edinburgh: T. & T. Clark, 1901 (1895, 1897)], 3-59; 'Epistolary Literature', in T.K. Cheyne and J.S. Black [eds.], *Encyclopaedia Biblica: A Critical Dictionary of the Literary, Political and Religious History, the Archaeology, Geography and Natural History of the Bible* [4 vols.; London: A. & C. Black, 1899–1907], 2.cols. 1323ff.; *Light from the Ancient East* [trans. L.R.M. Strachan; London: Hodder & Stoughton, 4th edn, 1927 (1910)], 224-46), but is now seen to be overdrawn, at least in much English-language scholarship. For representative recent examples, see D.E. Aune, *The New Testament in its Literary Environment* (LEC; Philadelphia: Westminster Press, 1987), 161; L.T. Johnson, *The Writings of the New Testament: An Interpretation* (Philadelphia: Fortress Press, 1986), 251. Trobisch does not seem to know of the English-language scholarship that has questioned Deissmann's categories, at least as reflected in his references in *Die Entstehung*.

[92] Trobisch himself distinguishes between a letter being sent and hand delivered by the author, a particularly doubtful distinction, in the light of letters being seen in epistolary studies as a substitute for the personal presence of the author. See H. Koskenniemi, *Studien zur Idee und Phraseologie des griechischen Briefes bis 400 n. Chr.* (Suomalaisen Tiedeakatemian Toimituksia B.102.2; Helsinki: Suomal-ainen Tiedeakatemia, 1956), esp. 88-127.

and family... The distinction between private friendly letters and public political letters is thus a distinction more appropriate to modernity than antiquity. Furthermore, many correspondences in antiquity that were either originally written or later edited with an eye toward publication have what we would call a private character: for example, Cicero, Ruricius, Seneca.[93]

There is also evidence that even private letters regularly had copies made (e.g. Cicero, *Fam* 9.26.1; 7.18.1; *Att* 13.6.3).[94]

The book of Hebrews is a recognizable problem for any analysis of the Pauline corpus, and Trobisch addresses it directly. His claim is that the flexibility of placement of Hebrews, along with other internal and external differences, indicates that Hebrews was not part of the original Pauline corpus, but was added later. However, Trobisch does not let other indications of flexibility in the canonical orderings affect his hypothesis. $\mathfrak{P}^{46}$ is, by Trobisch's admission, 'the oldest manuscript of the letters of Paul'.[95] Not only does it have Hebrews after Romans and before 1 and 2 Corinthians, but it has Ephesians before Galatians, and, of course, breaks off in 1 Thessalonians. Even though many scholars, including its original editor, Kenyon, and many since, believe that $\mathfrak{P}^{46}$ originally also included only 2 Thessalonians and Philemon,[96] other scholars (as noted above) believe that the Pastorals were included as well.[97] Trobisch must believe that this is the case, because he makes the claim that 'There is no manuscript evidence to prove that the letters of Paul ever existed in an edition containing only some of the thirteen letters'.[98] He must have this scenario in order to make his case. However, $\mathfrak{P}^{46}$ may well be just such an abbreviated instance, and be the earliest besides. This says nothing of the fragmentary papyri that only have a portion of a single Pauline letter (these include $\mathfrak{P}$10, 11, 14, 15, 16, 26, 27, 31, 32, 34, 40, 49, 51, 65, 68, 87, 94), or a few that have only a couple of letters (e.g. $\mathfrak{P}^{30}$ with parts of 1 and 2 Thessalonians,

---

[93] S.K. Stowers, *Letter Writing in Greco-Roman Antiquity* (LEC; Philadelphia: Westminster Press, 1986), 19.
[94] Murphy-O'Connor, *Paul*, 12-13.
[95] Trobisch, *Paul's Letter Collection*, 13, who dates it to around AD 200. Trobisch appears to have modified his position since *Die Entstehung* (pp. 26-27 and n. 60), where he contends that the 200 date is not so certain and argues instead for the third century.
[96] See F.G. Kenyon, *The Text of the Greek Bible* (rev. A.W. Adams; London: Duckworth, 3rd edn, 1975 [1936]), 70-71.
[97] See Duff, '$\mathfrak{P}$46 and the Pastorals', 578-90.
[98] Trobisch, *Paul's Letter Collection*, 22.

𝔓⁹² with Ephesians and 2 Thessalonians). This raises the further question of why Trobisch is content to accept variation in the arrangement of the ordering of Hebrews, as well as of some of the other letters (e.g. Philippians and Colossians in D 06 Codex Claromontanus, and Ephesians and Galatians in 𝔓⁴⁶), but not to accept the kind of evidence that, for example, Schmithals has marshalled that Romans belonged elsewhere, rather than at the beginning of the canon, a hypothesis that is also based upon early evidence.[99]

There are a number of further problems with Trobisch's analysis that relate to traditional critical issues in New Testament scholarship. For example, not everyone will be convinced by his dividing of the two Corinthian letters into seven original fragments. This is required in order to account for what Trobisch and others have seen as the shifts within the letters. However, there is also much recent scholarship that wishes to argue for the integrity of each of the Corinthian letters. There is also much critical scholarship that wishes to see fragmentary letters in the expanded portion of Trobisch's collection, such as in Philippians. Trobisch does not explain this later process of formation in any kind of detail, but it would seem unnecessary to have fragmentary letters found in the later pseudepigraphic letters. But there is apparently nothing in Trobisch's analysis that prevents the same criteria that he uses on the Corinthian letters from being applied to other letters, such as Philippians. Trobisch's analysis of Romans 16, which he takes as a cover letter being sent with a copy of Romans, is also out of keeping with much recent research. Much recent scholarship has argued for the unity of the letter,[100] a conclusion that jeopardizes Trobisch's analysis since this chapter introduces a distinctly personal element that he finds unsuitable for the four public letters of Paul.[101] Further, for Trobisch, to admit that there are any authentic letters in the rest of the thirteen threatens his theory, since it

---

[99] Schmithals, *Paul*, 254, citing the Muratorian canon (is this evidence for its early date?), Marcion, and Tertullian, *Marc* 4.5 and *Haer* 36.

[100] See Gamble, *Textual History, passim*; J.A. Fitzmyer, *Romans* (AB 33; New York: Doubleday, 1993), 55-68.

[101] Trobisch's argumentation (*Paul's Letter Collection*, 71) is difficult to grasp. He seems to assume that Romans 16 is a cover letter on the basis of there being many ancient examples of such letters (the one example he cites is from the third century AD). He then gives two characteristics of the cover letter, one that it is not addressed to the same place as is the original letter, and the other that it most often would mention the enclosed copies of the letter. Thus, he must take Rom 16:22 as 'I [Tertius] copied the letter for you'.

alters the symmetry that he sees between the three major parts. However, the critical consensus today is that at least seven of the letters are authentic, including 1 Thessalonians and Philippians in the church letters and Philemon in the personal letters. To allow for any of these letters to be authentic would indicate that, contrary to Trobisch, it was not necessary for Paul to be involved with the authentic letters for them to be collected, the heart of Trobisch's scheme; or that his rigidly following the principle of decreasing length within each section does not, in fact, hold as a means of dividing the three sections of the Pauline canon. There is also difficulty with the part of Goodspeed's hypothesis that Trobisch claims to have inadvertently supported. Again, many scholars of the book of Ephesians do not see this letter as forming any kind of an introductory letter suitable for the Pauline canon—in this case, even a reduced canon of nine letters—nor is it found at the head (or foot) of any Pauline letter list.[102] Lastly, the criterion of the collection has already been used by some scholars to establish the supposedly authentic letters.[103] However, most scholars do not think of this as a sufficient criterion. Once this is admitted, and the possibility of other letters broached, then the unity of Trobisch's group is lost, and with it, his theory.

4. CONCLUSION

This paper may appear to be simply a repetition of previously proposed views, with critical responses that leave each position seriously if not fatally wounded. If such is the case, then that is in itself a positive result of sorts—there is no entirely satisfactory theory as to the origins of the Pauline letter collection. That may well be the case—that critical scholarship at this point cannot agree on a convincing explanation of how it is that the Pauline letter collection emerged. Emerge it did, however, though not without plenty of controversy and confusion from virtually the earliest lists to the pre-

---

[102] Best, *Ephesians*, 66; Zuntz, *Text of the Epistles*, 276. It would be a dubious argument to claim that once the first four letters are removed, then Ephesians stands at the head of a collection. There is still the objection that the content of Ephesians itself it not appropriate as such a letter.

[103] See M. Kiley, *Colossians and Pseudepigraphy* (BibSem; Sheffield: JSOT Press, 1986), 46-47, who argues that Paul mentions 'financial transactions on behalf of his mission' in the seven authentic letters.

sent over the timing of such formation, the limits and ordering of such a collection, what constitutes the authentic letters in such a collection, and what were the later pseudepigraphic additions.

Perhaps it is most appropriate in conclusion to sift and analyze some of what I see as the common ground upon which all of the theories above rest. The first conclusion is that virtually all are agreed that the gathering of the Pauline corpus required personal involvement at some level. The Pauline school theory has been suggested, but even it appears most convincing if one can find recognizable and named people in that school. As a result, the proposals range from Paul himself to early followers (e.g. Luke, Timothy or Onesimus), to his opponents (e.g. Marcion), to later followers and supporters. Despite the diversity of possibilities and extent of time, it would appear that future proposals should concentrate on establishing reasonable procedures to determine who such people might have been and the kinds of actions that such individuals could have taken. A second conclusion is that theories that require the least dissection of the individual letters have a better chance of being accepted as probable. The more fragmentary hypotheses, it seems, offer less ground for establishing firm conclusions. This is especially seen in dealing with the Corinthian letters. The fact of two Corinthian letters is a strong argument against extravagant multiple letter hypotheses (this says nothing about how such fragmentary hypotheses are arrived at). A third point of common conception is that—whenever it may have happened—the letters were probably gathered in a particular place. This goes along with an individual being involved, and probably points away from there being many Pauline letter collections existing for very long in separate places. The amount of commonalty between the early manuscripts, as both Trobisch and Murphy-O'Connor have shown, clearly supports this. In any event, the geographical distribution of the letters of Paul is not very wide. Even if one includes the Pastoral Epistles as letters addressed to individuals located in the Asia Minor Mediterranean area, we have all of the letters confined to a stretch from Galatia in the east (probably Roman provincial Galatia) to Rome in the west, with Colossae, Laodicea/ Ephesus, Philippi, Thessalonica, and Corinth in between (a distance of roughly 1100 miles). Most of the letters were sent to destinations within a radius of not more than about 150 miles around the Aegean

Sea, all of them places where there were some Pauline supporters.[104] In the light of the travelling possible during that time (Paul himself serves as an excellent example), it is not unlikely that someone could have gathered the letter collection that resulted (missing out some letters that were either no longer extant or thought not to be of value, perhaps because of their particularistic nature).[105] It appears that such a process would have occurred early, resulting in the relative fixity of the contents of the manuscripts that contained Paul's letters and their order.

In the light of this, it is not surprising that variation in the Pauline corpus occurs within relatively narrow parameters, revolving around Hebrews, the alternating of Ephesians and Galatians, some uncertainty over Colossians and Ephesians, and of course whether the Pastorals are included.[106] As to Hebrews, I think that Trobisch is probably right that the amount and type of variation with Hebrews indicates that it was a later addition to a relatively fixed corpus of Paul's letters.[107] As Murphy-O'Connor has shown, however, if one does not rely only upon counting characters, but uses other evident ancient forms of measurement, such as the indicated stichoi, the fluctuation in placement of Hebrews is the only real variable—there is otherwise virtual fixity to the manuscript ordering.[108] The placement of Colossians before Philippians in a few manuscripts is understandable since they are within 200 characters of each other, and have similar stichoi in some traditions. In any event, this transposition only occurs in D 06 Codex Claromontanus and a fourteenth-century minuscule (5).[109] The placement of Ephesians before Galatians only occurs in $\mathfrak{P}^{46}$. This ordering does reflect actual length, with Ephesians 700-900 letters longer, depending upon whose count is followed. But again, the number of stichoi in some traditions is similar.[110] In other words, the

---

[104] See Murphy-O'Connor, *Paul*, 128, who uses such information in terms of his collection B.

[105] On the issue of the particularity of the letters and the problems related to collecting the Pauline letters, see Dahl, 'Particularity'.

[106] Schmithals, *Paul*, 256.

[107] Trobisch, *Paul's Letter Collection*, 20.

[108] Murphy-O'Connor, *Paul*, 125.

[109] Murphy-O'Connor (*Paul*, 123) dismisses this as 'an error without historical significance'.

[110] Murphy-O'Connor (*Paul*, 124) again dismisses this transposition as 'an insignificant error'. Cf. Trobisch, *Paul's Letter Collection*, 17, where he claims

evidence seems to point towards consistency in the composition and ordering of the entire Pauline corpus, not just within three groups of letters. Further, apart from 𝔓⁴⁶ (a manuscript that is important but should not necessarily be overvalued, as Zuntz's study of its peculiarities has indicated),[111] Hebrews only appears either at the juncture of the church and personal letters (that is, between 2 Thessalonians and 1 Timothy), or at the end of the Pauline corpus (or at the beginning).[112] If one accepts that this variation indicates that Hebrews was a later addition, it appears to have been added at the end of the corpus to indicate ambivalence over its authorship, or at the end of the church letters (after 2 Thessalonians) because it is not a personal letter, but in this case still reflecting indecision over authorship. In other words, if one removes Hebrews from the Pauline canon, there is a clearly established Pauline corpus that essentially follows the principle of decreasing size[113] from Romans to 2 Thessalonians, what might be called the church letters, and then begins again with an ordering in decreasing size from 1 Timothy to Philemon, what might be called the personal letters.[114]

---

that 𝔓⁴⁶ in its entirety is arranged according to length, with Hebrews placed before 1 Corinthi-ans so as not to separate the two Corinthian letters.

[111] Zuntz, *Text of the Epistles*, 263-83.

[112] A possible exception is the numbering of the chapters in B 03 Codex Vaticanus. But, as Trobisch notes (*Paul's Letter Collection*, 21-22), it is only the numbering of the chapters that places Hebrews after Galatians, since the books themselves are written with Hebrews after 2 Thessalonians. *Contra* Murphy-O'Connor, *Paul*, 123-25.

[113] This pattern is thus found not only in modern arrangements of the Pauline canon (Bruce, *Canon*, 130 n. 50), but in ancient times as well.

[114] This is not the place to defend at length the hypothesis that all of these letters qualify as personal letters of sorts, except to note that Philemon is typically considered a personal letter even if it is more than that (J.A. Fitzmyer, *The Letter to Philemon* [AB 34C; New York: Doubleday, 2000], 23), and that much of the dispute over authenticity of the Pastoral Epistles concerns the personal elements found in the letters and the fact that they are addressed to individuals associated with Paul's mission (see E.E. Ellis, *Paul and his Recent Interpreters* [Grand Rapids: Eerdmans, 1961], 49-57, for an older but representative survey of opinion). See now also J.T. Reed, 'To Timothy or Not? A Discourse Analysis of 1 Timothy', in S.E. Porter and D.A. Carson (eds.), *Biblical Greek Language and Linguistics: Open Questions in Current Research* (JSNTSup 80; Sheffield: JSOT Press, 1993), 90-118, who notes the clear indications of the personal nature of the correspondence addressed to Timothy.

Viewing the Pauline corpus in this way, I think, opens up further possibilities regarding its formation. We do not need to divide the corpus into three groups, reflecting three stages of formation. It is possible to view it as two groups, but two groups each united according to principles of organization and orientation of the letters within it. It is possible that Paul was involved in this process by virtue of his having produced copies of his letters,[115] even if some of them are seen to be more personal than strictly public letters, since such a firm disjunction between letter types does not seem to hold. If the corpus of authentic Pauline letters extends beyond the four Trobisch posits—as I (and most scholars) think is virtually certain,[116] and as the organization noted above seems to suggest—then Paul's chances of being involved are quite possibly increased, as he would have perhaps been the only person, possibly apart from his few closest associates, who would have had access to the many copies produced by his scribe. The only other person or persons who would have had such access would have been his closest followers, such as Luke, or possibly Timothy.[117] If Paul were not the initiator of the collecting process, and if there were not copies of the letters readily available, then the act of instigating the Pauline collection must have fallen to one of these close companions. As Guthrie says, and as virtually all of the theories noted above except for that of Goodspeed acknowledge, there is no evidence that Paul's reputation fell into disrepute. Thus, the collecting process must have involved a close follower or advocate of Paul, who perhaps undertook such action near the end of Paul's life, possibly when he was in prison in Rome, or very soon after his death. Luke is the most likely figure for such a scenario, on the basis of the internal Pauline evidence (Col 4:14; Phlm 24; 2 Tim 4:11), Church tradition

---

[115] I find Richards's theory very plausible, in the light of practice in the ancient world, the nature of the Pauline correspondence, and the indications from the Pauline corpus as a whole. See also O. Roller, *Das Formular der paulinischen Briefe: Ein Beitrag zur Lehre vom antiken Briefe* (BWANT 4.6; Stuttgart: Kohlhammer, 1933).

[116] Critical scholarship would, as noted above, endorse seven letters, but the above formulation suggests that there are structural reasons regarding the shape of the Pauline corpus for seeing all thirteen as authentic. Less likely is that nine letters are authentic, since that requires bracketing out an entire category of letters, the personal letters, in which at least one letter is acknowledged to be genuine.

[117] See Guthrie, *New Testament Introduction*, 655-57, for defence of Timothy. The relationship of this theory to the issue of the authenticity of the Pastoral Epistles is unavoidable.

regarding Luke's relation to Paul (especially in Acts, but also in Irenaeus, *Haer* 1.23.1; 3.10.1; 3.14.1; etc.), and even much critical scholarship regarding authorship of Acts.[118]

The major limitation here is the notion that Luke supposedly gives no direct evidence of knowing Paul's letters in Acts.[119] A useful analogy can be drawn between how Luke handles Jesus tradition in his Gospel and in Acts.[120] In the Gospel, Luke cites the words of Jesus extensively, and there is no question that (as the prologue says, Luke 1:1-4) he has used sources such as Mark and others that contained the words of Jesus. However, in Acts apart from the ascension and the words of Jesus in 1:4-5, 7-8, there is no other explicit indication of Luke's knowledge of Jesus tradition. In other words, here we have proof that, even though Luke knew important facts, he did not feel compelled to relate them. The same is perhaps true regarding knowledge of Paul's letters. What saves this from being sheer hypothesis are indicators throughout Acts that, although Luke does not depict Paul as a letter-writer or quote his letters explicitly, he seems to know what Paul had written in some of his letters. This is shown by numerous verbal, conceptual and perspectival factors, as Walker has shown.[121] Of course, if the compiler was Timothy, the problem of Acts does not emerge. In any case, there is reasonable evidence to see the origin of the Pauline corpus during the latter part of Paul's life or

---

[118] See C.-J. Thornton, *Der Zeuge des Zeugen: Lukas als Historiker der Paulusreisen* (WUNT 56; Tübingen: Mohr Siebeck, 1991); Porter, *Paul of Acts*, 187-206. It is even possible to accommodate the objection that this close companion assembled a number of smaller letters into larger ones, especially if he had been close to Paul and knew his mission strategy—this assumes that such a hypothesis is necessary.

[119] See Dahl, 'Particularity', 265-66, who recognizes the problem.

[120] I must confess to having lost sight of who first originated this analogy, and apologize for not making explicit reference to its source. The analogy, I believe, is so pertinent that I think it merits inclusion in any case, and I would welcome being informed of its originator so that I can include reference in any future reprint or use of it.

[121] Walker, 'Acts and the Pauline Corpus Reconsidered', 63-70, following especially M.S. Enslin, '"Luke" and Paul', *JAOS* 58 (1938), 81-90; *idem*, 'Once Again, Luke and Paul', *ZNW* 61 (1970), 253-71; and now with further evidence in W.O. Walker, Jr., 'Acts and the Pauline Corpus Revisited: Peter's Speech at the Jerusalem Conference', in R.P. Thompson and T.E. Phillips (eds.), *Literary Studies in Luke–Acts: Essays in Honor of Joseph B. Tyson* (Macon, GA: Mercer University Press, 1998), 77-86.

shortly after his death, almost assuredly instigated by a close follower if not by Paul himself, and close examination of the early manuscripts with Paul's letters seems to endorse this hypothesis.

DISPUTED AND UNDISPUTED LETTERS OF PAUL

MARK HARDING

Australian College of Theology
Kingsford, New South Wales, Australia

1. THE PAULINE CORPUS

Paul wrote letters. As one scholar has recently and rightly affirmed, they are the 'oldest written testimonies of Christianity'.[1] The New Testament contains thirteen letters that bear his name. It is also clear from the New Testament that this is not the extent of his output. 1 Corinthians 5:9 refers to a letter of Paul, now lost. 2 Corinthians 2:4 and 7:8 refer to a 'painful' letter, also lost.

Early Christian writers are aware of Paul's letters. Clement knows that Paul wrote a letter to the Corinthians (*1 Clem* 47.1-3). Ignatius speaks, albeit vaguely, of Paul remembering the Ephesians 'in every letter' (Ignatius, *Eph* 12.2).[2] The author of 2 Peter knows that Paul

---

[1] J. Becker, *Paul Apostle to the Gentiles* (Louisville: Westminster/John Knox, 1993), 8. Cf. H. Koester, *Introduction to the New Testament* (2 vols.; Philadelphia: Fortress Press; Berlin: de Gruyter, 1982), 2.1-2.

[2] See J.B. Lightfoot, *The Apostolic Fathers* (2 parts in 5 vols.; London: Macmillan, 1885–90; repr. Peabody, MA: Hendrickson, 1989), 2.2.65. Lightfoot points out that Ephesian Christians are actually mentioned in a number of Pauline letters, namely, Romans (16:5), 1 Corinthians (15:32; 16:8, 19), 2 Corinthians (1:8), and 1 and 2 Timothy, both of which he believed were genuine. However, W.R. Schoedel (*Ignatius of Antioch* [Philadelphia: Fortress Press, 1985], 73 and n. 7) believes that the remark is an instance of hyperbole (cf. 1 Thess 1:8; 1 Cor 1:2; Col 1:23; Polycarp, *Phil* 11.3). Andreas Lindemann (*Paulus im ältesten Christentum* [Tübingen: Mohr Siebeck, 1979], 84-85), who sees little evidence of the knowledge and use of letters of Paul in Ignatius, suggests that in *Eph* 12.2 Ignatius is articulating a belief that Paul must have written to the Ephesians often, since he clearly knew them well, having spent so much time among them, or that he would have occasionally thought of the Ephesians in his letters.

wrote letters (3:16). Polycarp also reminds his addressees, the Philippians, that Paul wrote 'letters' to them which they should study in order to progress in the faith (Polycarp, *Phil* 3.2).[3]

The extent to which Christian writers of the sub-apostolic period cite passages from Paul is keenly debated. Nearly 60 years ago, Albert Barnett produced an extensive examination of the degrees and shades of putative literary dependence of early writers prior to Irenaeus on the letters of Paul. Barnett's analysis invites the observation that *Romans* is cited with 'practical certainty' by Clement and Justin, *1 Corinthians* by Clement, Ignatius, Polycarp, and Justin, *Galatians* by Justin, *Philippians* by Polycarp, and *Colossians* by Justin.[4]

---

[3] One need not conclude that there were several letters of Paul to the Philippians known to Polycarp. See discussion in A.E. Barnett, *Paul Becomes a Literary Influence* (Chicago: University of Chicago Press, 1941), 174; E. Dassmann, *Der Stachel im Fleisch: Paulus in der frühchristlichen Literatur bis Irenäus* (Münster: Aschendorff, 1979), 154-55; J.B. Lightfoot, *Philippians* (London: Macmillan, 1881), 138-42. Lightfoot does consider the possibility that there were once several letters to the Philippians but prefers the view that ἐπιστολαί can be used of a single letter. However, see W. Schneemelcher, 'Paulus in der griechischen Kirche des zweiten Jahrhunderts', *ZKG* 75 (1964), 7 (following W. Bauer), for the view that that Polycarp has Phil 3:1 in mind, which might be read as implying on Paul's part that he had written to the addressees on other occasions. It is also possible that Polycarp is mirroring the view that Paul's letters to individual churches are tantamount to letters written to all, a point of view articulated in the Muratorian canon (see ll. 56-59).

[4] See the tables throughout Barnett, *Literary Influence*. Barnett is 'practically certain' that 1 Peter cites Romans and Ephesians, the Fourth Gospel cites Romans, Galatians and Ephesians, and the Pastoral Epistles cite Romans, 1 Corinthians, and Philippians. The 'practically certain' evaluation is indicated in Barnett's book by the letter symbol 'A'. Passages from Paul cited with a 'high degree of probability' receive the symbol 'B'. 'C' denotes passages cited with a 'reasonable degree of probability'. There is also a category of Pauline passages early writers may be alluding to entitled 'unclassed'. See Barnett, *Literary Influence*, x. When the 'A', 'B' and 'C' passages are grouped together, Clement of Rome appears to know seven Pauline letters (Romans, 1 and 2 Corinthians, Galatians, Ephesians, Philippians, Colossians), Ignatius eight letters (2 Thessalonians and Philemon may be alluded to, but the Pastorals appear not to be known by Ignatius), Polycarp nine (but not the Pastorals and Philemon), Justin six (Romans, 1 Corinthians, Galatians, Ephesians, Colossians, and 2 Thessalonians [2 Corinthians and 1 Thessalonians may be alluded to]), Ephesians nine (but not the Pastorals), the Pastorals a ten letter Pauline corpus, 1 Peter five (Romans, 2 Corinthians, Galatians, Ephesians, and 2 Thessalonians), the Fourth Gospel nine (but not Philemon and the Pastorals) and Hebrews eight (but not 2 Thessalonians,

However, it has been countered that, at best, these writers cite mere snatches and fragments of Pauline letters. Wilhelm Schneemelcher concluded that there are no unambiguous citations of Paul in early Christian writers before Irenaeus. Rather, these writers were more likely citing formulae and echoing traditions which happen to be present in the Pauline letters, not signalling their literary dependence on Paul.[5] In support of Schneemelcher's scepticism, it might be noted that no writer before Irenaeus cites any Pauline passage with clear ascription of authorship with the exception of Clement of Rome's citation of 1 Cor 1:11-13 (see *1 Clem* 47.1-3). By contrast, Irenaeus, unlike his predecessors, frequently cites Paul. He does so quite intentionally. Nevertheless, it is difficult to avoid the literary evidence that some Pauline letters are known to many of the early Fathers, though it is unlikely that collections of letters appeared as early as Harnack and Barnett had propounded.[6]

Philemon, and the Pastorals). Some scholars are prepared to argue that the Pastorals are cited or alluded to in *1 Clement* and Ignatius. For a positive evaluation of the evidence that the Pastorals are cited or alluded to in Polycarp, see A Committee of the Oxford Society of Historical Theology, *The New Testament in the Apostolic Fathers* (Oxford: Clarendon Press, 1905), 95-96. However, Barnett (*Paul*, 182-83) argues that, in the case of Polycarp, *Phil*, it is much more likely that the Pastorals are dependent on Polycarp (cf. W. Bauer, *Orthodoxy and Heresy in Earliest Christianity* [Philadelphia: Fortress Press, 1971], 217). I believe Polycarp and the author of the Pastorals are citing widely attested maxims. See M. Dibelius and H. Conzelmann, *The Pastoral Epistles* (Hermeneia; Philadelphia: Fortress Press, 1972), 85-86; N. Brox, *Die Pastoralbriefe* (RNT; Regensburg: Pustet, 1969), 26-28. Finally, it should be noted that Barnett does not register the possible citation of passages from the Pastorals in the apologists Theophilus (*Letter to Autolycus* 3.14) and Athenagoras (*A Plea for the Christians* 37) (both written in ca. 170–180 CE). For texts, see *ANF* 2.115 and 148 respectively.

[5] Schneemelcher, 'Paulus', 4-13. He gives as an example of the use of traditional material Ignatius, *Eph* 18.2; 20.2. Ignatius, Schneemelcher contends, is not dependent on Rom 1:3 ('Paulus', 5 and n. 11). Incidentally, Barnett (*Literary Influence*, 157, 159) assigns the classification 'B' ('high degree of probability') to the degree of literary influence of Paul on these two passages.

[6] Lindemann, *Paulus*, 30. Harnack argued that the thirteen-letter Pauline corpus was available to Polycarp. Barnett contends that Ephesians was written as the preface of a nine-letter collection, and that the author of the Pastorals knew a ten-letter Pauline corpus (*Literary Influence*, 2-3, 277). For an overview of the evidence for the knowledge of Pauline letters in each writer, see Dassmann, *Stachel*, 79-83 (Clement), 129-35 (Ignatius), 153-55 (Polycarp), 244-48 (Justin), 250-51 (Athenagoras), 251-54 (Theophilus).

The earliest list or canon of Pauline epistles of which we know is that of Marcion (ca. 140 CE), as attested by Tertullian (ca. 200 CE) and Epiphanius (ca. 375 CE). Based on the order in which he cites the letters of Paul in his refutation of Marcion in book five of his *Adversus Marcionem*, Marcion's canon of Paul's letters (the *Apostolikon*) comprised ten letters in the order Galatians, 1 and 2 Corinthians, Romans, 1 and 2 Thessalonians, Laodiceans, Colossians, Philemon and Philippians.[7] The letter to the Laodiceans, Tertullian writes, is none other than canonical Ephesians, which Marcion included, albeit 'mutilated', in his collection, having also changed its name.[8] The Pastoral

---

[7] See A. von Harnack, *Marcion: Das Evangelium vom fremden Gott* (repr. Darmstadt: Wissenschaftliche Buchgesellschaft, 1985), 43*, 168-69*. See also Epiphanius, *Panarion* 42.9.4. F.C. Baur (*Paul the Apostle of Jesus Christ: His Life and Work, his Epistles and his Doctrine. A Contribution to a Critical History of Primitive Christianity* [2 vols.; London: Williams and Norgate, 1875, 1876], 1.247) argues that the list as preserved in Epiphanius reveals two distinct collections arranged chronologically in order of composition—the collection of genuine letters, Galatians–Romans, followed by the pseudepigrapha, Thessalonians–Philippians. Baur's book was originally published in German in 1860.

[8] See Tertullian, *Marc* 5.11, 17 (*ANF* 3.454, 464-65). Cf. Epiphanius, *Panarion* 42.9.3-4. Epiphanius includes Ephesians in Marcion's canon, but adds that Marcion 'also has parts of the so-called *Epistle to the Laodiceans*' (text in F. Williams [trans.], *The Panarion of Epiphanius of Salamis* [2 vols.; Leiden: Brill, 1997], 1.278-79). It is much more likely that Marcion's copy of the letter did not identify the place of destination as 'Ephesians'. For an analysis of the relationship between Ephesians and Marcion's *Laodiceans*, see R.J. Hoffmann, *Marcion: On the Restitution of Christianity* (AARDS 46; Chico, CA: Scholars Press, 1984), 254-59. The confusion over the title of the letter is understandable given the fact that the earliest and best manuscripts do not in fact nominate the destination of the letter ($\mathfrak{P}^{46}$ ℵ* B* *et al.*). See further B.M. Metzger, *A Textual Commentary on the Greek New Testament* (London: United Bible Societies, 1971), 601; C.L. Mitton, *Ephesians* (NCB; London: Marshall, Morgan & Scott, 1973), 40. Mitton suggests that the letter may have carried the name of some other destination (like 'Laodiceans') or that the letter was intended to be a circular. Perhaps, he suggests, 'Ephesians' was added in the knowledge of Paul's extensive dealings with the church there. A.T. Lincoln (*Ephesians* [WBC 42; Waco: Word Books, 1990], 1-4), seeking to make sense of the difficult syntax of the superscript, argues that the letter might have been originally written for congregations in Hierapolis and Laodicea. The place names were deleted by a scribe in the interests of universalizing 'the sphere of the letter's influence' (p. 4). The superscription 'To the Ephesians' was added at a later date (pp. lxxxi-lxxxii).

Epistles, however, were not present in Marcion's canon. Indeed, Marcion, Tertullian reports, rejected them.⁹

In his *Adversus Haereses*, Irenaeus cites each letter of the New Testament Pauline corpus, except Philemon, including the Pastorals. Moreover, he attests Romans, Galatians, Colossians, Ephesians, and Philippians by name, though not differentiating the letters to the Corinthians and Thessalonians, and not distinguishing between the three Pastorals. His biblical canon unambiguously encompasses twelve of the canonical New Testament Pauline letters.¹⁰ The earliest New Testament manuscript of what appears to be the Pauline corpus, namely, 𝔓⁴⁶ (ca. 200), includes Hebrews second after Romans, but probably did not include the Pastorals.¹¹ The Muratorian canon (ca. 200) lists a thirteen-letter corpus, noting Philemon and the Pastorals, letters addressed to individuals, as different in kind from the public letters Paul wrote to churches (ll. 59-63).¹²

---

⁹ *Marc* 5.21. Tertullian suggests that Marcion rejected the letters because he did not believe that Paul wrote to individuals.

¹⁰ For the use of Paul's letters in Irenaeus, see E. Aleith, *Paulusverständnis in der alten Kirche* (Berlin: Töpelmann, 1937), 70; Dassmann, *Stachel*, 295-97. According to W.W. Harvey (see Dassmann, *Stachel*, 295), there are 324 citations of Paul in *Haer.*

¹¹ 2 Thessalonians and Philemon are not extant in the papyrus either. See discussion in F.G. Kenyon, *The Chester Beatty Biblical Papyri: Descriptions and Texts of Twelve Manuscripts on Papyrus of the Greek Bible. Fasciculus III Supplement: Pauline Epistles* (London: Emery Walker, 1936), xii. For a rejection of the argument that the absence of the Pastoral Epistles in the papyrus indicates a lack of their wide acceptance in the church of ca. 200 and for the possibility that the papyrus might have originally included the Pastorals after all, see J. Duff, '𝔓46 and the Pastorals: A Misleading Consensus', *NTS* 44 (1998), 578-90. In ℵ A B C Hebrews appears after 2 Thessalonians and before the Pastorals (see B.F. Westcott, *The Epistle to the Hebrews* [London: Macmillan, 1892], xxx; G.M. Hahneman, *The Muratorian Fragment and the Development of the Canon* [Oxford: Clarendon Press, 1992], 122-23). Hebrews was accepted by gnostic exegetes as a letter of Paul. Indeed, E.H. Pagels (*The Gnostic Paul* [Philadelphia: Fortress Press, 1975], 5) surmises that 𝔓46 exactly corresponds to the Valentinian canon of Pauline letters as deduced by the usage of the Pauline corpus in Valentinian writings.

¹² For discussion of the Muratorian canon's relating of the seven letters to the churches in Revelation 1-2 and the seven churches to which Paul wrote, see Barnett, *Literary Influence*, 41; Hahneman, *Muratorian Fragment*, 117-19. Nevertheless, it is not strictly accurate to describe these four letters as 'private'. Each one concludes with blessings in the plural. See M. Harding, *Tradition and Rhetoric in the Pastoral Epistles* (New York: Peter Lang, 1998), 100.

The case of Hebrews requires explanation. According to Eusebius, Hebrews was regarded as a letter of Paul by Clement of Alexandria. Clement sought to reconcile the stylistic differences between Hebrews and the Pauline letters by contending that Luke translated the original Hebrew of the letter into Greek, hence the Lukan style of the letter.[13] Origen, also alert to matters of style, regards the content of the letter as Pauline, but argues that the letter was not written by Paul but by a later interpreter.[14] Eusebius himself commends a thirteen-letter Pauline corpus with Hebrews as a fourteenth letter. However, he knows that Pauline authorship is doubted by some.[15] The Western church held out against Pauline authorship. The letter is first known from allusions to it in Clement of Rome.[16] Many in the East, including Athanasius, championed a fourteen-letter Pauline corpus.[17] It was formally declared one of the fourteen letters of Paul at the Second Council of Carthage in 419.[18] Over the next 1100 years Hebrews

---

Incidentally, the Muratorian canon appears to reflects doubts about the authorship of the Pastorals, which were 'written out of goodwill and love' (ll. 60-61; cf. l. 70 on the attribution of Wisdom to Solomon though it was actually written by his 'friends'), by commending their canonicity on the grounds that the catholic church values them 'for the ordering of ecclesiastical discipline' (ll. 62-63). See also M. Rist, 'Pseudepigraphy and the Early Christians', in D.E. Aune (ed.), *Studies in New Testament and Early Christian Literature: Essays in Honor of Allen P. Wikgren* (Leiden: Brill, 1972), 84. Rist argues that 'usage', that is, their witness to the current shape of ecclesiastical structure, rendered the Pastorals acceptable in the early church.

[13] Eusebius, *Hist eccl* 6.14.2. Pantaenus is probably the 'blessed presbyter' to whom Clement refers in the excerpt cited by Eusebius (*Hist eccl* 6.14.4). Pantaenus also believed that Paul wrote Hebrews.

[14] Eusebius, *Hist eccl* 6.25.11-14 (citing Origen). Origen leans towards Luke or Clement of Rome as author (see also *Hist eccl* 3.38).

[15] Eusebius, *Hist eccl* 3.38.2-3. Gaius of Rome was one who disputed Pauline authorship of Hebrews (*Hist eccl* 6.20).

[16] See the arguments for a Roman destination of the letter to the Hebrews in W.L. Lane, *Hebrews* (2 vols.; WBC 47A, B; Waco: Word Books, 1991), 1.lviii–lx.

[17] See Athanasius, 39th Festal Letter (written in 367), excerpted in *NPNF* (Series 2), 4.551-52. See also Westcott, *Hebrews*, lxxii. Hahneman (*Muratorian Fragment*, 121) observes that 'there is no evidence of a Pauline collection in the East which excluded Hebrews'. Pagels demonstrates that Hebrews was accepted as Pauline in gnostic circles (*Gnostic Paul*, 141-53).

[18] See Westcott, *Hebrews*, lxxiii.

enjoyed status as the fourteenth canonical Pauline letter.[19] However, scholars such as Erasmus, Luther, and Calvin were quite prepared to exercise independent judgment on this matter. Luther argued famously that Apollos wrote Hebrews. Calvin believed that Luke or Clement of Rome wrote it. Today no scholar argues that Paul was its author. That Hebrews emanates from the Pauline circle is quite possible (cf. 13:23).[20]

In a time when doubts were expressed as to the authorship of Hebrews, its early champions gave it an excellent pedigree in ascribing it (quite falsely) to the apostle. Here we are afforded an insight into an important criterion for determining the extent of the canon in the early church. An anonymous document, long used in the church and considered to be apostolic in its teaching, was ascribed to an apostle or to an associate of the apostles lest it be consigned to the extra-canonical margins. This factor also partly explains the attribution of the four (anonymous) Gospels to Matthew (an apostle), Mark (closely associated with Peter), Luke (closely associated with Paul) and John son of Zebedee (an apostle).[21] We should not underestimate the fact that in the case of Hebrews, and the four Gospels for that matter, the early church knew that it was dealing with an ancient document,[22] one that spoke in eloquent defence of the apostolic faith,

---

[19] See Westcott, *Hebrews*, lxxii-lxxiv. The Fourth Session of the Council of Trent (1546) re-affirmed Pauline authorship of Hebrews. See J. Neuner and J. Dupuis (eds.), *The Christian Faith in the Doctrinal Documents of the Catholic Church* (London: Collins Liturgical, 1983), 74.

[20] See Aleith, *Paulusverständnis*, 7 (including n. 41), for the influence of Pauline expressions. Koester (*Introduction*, 2.273) regards the echoes of the Pauline epistolary framework in Hebrews 13 as 'part of a pseudepigraphical frame'.

[21] This is not to deny that there were venerable traditions associating apostles and their associates with the Gospels. On the attribution of the Gospels to apostles or their associates, see Irenaeus, *Haer* 3.1.1. Cf. the fragments of Papias recorded in Eusebius, *Hist eccl* 3.39.15-16 (cf. 6.14.6); Tertullian, *Marc* 4.5. For the suspicion in which anonymous documents were held, see Tertullian, *Marc* 4.2 (*ANF* 3.347); W. Speyer, *Die literarische Fälschung im heidnischen und christlichen Altertum: Ein Versuch ihrer Deutung* (Munich: Beck, 1971), 175. On the significance of the long use of writings emanating from apostolic times as the crucial test of scriptural canonicity, see Koester, *Introduction*, 2.10-11; L.M. McDonald, *The Formation of the Christian Biblical Canon* (Peabody, MA: Hendrickson, 1995), especially 246-49.

[22] See Eusebius, *Hist eccl* 3.38.1, noting the use of Hebrews in *1 Clement*. Note also Origen's appreciation of the letter's antiquity (*Hist eccl* 6.25.13). Hebrews is cited and alluded to in *1 Clem* 36.2-5. See also other allusions in

and one that was no doubt very useful for countering the persistent influence of the venerable tradition of the Jews.[23] The impulse to ascribe anonymous works to apostles or their associates is consistent with the tendency of late first century New Testament documents, especially Luke–Acts, to regard the apostles as the guarantors of the practice and doctrine of the church.[24]

There are other extant letters in the Pauline corpus outside the New Testament. These are the letter to the Laodiceans and a letter known as *3 Corinthians*, as well as a collection of fourteen brief letters of Paul and Seneca, six of which claim Paul as the author. There are other non-canonical Pauline letters now lost. The Muratorian canon mentions a letter to the Laodiceans, one to the Alexandrians 'and several others [*et alia plura*] forged in Paul's name for the sect of the Marcionites, which cannot be received into the catholic church' (ll. 64-66). Adolf von Harnack identified the extant *Letter to the Laodiceans* with the Marcionite *Laodiceans* mentioned by the author of the Muratorian canon. In addition, Clement of Alexandria cites a passage recalling Phil 4:5 which he identifies as belonging to a letter of Paul to the Macedonians.[25]

We can thus speak of an extant corpus of some thirteen New Testament Pauline letters plus Hebrews (14), the extant *Laodiceans* (15), *3 Corinthians* (16), and the six letters of Paul to Seneca (22). We can rule out Hebrews since its Pauline authorship is the result of misattribution by many of the Fathers and by Councils and decrees of the Church. This leaves us with an extant corpus of twenty-one letters.

---

1 Clem 17.5; 36.1 and, less probably, 17.1; 19.2; 21.9; 27.1, 2; 56.4. For discussion, see *The New Testament in the Apostolic Fathers*, 44-48.

[23] Contra Koester, *Introduction* 2.272-76, who argues that the epistle counters gnostic denial of the salvific efficacy of the death of Christ.

[24] See W.A. Bienert, '"Apostolic" as a Norm of Orthodoxy', in W. Schneemelcher (ed.), *New Testament Apocrypha* (2 vols.; Cambridge: James Clarke; Louisville: Westminster/John Knox, rev. edn, 1990, 1992), 2.25-27.

[25] See Clement of Alexandria, *Protreptikos* 9.87.19-21; *New Testament Apocrypha* 2.31. Clement cites the following: ὁ κύριος ἤκκικεν λέγων, εὐλαβεῖσθε μὴ καταληφθῶμεν κενοί. While the first part of the citation recalls Phil 4:5, the second part is not attested.

2. Categories of Pauline Letters

In his great work on Paul, F.C. Baur appropriated the terms used by Eusebius in his discussion of the degrees of recognition of the canonical status of early Christian literature (*Hist ecc* 3.25) for his own classification of the New Testament Pauline deposit.[26] Baur argued that there were three categories of extant Pauline letters. The first class of Pauline letters included the four 'great epistles', namely, Romans, 1 and 2 Corinthians and Galatians. These were the Pauline *homologoumena*—the 'undisputed' letters. The letters of the second class, the remainder of the thirteen letters, Baur termed *antilegomena*, 'disputed' letters, because their authenticity had been called in question. However, in the case of the Pastoral Epistles, Baur added, doubt 'passes into an overwhelming probability of actual spuriousness'. Hence, Baur reserved Eusebius's term *nōtha*, 'spurious', for these three. I have also chosen to adopt these terms in the presentation below, though with some changes.

1. There are 'undisputed' letters—the *homologoumena*. All of these are found in the New Testament. Modern scholars are agreed that the following seven letters were written by Paul—Romans, 1 and 2 Corinthians, Galatians, Philippians, 1 Thessalonians and Philemon.

2. There are 'disputed' Pauline letters—the *antilegomena*. A majority of modern scholars argue that all or some of the remaining six letters of the New Testament Pauline corpus—Ephesians, Colossians, 2 Thessalonians, the Pastorals—are not genuine Pauline letters, and that they are pseudonymous. These might be termed *New Testament Pauline antilegomena*. A minority of modern scholars contend that all thirteen New Testament letters ascribed to Paul are genuine.

3. There are 'spurious' letters, *nōtha*. All Pauline letters outside the New Testament canon belong to this category. No modern scholar argues that one or more of these letters are genuine. These might be further categorised as *non-canonical Pauline Pseudepigrapha*.

---

[26] See his *Paul*, 1.245-49.

3. The Spurious Letters of Paul—The Non-Canonical Pauline Pseudepigrapha

There are eight extant letters in this category—*Laodiceans*, *3 Corinthians*, and the collection of six letters of Paul to Seneca.

Laodiceans[27]
Extant *Laodiceans* was accepted by Latin-speaking Christendom, as Vulgate and early Italian manuscript evidence bear witness. The letter found its way into the early vernacular European Bibles, including early English Bibles.[28] It is likely to have been penned originally in Greek. However, only the Latin text is extant.[29] The earliest manuscript of the letter is contained in the Fulda MS, written in 546. It is first cited in the fifth or sixth century pseudo-Augustinian *Speculum*.

Laodiceans is a cento of Pauline phrases drawn from several New Testament Pauline letters, Philippians overwhelmingly, though there are a couple of citations from Colossians and Galatians. Many commentators, such as James and Schneemelcher—editors of separate editions of the New Testament Apocrypha—dismiss it as 'wholly uninteresting' (James) or a 'clumsy forgery' (Schneemelcher).[30] Pink calls it 'paltry' (*armselig*).[31]

Most scholars doubt that this letter is the same as the Marcionite *Laodiceans* of the Muratorian canon. It does not articulate any of the distinctive tenets of Marcionite theology. Thus James, Schneemelcher, and other scholars argue that the pseudepigrapher was simply motivated to round out the Pauline corpus. Colossians 4:16 mentions a

---

[27] For discussion, text, and analysis, see J.B. Lightfoot, *Saint Paul's Epistles to the Colossians and to Philemon* (London: Macmillan, rev. edn, 1900), 272-98; L. Vouaux, *Les Actes de Paul et ses lettres apocryphes* (Paris: Letouzey & Ane, 1913), 315-26; K. Pink, 'Die pseudo-paulinischen Briefe II', *Bib* 6 (1925), 179-92; Harnack, *Marcion*, 134-49*; Schneemelcher, *New Testament Apocrypha*, 2.42-45; Hahneman, *Muratorian Fragment*, 196-200.

[28] See Harnack, *Marcion*, 134-35*; M.R. James, *The Apocryphal New Testament* (Oxford: Clarendon Press, 1924), 478; B.M. Metzger, *The Canon of the New Testament: Its Origin, Development, and Significance* (Oxford: Clarendon Press, 1987), 183.

[29] Lightfoot rendered the Latin text into Greek in his *Colossians*, 291-92.

[30] James, *Apocryphal New Testament*, 478; Schneemelcher, *New Testament Apocrypha*, 2.44.

[31] Pink, 'Die pseudo-paulinischen Briefe II', 190. Cf. Aleith, *Paulusverständnis*, 31, who describes the letter as being 'inhaltlich ohne jeden Wert'.

letter to (ἐκ, from) the *Laodiceans* that was also to be read to the Colossian community. Our pseudepigrapher, not finding such a letter in his Pauline corpus, created it from other Pauline letters in scissors and paste fashion. He did so without literary pretensions or attempt at rhetorical flair. However, Harnack argued that the two letters were in fact identical. He observed that Marcion's *Apostolikon* began with Galatians, and that extant *Laodiceans* begins with the citation of Gal 1:1. Moreover, there are subtle underscorings of Marcion's teaching. It was composed, Harnack surmised, by a Marcionite once the title 'Ephesians', championed by the orthodox, had been restored to the letter Marcion had known as *Laodiceans*.[32]

Nevertheless, Lewis Donelson, while rejecting the arguments advanced by Harnack for the identity of the two letters, contends that the author of *Laodiceans* should not be regarded as artless. Extant *Laodiceans*, he contends, might well have been penned by an orthodox believer in an attempt to put an end to the deceptive and subversive influence of 'heretics' among the churches. The author enlists the powerfully persuasive character of Paul—the Paul who suffers and perseveres—in order to promote his vision of orthodoxy and morality. Thus the letter warns its addressees to be wary of 'vain talk' (v. 4a), exhorts the readers to perseverance in the faith taught by Paul (vv. 4b, 16), and to devote themselves to the godly life in the expectation of eternal life (v. 10). It is possible that the letter was only finally rejected because it was confused with the letter associated with Marcion.[33]

3 Corinthians[34]

3 Corinthians found its way into the early versions of the Armenian Bible. It was also highly regarded in the Syrian church. Ephrem the

---

[32] For Harnack's arguments for the Marcionite provenance of extant *Laodiceans*, see his *Marcion*, 141-45*. However, it is difficult to account for a Marcionite provenance if Ephesians had been included as *Laodiceans* in Marcion's canon. See Hahneman, *Muratorian Fragment*, 198.

[33] L.R. Donelson, *Pseudepigraphy and Ethical Argument in the Pastoral Epistles* (HUT 22; Tübingen: Mohr Siebeck, 1986), 43. Donelson rightly notes the similar ethos of Paul brought to speech in the Pastoral Epistles.

[34] See discussion, text, and analysis in K. Pink, 'Die pseudo-paulinischen Briefe I', *Bib* 6 (1925), 68-91; James, *Apocryphal New Testament*, 288-91; M. Rist, 'Pseudepigraphic Refutations of Marcionism', *JR* 22 (1942), 46-50; A.F.J. Klein, 'The Apocryphal Correspondence Between Paul and the Corinthians', *VC* 17 (1963), 2-23; Dassmann, *Stachel*, 271-99; Schneemelcher and R. Kasser, *New Testament Apocrypha*, 2.217, 228-29, 255-56.

Syrian wrote a commentary on the Pauline corpus including *3 Corinthians*. That commentary, however, is only known in Armenian. The earliest extant text is that found in the third-century Papyrus Bodmer X. The letter is presented as Paul's studied response to a letter he has received from the Corinthians, who are troubled by the teachings of two false teachers Simon and Cleobius. The concerned Corinthians know that the teaching of these two did not have apostolic sanction.

Intriguingly, *3 Corinthians*, together with the letter sent by the Corinthian presbyters, has been incorporated into one of the best known of the books of the New Testament Apocrypha, namely, the *Acts of Paul*.[35] Hippolytus and Origen used this work without hesitation.[36] Eusebius, however, is not convinced. He lists it not among the 'disputed' works of the New Testament, namely, Jude, 2 Peter, James, 2 and 3 John, but among those writings which are 'spurious', though, in the case of this work, orthodox.[37]

The *Acts of Paul* is one of several extant apostolic *Acts* written in the period 160–220.[38] It is an anonymous romance in which traditions that might stem from apostolic times and were sustained in Pauline circles find expression.[39] Paul is presented as a wandering proponent of a counter-cultural, celibate life-style—not far from the picture of Paul encountered in, say, 1 Corinthians. Among those he meets in

---

[35] Arguments for incorporation of an already existing document are summarised by Klein, 'Apocryphal Correspondence', 13, 16.

[36] Schneemelcher and Kasser (*New Testament Apocrypha*, 2.215) cite Hippolytus, *Comm Daniel* 3.29; Origen, *Principiis* 1.2.3; *Comm Joh* 20.12. See also Dassmann, *Stachel*, 272 n. 43.

[37] Eusebius, *Hist eccl* 3.25. Some, writes Eusebius, place the book of Revelation in this category as well (3.25.4). Eusebius has no doubt that the *Acts of Paul*, the *Shepherd of Hermas*, the *Apocalypse of Peter*, the *Letter of Barnabas*, and the *Teachings of the Apostles* (*The Didache*) are 'spurious', yet orthodox. The following he nominates as both 'spurious' and unorthodox: the *Gospels of Peter, Thomas*, and *Matthias*, and the *Acts of Andrew, John* and other apostles.

[38] See S. Davies, *The Revolt of the Widows: The Social World of the Apocryphal Acts* (Carbondale and Edwardsville: Southern Illinois University Press, 1980).

[39] So Davies, *Revolt*, 30, 32; D.R. MacDonald, *The Legend and the Apostle: The Battle for Paul in Story and Canon* (Philadelphia: Westminster Press, 1983), 15, 89, 97; Bienert, *New Testament Apocrypha*, 2.22; M.Y. MacDonald, *Early Christian Women and Pagan Opinion: The Power of the Hysterical Woman* (Cambridge: Cambridge University Press, 1996), 170.

Iconium is a young affianced woman called Thecla. Her chance hearing of his preaching brings about her conversion to Paul's revolutionary way of life marked by devotion to Christ and rejection of cultural expectations of submissive domesticity. Her mother, who is sorely shamed by this wilful independence and repudiation of cultural mores, advocates her condemnation to death in the arena. However, Thecla miraculously escapes execution at the stake, and sets out to find Paul. After travelling with Paul to Antioch, Thecla is again sentenced to die in the arena, having spurned the attentions of one Alexander. Once again she escapes death, this time death by beasts. She baptizes herself in the arena in a pool of seals, and is ultimately released. Once more she finds Paul, who 'ordains' her to preach and teach (*Acts of Paul* 3.41). 'After enlightening many with the word of God', she dies (3.43).

The *Acts of Paul* is mentioned incidentally by Tertullian. His tract *On Baptism* is a work written to counter a certain Quintilla who has usurped the ecclesiastical authority that customarily resides in the episcopal office. Tertullian rejects the notion that women might presume to baptize, preside at the Eucharist and teach in the congregation, having been emboldened to claim such rights by the precedent supplied by Thecla's self-baptism and Paul's commissioning of Thecla to preach in *Acts of Paul*. This work, he asserts, was lately authored by a presbyter in Asia. The author's defence, Tertullian informs us, is that he wrote the *Acts* 'out of love for Paul'. We can further surmise that the work was written to counter false teaching in which the authority of Paul was invoked.[40] The offender was consequently removed from his office, though not excommunicated. Tertullian is rather more incensed by the potential for presumption on the part of some women to exercise leadership independently of episcopal oversight within the church (since that is the occasion of his writing of the tract)—a presumption already assumed by the troublesome Quintilla—than the origin of the *Acts*. Yet, the fact that it is a recent work, and not from apostolic times, only underscores what Tertullian already believes about the work. It does not contain apostolic teaching and most certainly does not provide any legitimate apostolic mandate for women to presume to teach and administer the sacraments. Yet many in the early church did not appear to regard the work as heretical.

---

[40] See Speyer, *Fälschung*, 210-12.

Strictly speaking, the *Acts of Paul* is not pseudonymous. We have no evidence that the work was being passed off as an apostolic pseudepigraphon.[41] However, *3 Corinthians* is pseudonymous. In all likelihood the letter was circulating separately when the *Acts* was written.

3 Corinthians is a self-consciously literary work. It explicitly counters a number of theological propositions consistent with a range of false teachings encountered in the second century.[42] Some of these are known to have been held by Marcion and by Gnostics. The tenets of the teaching are: angels, not God, made the world; God does not care for the world; God did not make the body; there is no resurrection of the body but of the spirit only; Jesus was not crucified but only appeared to be; Jesus was born neither of Mary nor of the seed of David.

Pseudo-Paul's response takes the form of a rebuttal of each proposition. The true, apostolic teaching is set forth concisely, creedally and dogmatically. The letter reads as a compendium of apostolic teaching, addressing each doctrinal query in turn before exhorting the addressees to 'abide by the rule' (3.36). Throughout the letter there is a decisive underscoring of the unity of the God revealed in the Hebrew Bible as creator and author of salvation and the God and Father of the Lord Jesus Christ. The note of eschatological urgency in 3.3, 36 is a nice piece of Pauline verisimilitude designed to underscore both the certainty of the resurrection and the coming judgment on

---

[41] Schneemelcher and Kasser, *New Testament Apocrypha*, 2.215.

[42] The affirmation of God as creator is a central concern of *3 Corinthians*. See Klein, 'Apocryphal Correspondence', 10, 22. Klein believes that the teaching of Bardaisan as interpreted by his followers is the heresy attacked. Rist ('Pseudepigraphic Refutations', 46-50) is convinced that Marcionism is the teaching attacked, and aligns it with other second- and third-century works designed to counter that teaching, namely, the Apostles Creed, the *Didaskalia Apostolorum*, the *Epistle of the Apostles*, and the Pastoral Epistles. It is difficult to see how the Pastoral Epistles could have been conceived as anti-Marcionite given Marcion's anti-Jewish stance and the Jewish tendencies of the false teachers attacked in the letters. For further general discussion, see Aleith, *Paulusverständnis*, 30-31; Lindemann, *Paulus*, 374; Dassmann, *Stachel*, 277. Note also G.W. MacRae, 'Why the Church Rejected Gnosticism', in E.P. Sanders (ed.), *Jewish and Christian Self-Definition. I. The Shaping of Christianity in the Second and Third Centuries* (London: SCM Press, 1980), 126-33. MacRae underscores the unity of God as creator of the flesh and as saviour come in the flesh in antignostic polemic.

those who reject the revelation. In summary, Pseudo-Paul responds to the challenge posed by reports of false teaching by appealing to the fixed rule of faith upon which apostles and prophets agree. In the light of Gal 1:12 and 1 Cor 15:3, line 4—'I delivered to you in the beginning what I received from the apostles who were before me...'—is particularly un-Pauline (contrast *Laodiceans* 1 [citing Gal 1:1]). Nevertheless, in the face of the championing of Paul by heretical groups such as the Marcionites, the author of *3 Corinthians* proceeds to affirm the unity of the faith delivered to the apostles, and the agreement of the apostle Paul with that teaching.

Letters of Paul to Seneca[43]
This disarming collection of fourteen letters purports to be the correspondence of two contemporaries—'the best of both worlds', 'Christian saint and pagan philosopher'[44]—who are developing their friendship through the conducive medium of the letter. Paul is awaiting capital punishment. He is deferential to Seneca, his social superior. Seneca responds warmly and sympathetically to the apostle and his plight. The first letter refers to letters of Paul which Seneca has read to Nero. Letter 7 finds Seneca observing that Paul's style in Galatians and in 1 and 2 Corinthians is uncultivated. The most interesting of the letters is no. 11 in which Seneca describes the Fire of Rome of 64, blaming Nero, and commiserating with Paul that the Christians were falsely accused of setting the fire and then horribly punished. This letter might well have been incorporated into the collection.[45]

In contrast to the albeit limited canonical status achieved by *Laodiceans* and *3 Corinthians* in some sectors of the early church, the correspondence of Paul and Seneca never enjoyed such esteem. They are not attested before the end of the fourth century. Lactantius, who wrote in ca. 324, does not seem to know them.[46] However Jerome did regard the letters as genuine.[47] Cornelia Römer conjectures that the

---

[43] For discussion, text, and analysis see Pink, 'Die pseudo-paulinischen Briefe II', 193-200; C. Römer, *New Testament Apocrypha*, 2.46-53.
[44] R. Syme, 'Fraud and Imposture', in K. von Fritz (ed.), *Pseudepigrapha. I. Pseudopythagorica, lettres de Platon, littérature pseudépigraphe juive* (Entretiens sur l'antiquité 18; Geneva: Fondation Hardt, 1972), 9.
[45] See Pink, 'Die pseudo-paulinischen Briefe II', 199-200.
[46] Lactantius, *Institutes* 6.24.13-14.
[47] Jerome, *Vir* 12. Cf. Augustine, *Ep* 153.14.

correspondence could have come into being as a counter to a recently published pseudepigraphon entitled 'Letter of the high priest Annas to the philosopher Seneca'.[48] The Paul and Seneca correspondence associates the famous and highly esteemed Seneca with the great apostle of the Christian mission. It is also possible that the letters are rhetorical exercises in which the student is required to capture the character of a great one from the past in epistolary form, an adaptation of what rhetoricians termed *prosopopoeia*—speech in character.[49]

In the case of these eight letters, none was written by Paul. This can be established by the following criteria. None is attested earlier than the late second century.[50] The theological distinctives of *3 Corinthians* do not commend themselves as distinctively Pauline. The dialogical theological strategies of Paul, certainly those we encounter in the *homologoumena*, are not present in the letter either. Yet these letters did persuade some that they were genuine. *Laodiceans* and *3 Corinthians* were included in some Bibles—versions of the Latin and Armenian respectively.

Do these letters further our knowledge of Paul? The answer, clearly, is No. Nevertheless, quite obviously, they do provide a window into the manner in which early proponents of the Pauline heritage made use of the apostle in the enterprise of defending and interpreting the faith. They are early testimonies of the esteem in which Paul was regarded such that his later followers sought to articulate the manner in which his legacy should be interpreted in terms their contemporaries might find intelligible. Moreover, these letters, *3 Corinthians* especially, constitute evidence that writing pseudonymously was a strategy used for ideological purposes in the keenly contested battle for the ownership of the Pauline heritage against those custodians considered false and subversive.

---

[48] See *New Testament Apocrypha*, 2.47.

[49] See Quintilian, *Inst* 1.8.3; 3.8.49-52; 6.1.25; 9.2.29-37; 11.1.41. For the practice of impersonation in letter-writing, see L.M. Stirewalt, *Studies in Ancient Greek Epistolography* (SBLRBS 27; Atlanta: Scholars Press, 1993), 21 and n. 66; A.J. Malherbe, *Ancient Epistolary Theorists* (SBLSBS 19; Atlanta: Scholars Press, 1988), 6-7.

[50] Klein ('Apocryphal Correspondence', 4) dates *3 Corinthians* to ca. 170 CE.

4. Pseudepigraphy in the Early Church

There always has been a concern and cause to discriminate between authentic Pauline and pseudonymous letters, that is, letters written in Paul's name. 2 Thessalonians 2:2 is already aware of the baneful influence of a letter circulating among the Thessalonian believers purporting to have been written by Paul. Some scholars contend that the author of 2 Thessalonians was identifying 1 Thessalonians as the 'false' letter.[51] There is considerable irony in the observation that many scholars regard 2 Thessalonians itself as pseudonymous. Regardless of positions taken on this issue, it is clear that the writing of Pauline pseudepigrapha was an early problem in the church, as Speyer has rightly observed.[52] If 2 Thessalonians is a genuine letter of Paul, at least one Pauline pseudepigraphon is circulating in the mid first century, in the apostle's lifetime!

Pauline pseudepigrapha continued to be a problem in the second century. Tertullian reports that Marcion excluded the Pastoral Epistles from his Pauline canon, though he is not quite sure on what grounds. In Tertullian's eyes, one can only assume, Marcion regarded the Pastorals as pseudonymous though it is by no means clear that Marcion even knew them. The Muratorian canon, as we have seen, neatly distinguishes between authentic and spurious letters of Paul, naming two of them authored pseudonymously by Marcionites in defence of Marcion's teaching and referring to others written for the same purpose.

The second century was a period in which competing and opposing theological points of view were vigorously and bitterly debated. Defenders of the faith against Marcionites and others adopted two strategies, namely, the writing of formal refutations and the generating of pseudepigrapha. Irenaeus and Tertullian are two who wrote major treatises mustering all the rhetorical wit of which they were capable in the enterprise of attacking and overthrowing the teaching of the

---

[51] See concise discussion in Rist, 'Pseudepigraphy', 82-83. There are examples of forgeries condemning other forgeries. In the mid-fourth-century *Apos Con* 6.16 (*ANF* 7.457), the writers (the 'Twelve') warn their readers that heretics have forged books in the names of Christ, the apostles, and worthies from the Hebrew Bible. See also *3 Cor* 3.3 (*New Testament Apocrypha*, 2.255); *Epistle of the Apostles* 29 (*New Testament Apocrypha*, 1.266).

[52] See Speyer, *Fälschung*, 180. He also instances Rev 22:18-19. See also Ps.-Clementine, *Contestatio* 5.2 (*New Testament Apocrypha*, 2.496).

'heretics'. The writing of pseudepigrapha, Martin Rist suspects, was perhaps a more effective means of defending the faith since this strategy allowed an apostle, and in some cases, Jesus himself, to condemn heretical teaching as though it was present to them.[53]

Building on the work of Speyer, Donelson's survey of second century epistolary pseudepigrapha in chapter one of his 1986 monograph, *Pseudepigraphy and Ethical Argument in the Pastoral Epistles*, demonstrates how frequently the names of apostles and other great figures of the apostolic era were invoked as the authorities behind the views being espoused in the documents of the orthodox and unorthodox alike. This is plainly evidenced in *3 Corinthians*. No one today believes that Paul wrote this letter. However it has been written in his name because the author, a custodian of the orthodox deposit, knows that to write in his own name will not gain him the hearing he believes the teaching deserves in the critical circumstances in which he writes. He is defending the apostolic faith against a range of heresies. It is not his teaching but that of the apostle to which he has given voice.[54] The writing of pseudepigrapha in the names of apostles or their close contemporaries was part of the process by which early believers—'orthodox' and 'heterodox' alike—sought to define and establish the boundaries between truth and falsehood.[55]

However, as Rist shows, we encounter in the pseudepigraphical writings of the 'orthodox', but by no means restricted to their pseudepigrapha, a dependence on the strategy designed to demonstrate the essential unity of the faith delivered in orderly succession by Jesus to the Twelve and from them to Paul and to their successors in the churches.[56] That faith was identical with the faith of the contemporary church. Indeed, Paul, according to Tertullian, the *Epistle of the Apostles*, and *3 Corinthians*, received the same faith—in the latter two works through the direct agency of the Twelve.[57] That faith Paul

---

[53] Rist, 'Pseudepigraphic Refutations', 39-62.
[54] See Syme, 'Fraud and Imposture', 8-9.
[55] See also Speyer, *Fälschung*, 278-85.
[56] Rist, 'Pseudepigraphic Refutations', 39-62. Cf. Speyer, *Fälschung*, 188, who observes this tendency with respect to the presentation in 2 Timothy of Paul as the possessor and imparter of true teaching, and Timothy, in turn, as one who transmits this teaching to trustworthy men (2 Tim 2:2).
[57] Tertullian, *Praescr* 13 (the doctrinal essence of the faith taught by Christ), 20-22 (Christ [taught by God] taught the Twelve who faithfully transmitted this teaching), 24 (the same apostolic faith imparted to Paul in the 'third heaven'), 25 (Paul imparted the whole deposit to Timothy) (*ANF* 3.249ff.); *Epistle of the*

bequeathed to Timothy, which faith Timothy is exhorted to pass on to 'faithful men' (2 Tim 2:2). Thus the unity of the faith together with the agreement of apostles and their successors is assured and tangibly demonstrated, and, more specifically, Paul himself is shown to agree with the apostles when he had been appropriated by Marcionites and Gnostics.

As I noted above, the Muratorian canon is aware that the Marcionites 'forged' letters in Paul's name. They did so for precisely the same reason as the orthodox. In an era with only a rudimentary and developing sense of orthodoxy, it was self-evidently important to the combatants in these disputes to enlist the undisputed weight of the great authorities from the era of the earliest church as the guarantors of the truth they were commending. The letters these disputants wrote, though pseudonymous, were accepted into some canons—Marcionite and 'orthodox'—because those who received them subscribed to the teaching they contained, believing it to be orthodox. Clement of Alexandria also testifies to the fact that the Gnostics, among whom Marcion was content to dwell, also believed in an apostolic succession from Paul to Theudas to Valentinus as a means of guaranteeing the continuity of the teaching of the School of Valentinus with the apostolic era.[58]

It was not easy in the early church consistently to distinguish between the genuine and the forged. The practice of rhetorical schools of requiring students to be competent in the practice of literary impersonation achieved through the epistolary-writing exercise known as *prosopopoeia* may have contributed to the expectation of the versatility of the letter writers. In the church, the test of authorship was based foremost on the test of doctrinal orthodoxy. Correctness of doctrine becomes the 'primary basis for judgment'.[59] This is highlighted in a number of instances. Tertullian, as we have seen, was probably more incensed by the encouragement given to women preaching and administering the sacraments than by the circumstances of the

---

Apostles 31 (Jesus anticipates the conversion of Paul and directs the Twelve to instruct him [*New Testament Apocrypha*, 1.267]); *3 Cor* 3.4 [*New Testament Apocrypha*, 2.255]. See discussion in Speyer, *Fälschung*, 188. Speyer draws attention to the same phenomenon in early Judaism in which there is posited an unbroken link between the rabbis and Moses (as in *m Abot* 1.1).

[58] See Clement of Alexandria, *Stromateis* 7.17. See also Pagels, *Gnostic Paul*, 5-6.

[59] Donelson, *Pseudepigraphy*, 16. Cf. *Apos Con* 6.16.

authorship of the anonymous *Acts of Paul*. However, it cannot be denied that the presbyter who wrote the work was de-frocked. Bishop Serapion of Antioch allowed the reading of the *Gospel of Peter* in one of his churches although he himself did not know it among the Petrine books 'delivered to us'.[60] However, when he finally had cause to read it he rejected it on the grounds of its docetic teaching. In ca. 440, the presbyter Salvian was rightly suspected of having forged a treatise on wealth written in the name of Timothy. This is clearly a serious charge. His bishop, Salonius, makes it clear that forgery will not be tolerated and that his work will be relegated to the apocrypha. Salvian's guarded and oblique defence is to argue (in his eighth letter), among other things, that it is the content of a book that should be determinative for assessing its value not the name of the author.[61]

Salvian's tortuous defence of himself alerts us to the fact that pseudepigraphers took considerable risks. Donelson, among others, observes, quite rightly, that if a document was found to be a pseudepigraphon it was rejected and its author castigated.[62] We know of no pseudepigraphon which was retained once it was demonstrated that it had been forged in order to be passed off as genuine. It is virtually certain that had the Armenian and Latin-speaking churches which accepted *3 Corinthians* and *Laodiceans* known that these documents were in fact pseudepigrapha they would have been excluded from their canons.

Nevertheless, the author of the Muratorian canon acknowledges Wisdom of Solomon as a pseudepigraphon, 'written by friends of Solomon in his honour' (l. 70). In this case, however, I conclude that the author of the Muratorian canon perceived no attempt to deceive on the part of the 'friends'. Mark Kiley, who appeals to the practice of generating pseudepigrapha in the philosophical 'schools' to articulate and further the teaching of revered masters, argues that the canon testifies to a 'practice which was perceptible and praiseworthy in parts

---

[60] Eusebius, *Hist ecc* 6.12.3.

[61] For a sympathetic treatment, see A.E. Haefner, 'A Unique Source for the Study of Ancient Pseudonymity', *ATR* 16 (1934), 8-15. See also Rist, 'Pseudepigraphy', 90-91; Donelson, *Pseudepigraphy*, 21-23. The *Apostolic Constitutions*, an orthodox pseudepigraphon, also subscribes to the point of view that the content of a book is more important than the name of its author (see 6.16 [*ANF* 7.457]).

[62] Donelson, *Pseudepigraphy*, 16; F.F. Bruce, *The Canon of Scripture* (Leicester: InterVarsity Press, 1988), 261; S.E. Porter, 'Pauline Authorship and the Pastoral Epistles: Implications for Canon', *BBR* 5 (1995), 122.

of the culture of the time'.⁶³ The author would have rejected the suggestion that Wisdom had been forged.

On what grounds could pseudepigraphers, both orthodox and heterodox, have justified their enterprise? A number of scholars, such as Norbert Brox, Petr Pokorny, and Lewis Donelson, have argued that the concept of the noble lie is crucial.⁶⁴ Plato contended that the telling of a lie was justified in the interests of maintaining the truth.⁶⁵ The principle pervades the classical and Greco-Roman eras, and is invoked by Christian writers.⁶⁶ In the early church, writers looked to the apostolic era for guidance and for vindication of their views. They appeal to those who heard the message directly from Christ.⁶⁷ From the perspective of the defenders of the faith, it was in the church's best interests to deceive it. When confronted by Gnostics, Marcionites or other 'heretics', it was understandable and natural that orthodox writers sought to defend the faith which they had inherited. The same is true on the part of the Marcionites and Gnostics when confronted by their opponents. Only by invoking an apostle as author could one guarantee a sympathetic hearing, even if that meant deceiving the faithful. This is precisely the argument put by Salvian, a known pseudepigrapher, for the practice. A lie was told in the cause of a great truth and in the service of a great cause.

---

⁶³ M. Kiley, *Colossians as Pseudepigraphy* (BibSem; Sheffield: JSOT Press, 1986), 19. See also n. 109 below regarding the possibility of the existence of a Pauline 'school' responsible for generating the Pauline pseudepigrapha. Also relevant is Tertullian's comment regarding the publication of the works of masters by their pupils (*Marc* 4.5): 'And it may well seem that the works which disciples publish belong to their masters' (*ANF* 3.350). Tertullian has the New Testament Gospels specifically in mind. For an accessible deposit of pseudepigrapha created in a philosophical 'school', see A.J. Malherbe (ed.), *The Cynic Epistles* (SBLSBS 12; Atlanta: Scholars Press, 1986).

⁶⁴ N. Brox, *Falsche Verfasserangaben: Zur Erklärung der frühchristlichen Pseudepigraphie* (Stuttgart: KBW, 1975), 83-87; P. Pokorny, 'Das theologische Problem der neutestamentlichen Pseudepigraphie', *EvT* 44 (1984), 493-94; Donelson, *Pseudepigraphy*, 18-23.

⁶⁵ *Republic* 2.376E–383C, 3.389B, 3.414C-E.

⁶⁶ Both Pokorny ('Problem', 493-94) and Donelson (*Pseudepigraphy*, 18-19) cite Clement of Alexandria, *Stromateis* 7.53 and Origen, *Contra Celsum* 4.19 (who appeals to *Republic* 3.389B [see previous note]).

⁶⁷ Donelson, *Pseudepigraphy*, 20. Cf. Rist, 'Pseudepigraphic Refutations', 39-62; Pokorny, 'Problem', 495-96.

By this very human and culturally conditioned means the early churches set about defining the content and the boundaries of the faith delivered to them. In time the great Councils of the church would do this definitively, but no less polemically engaged with the trajectories of the deposit of faith adjudged heterodox. What we encounter in the second and third centuries, and in the New Testament era itself, is a variety of Christian traditions.[68] There is no one faith, but rather a plurality of voices. There are independent and intersecting trajectories of faith and practice. The writing of pseudepigrapha is an attempt to legitimate one's own custodianship of the deposit of faith. The writing of Pauline pseudepigrapha extends back to the first century, and, if 2 Thessalonians is genuine, to Paul's lifetime.

5. The Undisputed Letters—New Testament Pauline Homologoumena

Literary Integrity
I have already outlined the extent of this corpus of Pauline letters. The literary integrity of several of the letters has been called into question by scholars over the last 200 years.

Some argue that Romans 1–15 only comprise the original letter Paul wrote to the Romans. Chapter 16, it has been argued, may be an addition to the letter, perhaps intended for Ephesus. There is considerable manuscript evidence for an unsettled text at the conclusions of both Romans 14 and 15. Marcion, so Origen tells us, removed chs. 15 and 16 from his text.[69]

2 Corinthians presents a significant challenge. There are a number of intriguing seams in the text. A commonly held view is that 2 Corinthians is largely comprised of two distinct sections—chs. 1–9, 10–13.

---

[68] Bauer's *Orthodoxy and Heresy* is the classic statement of this point of view.
[69] See the discussion of the textual challenges posed by the final two chapters of Romans in Metzger, *Textual Commentary,* 533-36. See also K.P. Donfried, 'A Short Note on Romans 16', in K.P. Donfried (ed.), *The Romans Debate* (Peabody, MA: Hendrickson, 1991), 44-52. He argues that ch. 16 was part of Paul's 'original edition of Romans' (p. 52). Donfried accepts the arguments that the doxology of Rom 16:25-27 was written by Marcion whose edition of Romans ended, otherwise abruptly, at 14:23 (p. 50). This form of the text is supported by some Western manuscripts (see W.G. Kümmel, *Introduction to the New Testament* [London: SCM Press, 1972], 222-24).

Chapters 1–9 may comprise as many as four discrete documents as follows: (1) 1:1–6:13 and 7:2-16—a conciliatory letter, (2) 6:14–7:1—a non-Pauline interpolation, (3) 8:1-24—a letter promoting the collection for the church in Jerusalem, and (4) 9:1-15—written to some other church, or to promote the collection. The passage 10:1–13:13 may, perhaps, incorporate part of the 'painful letter' referred to in 2 Cor 2:4 and 7:8.[70]

1 Corinthians 14:33-36 looks suspiciously like an interpolation. It interrupts the flow of the context and appears to contradict what Paul has been saying about women prophesying and praying in the congregation.[71] Another seam appears at the juncture of Phil 3:1 and 2. Philippians 3:2–4:1 might well have been written earlier than the first two chapters as part of a letter thanking the Philippians for the generous financial gift Paul had received through the agency of Epaphroditus.[72] Some scholars argue that 1 Thess 2:(13)14-16 is an interpolation. The astringency of the remarks about the Jews in this passage seems to presuppose the horrors of the First Jewish Revolt (or the second), and contradict the thrust of Paul's later discussion of the role of God for the Jews in Romans 9–11.[73]

What we are encountering here, I believe, is evidence that fragments of Pauline and some non-Pauline material were folded into

---

[70] See the presentation in B.D. Ehrman, *The New Testament: A Historical Introduction to the Early Christian Writings* (New York and Oxford: Oxford University Press, 1997), 280-84.

[71] See Koester, *Introduction*, 2.125; Becker, *Paul*, 9. Contra J.D.G. Dunn, *The Theology of Paul the Apostle* (Grand Rapids: Eerdmans, 1998), 589-93. Arguing that the passage is an interpolation, Ehrman (*New Testament*, 346-47) neatly demonstrates the verbal and thematic parallels between 1 Tim 2:11-13 and 1 Cor 14:34-35.

[72] See Ehrman, *New Testament*, 293-94, who highlights the difference in tone between the two sections of the extant letter.

[73] Baur nominated this passage as an un-Pauline interpolation in *Paul*, 2.86-88. He argued that the 'polemic is so external and so vague that the enmity of the Jews to the Gospel is characterized solely in terms of that well-known charge with which the Gentiles assailed them, the *odium generis humani*'. See also the discussion in F.F. Bruce, *1 and 2 Thessalonians* (WBC 45; Waco, TX: Word Books, 1982), 43-51. However, J.C. Beker (*Paul the Apostle: The Triumph of God in Life and Thought* [Philadelphia: Fortress Press, 1980], 331) regards 2:14 as genuine, though an 'outburst'. Becker (*Paul*, 133, 461-63) is also prepared to argue that the passage is genuine, as are R. Jewett (*The Thessalonian Correspondence: Pauline Rhetoric and Millenarian Piety* [Philadelphia: Fortress Press, 1986], 40-41) and Dunn (*Theology*, 507 n. 40).

the letters at the time when Pauline letter-collections were being made at the end of the first century or beginning of the second. Some scholars argue that the Pastorals comprise genuine Pauline fragments combined with later non-Pauline materials.[74] Here there may be an analogy with the process by which the Fourth Gospel came into being. It is widely conceded that John 21 is a non-Johannine appendix. John 7:53–8:11 may well have been a piece of Johannine tradition incorporated into the Gospel at a late stage in its documentary history.[75] In the Hebrew Bible the composition history of most of the books is likely to have been as complex. Amos and Isaiah are two examples of books that grew by supplementation and addition.

Theological Integrity
F.C. Baur contended that there were profound theological differences between the four letters of Paul he considered genuine and the remainder of the New Testament Pauline corpus. At stake in the 'great' four was the defining issue of Paul's apostolate, namely, whether or not there was to be a Christianity free from Judaism and essentially different from it.[76] In the *antilegomena*, the remaining nine letters of the corpus, Baur argued that we encounter the 'double of the Apostle', an Apostle working for the reconciliation and unification of Jewish and Pauline Christianity, and who had completely supplanted the genuine Paul in the Acts of the Apostles.[77] While the bold particulars of Baur's thesis have long since been successfully challenged, he was correct in perceiving the New Testament Pauline corpus as the witness to two distinct historical movements, namely, the apostolate of Paul and the dealings of the Pauline party after the death of the apostle.

The seven letters—Romans, 1 and 2 Corinthians, Galatians, Philippians, 1 Thessalonians and Philemon—currently and justly commend themselves to most modern scholars as genuine works of the apostle, notwithstanding questions about their literary integrity. There are good reasons for accepting these letters at face value as genuine.

---

[74] See P.N. Harrison, *The Problem of the Pastoral Epistles* (Oxford: Oxford University Press, 1921); J.D. Miller, *The Pastoral Epistles as Composite Documents* (SNTSMS 93; Cambridge: Cambridge University Press, 1997).

[75] For an attractive hypothesis concerning the composition history of the Fourth Gospel, see R.E. Brown, *The Gospel According to John* (2 vols.; AB 29, 29A; New York: Doubleday, 1966, 1972), 1.xxxiv-xl.

[76] See Baur's comment on Galatians in his *Paul*, 1.253.

[77] Baur, *Paul*, 1.245.

Their common style and vocabulary are two markers identifying their common authorship, but these are matters I have chosen not to highlight.

The theological distinctives of the *homologoumena* also suggest a single author. The thesis of J. Christiaan Beker, who argues that Paul is an apocalyptic thinker whose worldview was dramatically affirmed by his encounter with the risen Christ, is an attractive one. For the sake of providing as clear a focus as possible in the presentation below, I acknowledge a considerable debt to Beker's analysis of the Pauline *homologoumena* and *antilegomena*.

According to Beker, the basic co-ordinates, or the 'deep structure', of the traditional apocalyptic worldview, a view shared by Paul, are (1) historical dualism, (2) universal cosmic expectation, and (3) the imminent end of the world.[78] Thinking much indebted to apocalyptic theology, suffused with a heightened conviction that the Christ-event, culminating in the resurrection, has hastened the coming of the end-time triumph of God, with Christ as the 'pledge of God's imminent self-vindication',[79] is present from the beginning of the series of genuine letters (1 Thessalonians) to the end (Philippians). It is this perspective which gives the *homologoumena* their consistent theological stamp.

Paul's apocalyptic worldview has been radically modified. He regards humankind as no longer dualistically divided between keepers and non-keepers of the Torah but between those who have put their trust in Christ proclaimed in the gospel, whose death on the cross becomes the 'focal point of God's universal wrath and judgment', and those who are disobedient to the gospel.[80] That disobedience can be expressed as much by insistence on Torah-keeping in the face of the preaching of the gospel as by persisting in the futility of idolatry. In

---

[78] Beker, *Paul*, 15-16, 136-37. In *Heirs of Paul: Paul's Legacy in the New Testament and in the Church Today* (Philadelphia: Fortress Press, 1991), 25, J.C. Beker observes that 'Paul's theology is permeated with an apocalyptic substrate'. However, one should not underestimate the transformation of Paul's apocalyptic outlook affected by the Christ-event. Note also the caveats of L.E. Keck, 'Paul and Apocalyptic Theology', *Int* 38 (1984), 229-41. Keck argues that the perspective of radical discontinuity of the present age and the age to come is the hallmark of Paul's apocalyptic thinking (cf. Beker, *Paul*, 137).

[79] See J.C. Beker, *Paul's Apocalyptic Gospel: The Coming Triumph of God* (Philadelphia: Fortress Press, 1982), 34.

[80] Beker, *Paul's Apocalyptic Gospel*, 35. Beker adds: 'The death of Christ signifies the apocalyptic judgment on all mankind.'

the light of the cross as God's indictment of all people, Beker insists, there can be no appeal to special status before God, no claim to special privilege, no elitism. The promises of God have been fulfilled respecting the deliverance of Israel and the inclusion of Gentiles in the end-time people of God.[81] Believers have already passed through what Beker calls the 'abyss of God's judgment', baptized into Christ's death and buried with him.[82] The power of sin and death has been broken. However, whereas the resurrection of Christ constitutes the assurance of the resurrection of believers, unbelievers (whether Jew or Gentile) who persist in living as though Christ had not already defeated the powers of this world will be overthrown in the coming final judgment. The believer lives very much in the tension of the present age and the age to come—between the 'now' and the 'not yet'. Jesus has been raised. In that sense the end-time resurrection is a reality. The risen Lord, the vindicated messianic agent of God, is the sign that the present order is about to pass away to be replaced by the Kingdom of God. For Paul the resurrection of Christ is *the* decisive eschatological event heralding the turn of the ages and the fulfilment of divine promise (see, for example, Rom 1:1-5; 1 Cor 10:11; 2 Cor 1:20).

In the meantime, in the midst of trouble and persecution, believers are to be ready and alert. Their life is shaped by the hope of the end-time triumph of God and by the expectation of participating in the *parousia* and the resurrection of the dead as imminent events (note 1 Thess 4:17; 1 Cor 7:29; 15:51; Rom 13:11-14). Indeed, Beker claims, the 'intensity of Paul's apocalyptic religion is characterized by hope'.[83] Paul's letters, then, are not only substitutes for his actual presence but are also affirmations of his apocalyptic interpretation of the Christ-event.

Furthermore, Beker underscores a certain dialogical energy and dynamic about each of these letters and the way Paul proceeds to engage his addressees. He is always seeking to bring into dialogue the 'deep structure' of his apocalyptic gospel, or what Beker calls the 'coherence' of his gospel, and the 'contingent' circumstances of his

---

[81] See Dunn, *Theology*, 318: 'An epoch characterized by Jewish privilege and protection under the law had reached its goal in the fulfilment of ancient promise and the possibility of new maturity before God for Gentile as well as Jew.'

[82] Beker, *Paul's Apocalyptic Gospel*, 35.

[83] Beker, *Paul*, 146.

addressees. The 'surface structure' of Paul's thought, comprising symbols such as 'justification', 'freedom', and 'reconciliation', interprets and mediates the 'deep structure' of Paul's thought to his addressees as it has been effected by the Christ-event.[84] Paul is committed to doing theology in dialogue with the life-situations of his addressees.[85] Paul reasons with and exhorts them in the light of his conviction that the resurrection of Jesus has confirmed his apocalyptic worldview. With the exception of the letter to the believers in Rome, believers whom he had never visited, Paul writes as pastor and nurturer. Only occasionally does he use the language of polemic and vilification.

Issues foundational to Jewish identity are broached frequently in the *homologoumena* in a manner which suggests that many of Paul's addressees are Jews and that these issues are live ones. They arise out of the historical mission of Paul to 'Jews first and also to the Gentiles' and reflect the Jewish/Gentile mix of the early Christian communities. Accordingly, a significant issue for Paul is that of the freedom of the believer in the Spirit and its corollary, justification by faith and not by works required by the law. These works operate as the badges of a Jewish profession and as determiners and sustainers of a Jewish identity.[86]

In general, therefore, it is not only the consistently apocalyptic tenor of his interpretation of the Christ-event but the dialogical method by which Paul makes his gospel a 'word on target' that gives the *homologoumena* their theological and hermeneutical consistency, and

---

[84] Beker, *Paul*, 17-18.

[85] Compare L.E. Keck, *Paul and His Letters* (Philadelphia: Fortress Press, 1988), 19-21; Dunn, *Theology*, 713-16. On the occasional nature of Paul's letters, see also Becker, *Paul*, 7-8, 373. However, this is not to say that Paul's letters are 'spontaneous' and 'private' (see Keck, *Paul*, 21).

[86] See J.D.G. Dunn, *Romans 1–8* (WBC 38A, B; Waco, TX: Word Books, 1988), lxiii-lxxii, and *Theology*, 354-79; Becker, *Paul*, 393; Ehrman, *New Testament*, 289. These writers argue that there is no evidence of legalism in early Judaism. Doing the 'works of the law' does not establish a claim on God's mercy. *Contra* J.A. Fitzmyer, *According to Paul: Studies in the Theology of the Apostle* (New York: Paulist, 1993), 18-35. While affirming early Jewish understanding of doing the works of the law generally not as 'merit-amassing' but as expressing faithfulness to the covenant, Fitzmyer argues that 4QMMT does support an interpretation of the 'works of the law' which has a 'legalistic connotation' (p. 23). However, it is doubtful that the passage cited by Fitzmyer (pp. 21-22) can bear this interpretation.

chiefly commends the common authorship of these seven letters as a corpus.

This brings us to the disputed New Testament Pauline letters, the Pauline *antilegomena*.

6. THE DISPUTED LETTERS—THE NEW TESTAMENT PAULINE ANTILEGOMENA

Doubts have been cast on the authenticity of the six remaining Pauline New Testament letters during the last 200 years. The case against the authenticity of each might be concisely summarized as follows.

Ephesians reads much more like a reflective, speculative treatise than a letter prompted by local, occasional concerns. As we have already had cause to observe, no destination is nominated in the earliest manuscripts of the letter. It does not appear to address a particular congregation but, rather, seeks to present the message of the apostle in general terms.[87] The 'church', which is the subject of the crucial content of Ephesians, is not the local congregation but consistently the church universal. The ecclesiology of Ephesians has, therefore, moved far from Paul's engagement with the local churches to which he writes. Thus, we do not encounter Paul's 'dialogical hermeneutic', to invoke Beker's terms, 'dislodged' as Ephesians is from any engagement with a local, contingent situation.[88]

Ephesians' portrait of Paul has moved beyond his self-presentation in the *homologoumena*. He has become the chief 'mystagogue' of the faith (see 3:3, 9). He is presented as the unique apostle to the Gentiles whose ministry definitively reveals the shape of God's saving plan for the world (3:8-9).[89] Moreover, the writer states that God has revealed 'the mystery' to Paul, the content of which is the unity of Jew and Gentile in the church (2:11-22; 3:3, 9). This constitutes the culmination of the work of God for the end time, a work superintended by

---

[87] See N.A. Dahl, 'The Particularity of the Pauline Epistles as a Problem in the Ancient Church', in *Neotestamentica et Patristica* (NovTSup 6; Leiden: Brill, 1962), 260-71 (esp. 266).
[88] *Heirs of Paul*, 88 (cf. 69).
[89] Beker, *Heirs of Paul*, 68, 71.

Christ and presented in Ephesians as an accomplished fact.[90] Indeed, as Beker observes, there exists in Ephesians a 'symbiosis' of church and Christ that resembles that between husband and wife (cf. Eph 5:31).[91] The apostle's radical contention that the cross undoes all claims to special status before God led to a ministry fraught with conflict between keepers and non-keepers of the law. In Paul's mind this was a conflict of apocalyptic proportions, a cosmic drama signifying the clash of the power of slavery, sin and death and the power of the dawning new age dramatically manifest in the Christ-event and the gift of the Spirit. However, the friction and unease that marked the historical Paul's ministry among Jews and Gentiles has given way in Ephesians to the contemplation of the accomplishment of peace between the two in the church. The law as a defining, even divisive, issue in the communal life of believers is no longer a live and crucial issue to the author of Ephesians.

In Ephesians and Colossians, Paul proclaims a Christ, who, Beker argues, is presented in a manner evocative of the *Christus Rex* of the Orthodox liturgical tradition and presides in triumph over the 'cosmic church', his body (see Eph 1:22-23).[92] Moreover, the church, not the created order, has become the arena in which the redemptive purposes of God are revealed (3:9-10; contrast, for example, the future orientation of God's triumph to be revealed in a new creation in Rom 8:18-25). The plan of God thus culminates in the church (see Eph 2:11-22; 3:6, 7-13). Eschatology has become synonymous with ecclesiology. The tension of the now and not-yet of Christian existence has been collapsed into a christocentric and ecclesiological triumphalism.

---

[90] Contrast the tortuous relationships between Jews and Gentiles encountered in the *homologoumena*. See R.F. Collins, *Letters That Paul Did Not Write* (Wilmington, DE: Michael Glazier, 1988), 146.

[91] Beker, *Heirs of Paul*, 70.

[92] See J.C. Beker, *The New Testament: A Thematic Introduction* (Minneapolis: Fortress Press, 1994), 60. Cf. *idem*, *Heirs of Paul*, 66. In the *homologoumena*, the church is the place for the celebration of the radical freedom of the people of God in the light of the Christ-event expressed in charismatically endowed ministries, and yet cultural proprieties should also be observed. The term 'church' (ἐκκλησία) is never universalized as in Ephesians, and is almost always used to refer to the local congregation (and sometimes of a group of congregations). By contrast, the term 'body' (σῶμα) is able to bear universalist implications since it implies 'the incorporation of all believers in Christ' (*idem*, *The Triumph of God: The Essence of Paul's Thought* [Minneapolis: Fortress Press, 1990], 102).

In Ephesians, believers are already raised with Christ, already saved (σεσῳσμένοι, 2:5),[93] and already seated with him in the heavenlies (2:5-6). The Paul of the undisputed letters does not use the language of resurrection to denote the life of believers in the present age.[94] In Ephesians, however, the resurrection of believers—an essential aspect of the coming apocalyptic triumph of God in Paul—has become a present experience. Moreover, a Christianized Household Code in Eph 5:22–6:9, matched in Col 3:18–4:1 (cf. 1 Pet 2:18–3:7), makes an appearance for the first time in the Pauline corpus. Such strategies for living were not employed by the historical Paul.[95] His vision of the ecclesiastical life abides in the tensions between the liberating program celebrated in Gal 3:28 and a concern for cultural proprieties in the conduct of church gatherings (see 1 Cor 11:3; 14:33b-36), gatherings in which women prophesy and pray.

Colossians and Ephesians share some material in common, a factor which contributes to the impression that the two letters share a similar outlook.[96] Yet Colossians is far more dialogical in its argumentative strategies than Ephesians. The author, in contrast to the author of Ephesians, appears to be committed to relating his gospel to the local situation of the addressees. However, we also encounter evidence that distances Colossians from the apocalyptic tenor of the theological outlook of the *homologoumena*. The Pauline stress on the end-time triumph of God has been swallowed up by a triumphant Christology, a Christology, moreover, highly indebted to 'wisdom' terminology in a way unprecedented in the *homologoumena*.[97] In Christ, the author

---

[93] See the discussion of the vocabulary of salvation in Ephesians and the *homologoumena* in Ehrman, *New Testament*, 331.

[94] See Ehrman, *New Testament*, 327.

[95] See, for example, Koester, *Introduction*, 2.266; Collins, *Letters*, 200-201; Ehrman, *New Testament*, 327-28; J.D.G. Dunn, *Unity and Diversity in the New Testament: An Inquiry into the Character of Earliest Christianity* (Philadelphia: Trinity Press International, 1990), 345-46.

[96] Barnett, *Literary Influence*, 2-40; Kiley, *Colossians as Pseudepigraphy*, 40-42; Collins, *Letters*, 143-44; Lincoln, *Ephesians*, xlvii-lviii. Ehrman (*New Testament*, 327) highlights the contrasting style of Colossians ('complex, involved') over against the more 'succinct' style evident in the *homologoumena*. Ehrman also contrasts the style of Ephesians and the *homologoumena* (*New Testament*, 330; cf. Collins, *Letters*, 141-43). It is also unexpected that Paul, if he were the author of Colossians and/or Ephesians, would have been content to reproduce material he had written earlier.

[97] Beker, *Heirs of Paul*, 65-67.

states, are hidden all the treasures of wisdom and knowledge of God (2:3). The assertion that believers are already 'raised with Christ' (see 2:12-13 [contrast Rom 6:5, 8]; 3:1-4) also represents a significant move away from the presentation of the Christian life in the *homologoumena* and corresponds, as noted above, to the presentation in Eph 2:5-6. The resurrection of believers is always a future prospect in the *homologoumena*. End-time expectation has receded in Ephesians and Colossians. The church faces an open-ended future in which the imminence of the apocalyptic closure has been eclipsed.

For many scholars, the chief difficulty in 2 Thessalonians is the eschatological timetable of 2:1-12. Assuming that 1 Thessalonians is a genuine Pauline letter, and given the eschatological views of Paul articulated in that letter and the *homologoumena* in general, this is a totally unexpected teaching. The author is seeking to defuse apocalyptic expectation not to stimulate and prepare for it as Paul does in 1 Thess 4:13–5:11.[98] There the Day of the Lord will overwhelm those unprepared like a 'thief in the night' (1 Thess 5:4). The author of 2 Thessalonians contends that the end is not yet in sight. There must first appear the 'man of sin', a figure perhaps modelled on *Nero redivivus*, an expectation current in the generation following Nero's suicide in 68.[99] Furthermore, as much as two-thirds of 2 Thessalonians comprises sentences and phrases taken from 1 Thessalonians.[100] The personal warmth of Paul in 1 Thessalonians is exchanged for a more didactic and commanding tone.[101] The tone of the letter to Philemon should also be contrasted with 2 Thessalonians in this respect.

There is much to commend the notion that the three Pastoral Epistles have a common post-Pauline author. After engaging the *homologoumena*, the reader of these letters is transported to a different world. Whereas we hear echoes and interpretations of the great theological themes of the undisputed letters in Ephesians and Colossians, in the Pastorals we suspect the author is less in touch with the precise issues and concerns that motivated the historical Paul. Scholars have frequently noted the contrasting vocabulary and style of the Pastorals

---

[98] Beker, *Heirs of Paul*, 73; cf. Becker, *Paul*, 424, 443-44.

[99] See Collins, *Letters*, 209-10 (citing the views of F.H. Kern, 1839).

[100] Beker, *Heirs of Paul*, 72. Beker further characterizes the strategy of 2 Thessalonians as an exercise in the adaptation of the Pauline tradition by 'imitation' of Paul (*Heirs of Paul*, 80).

[101] Collins, *Letters*, 222-23; Beker, *Heirs of Paul*, 73.

when compared with the *homologoumena*.¹⁰² Moreover, the letters cannot be fitted into the career of Paul as that is known from the Acts and from the undisputed Pauline corpus. Accordingly Paul, who had declared his career in the east over (see Rom 15:23-24, 28), is now pictured as having had a subsequent mission in the Greek east (Ephesus, Crete) that issued in what we can only assume to be a second imprisonment.

At significant junctures the theology of the Pastorals does not compute with the *homologoumena*. The law, observes the author at 1 Tim 1:8-11, is not meant for the just but for the unjust (contrast Rom 3:19; 7:7-25). The law has become a kind of moral 'policeman'. The ungodly need its injunctions to rein them in. The godly already keep it. Nevertheless, the writer has sought to make sense of two Pauline injunctions, namely, that Christ has brought about the end of the law (see Rom 10:4) and that the law is 'good' (see 7:16).¹⁰³ In contrast with Ephesians and Colossians, there is a keen eschatological expectation in the Pastorals, especially with respect to the judgment to come, though not perhaps as urgent as it is in the *homologoumena* insofar as there is an anticipation of successive generations of believers (see 2 Tim 2:2).¹⁰⁴ Indeed, the author insists on a future eschatology which runs counter to expressions of a more realized conception in Ephesians and Colossians, and rebuts any thought that believers might consider their resurrection to be a present reality.¹⁰⁵ We hear no more of the cross in these letters. The author uses the language of baptismal

---

¹⁰² See, for example, Collins, *Letters*, 94-96.

¹⁰³ Lindemann, *Paulus*, 145-46. Cf. A.T. Hanson, *The Pastoral Epistles* (London: Marshall, Morgan & Scott, 1982), 58-59.

¹⁰⁴ The eschatology of the Pastorals is much more attuned to that of the Acts of the Apostles. The stress on the certainty of judgment is a mark of the letters' anti-Marcionite stance, according to Rist, 'Pseudepigraphic Refutations', 60. Cf. *3 Cor* 3.37 (*New Testament Apocrypha*, 2.256).

¹⁰⁵ Contrast 2 Tim 2:17-18 with Eph 2:5-6; Col 2:12-13; 3:1. The *Treatise on the Resurrection* (also known as the *Epistle to Rheginus*), a work discovered in the Nag Hammadi Corpus and which belongs to the Valentinian 'school', contends that those who begin to contemplate divine things can consider themselves raised already. This doctrine is attributed to 'the apostle', namely, Paul. The realized eschatology of Ephesians and Colossians has been articulated by the author, who, at *Treatise on the Resurrection* 45.23, 25 draws on Rom 8:17; Eph 2:4-6; Col 2:12; 3:1-3 (see B. Layton, *The Gnostic Scriptures* [Garden City, NY: Doubleday, 1987], 321 n. 45i). 2 Timothy 2:17-18 is polemically engaged with a trajectory of thought which is possibly deutero-Pauline in origin.

regeneration and renewal (Titus 3:5). Women will be saved by bearing children (διὰ τῆς τεκνογονίας; 1 Tim 2:15) if they also fulfil some basic ethical requirements. The Household Code ethic of much of 1 Timothy and Titus expresses the author's commitment to inculcating conventional moral and social mores.[106]

Paul's method of engaging his addressees is not encountered in the Pastorals. The author issues mandates and directives. The most necessary thing is for the addressees to 'guard the deposit' (1 Tim 6:20), to pass it on undiminished, and to choose faithful successors who will be apt to teach others (see 2 Tim 2:2). The flexible, dialogical method of Paul's interpretation of the Christ-event has not been actualized by the author.[107]

The ecclesiastical organization of the Pastorals has moved significantly beyond the charismatically-ordained ministries glimpsed in, say, 1 Corinthians 12–14. Elders and deacons are required to be up-standing members of the wider society, sober and respectable male heads of households who are apt to teach and lead the 'household of God' (1 Tim 3:15).

Paul is presented in hagiographical and heroic terms. He is the sole apostle. In 2 Timothy he is portrayed as a transparently good man, unjustly condemned. Now he faces death alone having been deserted by false colleagues. Yet he is faithful and unbending, confident that God will preserve his ministry (2 Tim 1:12).

The false teachers appear to be proto-Gnostics of an ascetic and Jewish bent. They and their dangerously subversive views are vilified by the author who seeks to create an aversion to their influence by invoking the traditional polemic used extensively by philosophers in their debates. By using such language, one undermined an opponent's influence by castigating his or her immorality or lack of self-control.[108] The author of the Pastorals scarcely engages the false teachers at the theological level. The argument for the sanctity of foods in 1 Tim 4:3-5 is the sole creative theological argument presented in the three letters.

---

[106] See the discussion of this issue in D.C. Verner, *The Household of God: The Social World of the Pastoral Epistles* (Chico, CA: Scholars Press, 1983), 166-71.

[107] Beker, *Heirs of Paul*, 39-43, 86.

[108] See A.J. Malherbe, 'Medical Imagery in the Pastoral Epistles', in his *Paul and the Popular Philosophers* (Minneapolis: Fortress Press, 1989), 121-36.

7. PSEUDEPIGRAPHA IN THE NEW TESTAMENT?

That there are Pauline pseudepigrapha outside of the canon is readily agreed. In the case of *3 Corinthians* and *Laodiceans*, otherwise unknown authors penned these letters in Paul's name. The author of the former did so because he believed that the defence of the faith warranted writing under a pseudonym. That both authors sought to deceive can be readily admitted. The practice of writing in Paul's name is already attested by 2 Thessalonians. Scholars have questioned the authenticity of the six letters on reasonable grounds. The arguments have all been rehearsed over the last 200 years, and are readily accessible. I have summarized them above.

What might have occasioned this literary activity and who might be responsible?[109] At the very least one might argue that literate followers of Paul, perhaps with access to some of his letters, sought to actualize the teaching of the apostle for new situations and to meet new challenges being faced by Pauline churches. In the case of Ephesians, I contend that a younger one-time associate of the now dead Paul wrote to extend the apostle's influence beyond his life-time by reflecting on the universal meaning of his gospel and work. The author of Colossians, I believe, sought to engage a particular kind of Jewish-Christian proto-gnostic influence operating in a Pauline church. The author of 2 Thessalonians endeavoured to defuse apocalyptic excitement among Paulinists. In the case of the Pastoral Epistles we have to do with pseudepigrapha written, like *3 Corinthians*, to combat the insidious influence of those considered to be false teachers. The authors of these six letters opted for the strategy of writing pseudonymously. This was warranted if the church was going to withstand attacks on its integrity and apostolic identity. In the case of the Pastorals the threat from false teachers is all the more urgent because it appears to manifest itself in the form of a system of thought and practice. In each case the author wrote in Paul's name because to

---

[109] Several scholars argue that the New Testament Pauline *antilegomena* are the product of a Pauline 'school', followers of the apostle based in Ephesus who committed themselves to re-minting and articulating the message of their master for times discontinuous with him. See, e.g., H.-M. Schenke, 'Das Weiterwirken des Paulus und die Pflege seines Erbes durch die Paulus-Schule', *NTS* 21 (1974–75), 505-18; Beker, *Heirs of Paul*, 67. However, see also the cautious response from Collins (*Letters*, 251-52) on the subject of the existence of a 'school'.

write in his own would not receive the desired effect. He would not gain a hearing. The voice of Paul would not be heard.

As I have already acknowledged, the stakes were high for pseudepigraphers. Orthodox and heterodox used the pseudepigraphical device knowing that to be discovered was to invite condemnation. With respect to Ephesians, Colossians, and 2 Thessalonians the authenticity of these letters seemed to have been affirmed almost everywhere among orthodox and heterodox alike. In the case of the Pastorals only is there some doubt due to late attestation and expressions of doubt as to their authenticity on the part of some early authorities.

In the early church whether books articulated orthodox teaching or not was of supreme moment. By the mid second century, the *antilegomena* had enjoyed a role in the shaping of what it meant to be orthodox among the writers of the sub-apostolic period, and among the early Fathers such as Irenaeus and Tertullian as well as their opponents.

For the Marcionites and Gnostics, the Pauline letters, at least the ten-letter corpus, affirmed their ascetic and celibate lifestyles and supported their particular theological convictions and ecclesiastical order. For the Fathers of the Great Church, these six letters mediated the particularity of the Pauline *homologoumena* and the angularity of the apostle to succeeding generations of believers who faced issues the historical Paul never encountered. Accordingly these letters reflect and inculcate conventional Greco-Roman social roles and hierarchical modes of living together.[110] 2 Thessalonians defuses apocalyptic speculation. Ephesians and Colossians supersede the language of the end-time triumph of God with a theology of resurrection life with Christ in the present. In Ephesians the church is revealed as the climax of God's saving purposes. In the case of the Pastorals the author represented Paul's last words, his testament, to his delegates. The author mandated a highly conducive vision of ecclesiastical life by stressing the need for the church to reflect Greco-Roman social values. In their teaching and proclamation, the leaders, and they alone, of the churches of the letters bear nothing less than the authority of the apostle himself. They, not the proto-Gnostics, are the true guardians of

---

[110] Note also G. Vallée, 'Theological and Non-Theological Motives in Irenaeus's Refutation of the Gnostics', in Sanders (ed.), *Jewish and Christian Self-Definition*, 174-85 (especially 181-85); MacRae, 'Why the Church Rejected Gnosticism', 128-30.

his legacy. To be in fellowship with them is to be in fellowship with Paul and to hear his words.

8. Objections to the Presence of Pseudepigrapha in the New Testament

Whether or not there are pseudepigrapha in the New Testament remains a contentious issue. It has been frequently argued that had early church authorities suspected or recognized that certain books of the New Testament had been authored pseudonymously the Fathers would have rejected them. I am claiming that the Fathers did not recognize these as pseudepigrapha because they were predisposed to accept their genuineness on the grounds of their orthodox content.

Another argument against the inclusion of pseudepigrapha in the New Testament supposes that the early Fathers were well-equipped by virtue of their education to differentiate pseudepigrapha from authentic texts, and for that reason were consistently discriminatingly alert to questions of style and content. Galen, we are reminded, produced a set of criteria to aid in the determination of what books were genuinely his and which ones were not.[111]

However, the evidence from the era of the early church suggests a more complex and ambiguous picture. It is true that criteria of style were invoked by early Fathers in considering the merits of attributing common authorship to 1 and 2 Peter (Jerome), Hebrews and the Pauline corpus (Origen), and Revelation and the Fourth Gospel (Dionysius of Alexandria). Yet, Jerome failed to recognize the pseudonymous nature of the *Letters of Paul and Seneca*. Origen insisted that the sixth century BCE Daniel was the author of Susanna, despite the eminently reasonable stylistic arguments for a more recent date advanced by Julius Africanus.[112] Hebrews, though not a pseudepigraphon, was widely accepted by the fourth century as a genuine letter of Paul, and

---

[111] See Speyer, *Fälschung*, 124 n. 1. Galen was not alone in his concern. See Speyer's discussion in *Fälschung*, 112-28.

[112] See discussion in Rist, 'Pseudepigraphy', 89-90. Julius Africanus's arguments that Susanna is a 'forgery' are contained in a letter to Origen (ca. 240 CE) (see text in *ANF* 4.385). Origen is much concerned to defend the integrity of Susanna because it is found in every (Greek) Bible used by the Church (*ANF* 4.386-92). The Church, Origen is arguing, has already decided in favour of its orthodoxy.

always seemed to have been accepted thus in the East. The considerable stylistic and linguistic differences between Hebrews and the Pauline corpus, acknowledged by many in the early church, were explained away.[113] *Laodiceans* and *3 Corinthians* were included in some early Christian canons. The Wisdom of Solomon continued to be accepted by Fathers, such as Augustine, who rejected Solomonic authorship implicitly claimed in 7:1-22a and 8:17-18.[114] It is also noteworthy that the Muratorian canon, claiming Wisdom for the (New Testament) canon, ascribes authorship to 'friends of Solomon writing in his honour' (l. 70). The author of the canon, as observed earlier, recognized the book as a pseudepigraphon.

Nevertheless, there are those who argue that the writing of pseudepigrapha is to be deplored as a fraudulent exercise, as an immoral and duplicitous enterprise designed to deceive. On the other hand, Brox, Pokorny, and Donelson appeal to the recourse by pseudepigraphers to the 'noble lie', the lie told for a good cause. This, I believe, was a strategy utilized by early Christians in order to defend the orthodox faith against the corrosive influence of false teachers. It is difficult to see how else in the late first and second century CE the rival custodians of the Pauline tradition could have otherwise successfully promoted and defended the cause of orthodoxy except through this means.

In theological terms, one might argue that God used the post-Pauline authors of Pauline pseudepigrapha to extend the authority and influence of the apostle—each author actualizing and re-presenting particular aspects of the Pauline tradition—in the post-Pauline era. Ephesians and the Pastorals especially are attempts to articulate the significance of the apostle's heritage for new times and situations. These writers sought to overcome the particularity of the historical Paul.[115] They also enlisted him for the orthodox cause, bringing Paul

---

[113] F.F. Bruce, *The Epistle to the Hebrews* (NICNT; Grand Rapids: Eerdmans, 1964), xxxvi-xxxvii, citing efforts by Clement of Alexandria and Origen to reconcile the data of the Pauline corpus with Hebrews. See also nn. 13, 14, above.

[114] W.E.O. Oesterley, *An Introduction to the Books of the Apocrypha* (London: SPCK, 1935), 196, who also notes that Jerome denied and Origen doubted Solomonic authorship.

[115] See Dahl, 'The Particularity of the Pauline Epistles', 260-71. Ephesians is a general letter articulating the thrust of the ministry of Paul for Gentiles in Pauline churches (pp. 266-67). 1 Timothy and Titus are church orders, 2 Timothy a testament (p. 266). Dahl also presents evidence that Romans and 1 Corinthians

to speech against rival guardians and interpreters of the Pauline tradition. For their part, the opponents were also engaged in the same enterprise.

The issue cannot be settled by recourse to theological presuppositions to the effect that God could not have caused 'fraudulent' or 'deceptive' Scripture to have been written. That would be to discount the humanness of the moment when early Christian writers were engaged in the urgent task of defining the apostolic faith in the midst of seemingly endless, even uncontrollable, diversity.[116] It will not do to argue that scholars who claim that the New Testament contains such writings should advocate their removal from the canon.[117] That would amount to identifying the revelation with the New Testament itself instead of perceiving it as a human witness of the revelation of God in Christ, as Pokorny aptly observes.[118] The issue cannot be settled by appealing to the critical acumen of the early Fathers. They brought into play their powers of critical analysis of texts only when they were either defending the prior inclusion of various books in their canons or were suspicious on theological grounds that a work under question was unorthodox.[119]

---

have been interpolated so as to present the message of each in more general ('catholic') terms (pp. 267-71).

[116] This point is ably argued by Donelson, *Pseudepigraphy*, 199-202. Note also his remark: 'Pseudepigraphy represents one mode of response to the predicament of second-generation theology. Theological warrants must come from somewhere, especially when the diversity of opinions about the character of the Christian life was, to some minds at least, out of control. The church's inability to adjudicate these debates created an urgent need for unimpeachable warrants' (p. 201).

[117] See E.E. Ellis, 'Pseudonymity and Canonicity of New Testament Documents', in M.J. Wilkins and T. Paige (eds.), *Worship, Theology and Ministry in the Early Church: Essays in Honour of Ralph P. Martin* (JSNTSup 87; Sheffield: JSOT Press, 1992), 212-24.

[118] Pokorny, 'Problem', 496. Pokorny also argues that the presence of pseudepigrapha in the canon is a testimony to God's grace: 'Wenn die Kirche auch pseudepigraphe Schriften als apostolisches Zeugnis aufgenommen und kanonisiert hat, so bedeutet das für uns...dass auch der biblische Kanon durch Gottes Gnade und nicht durch das Werk der Menschen in Geltung ist. *Sola gratia* gilt auch hier.'

[119] Pokorny, 'Problem', 490.

9. Conclusion

The Pauline corpus is a comparatively small collection. Outside of the New Testament no authentic letters are extant. Within the New Testament all are agreed that there are seven authentic letters. The other six are 'spoken against', *antilegomena*. These six command the attention of many scholars intrigued by the problems of authorship they generate.

In all the New Testament Pauline *antilegomena* I conclude that the authors have moved away appreciably from the hermeneutic, theology, and vocabulary of the *homologoumena*. This is chiefly evident in the Pastorals. The very *particularity* of Paul bequeathed to successive generations in the letters rendered him opaque. Yet, it is also true that he is greatly revered by many in the early church—orthodox and heterodox alike.[120] His authority was invoked by both sides in the bitter quests for orthodoxy and ownership of the faith delivered by Christ to the apostles.

It would be fruitless, I believe, for the church to re-draw its canon today on the basis that had the early church known it was dealing with documents many scholars today regard as pseudepigrapha it would have rejected them. Pseudepigrapha were accepted because they bore a confirming testimony to the significance of the Christ-event as that was interpreted, and as such were believed to be authentic. Anonymous books were erroneously attributed lest their witness be lost to the church. These books enhanced the apostolic witness to the tradition articulated in the church from early times. That tradition had been accepted unquestionably as apostolic and was now inscripturated and in the process of being canonized.

It is my contention that those who wrote in Paul's name were engaged in the defence of the faith in the face of those they considered detractors and heretics, even rival Paulinists. *3 Corinthians* is an

---

[120] See n. 105 above and the discussion there of the invocation of Paul in *Treatise on the Resurrection* 45. Note also the comments of Irenaeus, *Haer* 4.41.4 and Clement of Alexandria, *Stromateis* 7.17 on the use of Paul by the Gnostics. Cf. Pagels, *Gnostic Paul*, 1-2 (see also her n. 10), 5-6 and *passim*, for evidence of the esteem in which Valentinians held Paul. In his *De Praescriptione Haereticorum* 5-6, Tertullian contests the use of Paul by heretical groups, arguing, for example, that the same Paul who counts 'heresies' (that is, 'factions' [NRSV]) as sins against the flesh in Gal 5:20 also castigates heretics in Titus 3:10, 11. Indeed, 'in almost every epistle' Paul condemns heresies (6) (*ANF* 3.245-46).

excellent example of the use of pseudonymity to defend the apostolic faith. Authors, both orthodox and heterodox, enlisted the authority of the apostle and articulated something of the force and dynamic of his personality. They actualized aspects of his teaching in the interests of protecting and guarding the faithful from presentations of the apostolic deposit that were considered misleading and false. They made Paul speak afresh. This enterprise can be traced to the first century itself, as 2 Thess 2:2 testifies. Authors wrote pseudonymously on the ground that the deception involved was in the interests of a holy cause. They wrote to confirm the content of the Pauline and apostolic faith for the salvation and eternal felicity of the faithful.

PAUL WROTE SOME OF ALL, BUT NOT ALL OF ANY

†J.C. O'NEILL

University of Edinburgh
Edinburgh, UK

Paul wrote some of all, but not all of any of the epistles that bear his name; even Philemon was glossed. The canonical epistles that name Paul in the opening greeting are all official letters from an apostle to a church or churches, or to an inferior minister or layman. They are often written not only in Paul's name but also in the name of other officials, called *brother* (Sosthenes, 1 Cor 1:1; Timothy, 2 Cor 1:1; Col 1:1; Phlm 1) or *brothers* (Gal 1:2) or a *fellow-servant* (Timothy, Phil 1:1) or simply named with him (Silvanus and Timothy, 1 Thess 1:1; 2 Thess 1:1).

Paul almost always wrote with authority as an apostle (Romans, 1 Corinthians, 2 Corinthians, Galatians, Ephesians, Colossians, 1 Timothy, 2 Timothy, Titus) or as a servant (like God's servants the prophets: Romans again, Philippians, Titus again). Where he gives himself no title, he is sure soon to remind his recipients that 'our word came to you...with power and the authority of the Holy Spirit' (1 Thess 1:5) and that they should remain in communion with him and his fellow-workers in order to escape judgment when the Lord Jesus shall be revealed in flame of fire (2 Thess 1:7-9).

As befits the writer of an official letter, Paul often employed an amanuensis, if not always. Tertius writes in his own voice in the final greetings in Romans (Rom 16:22), and Paul sometimes takes up the pen himself at the end of an epistle (1 Cor 16:21; Gal 6:11; Col 4:18; 2 Thess 3:17; Phlm 19). The greetings and final benedictions follow the model of official letters.

However, all the canonical letters with Paul's name in the opening greeting are, in their present form, books. That is, they were originally made up of sheets of papyrus, folded, and gathered together to make a codex or book. This is evident when we observe the ratio of the length of any one compared with each of the others, as A.Q. Morton has discovered.[1] In fact, this is true of every book in the New Testament, but in this article I restrict attention to the Pauline corpus, which probably existed separately before being united with Hebrews, the Gospels, Acts, the Catholic Epistles, and Revelation.

The fact that the books of the Bible were divided into chapters—early on in the Codex Vaticanus and later, according to the system we now follow, by Stephen Langton of Paris, later Archbishop of Canterbury—shows an intuitive grasp of each book as a compilation rather than as a tract written by one author. Morton suggested that the Gospels were compilations constrained by the physical limits of the quires that made up the codex. Thus he argues that the Gospel of John was a codex of one hundred and twenty pages comprising six sections written as one quire of five sheets, the average content of the page being 588 letters, the pages having 28 lines and 22 letters.[2]

It looks as though the epistles were subject to the same constraints, for the lengths of the epistles in number of characters do not form a smooth series. Rather, they are stepped, and each step seems to be related to the others by being a different multiple of a unit comprising one sheet of papyrus folded into two, giving two leaves and four pages, each page containing roughly the same number of characters. These hypothetical four-page quires contain roughly the same number of characters as the chapters intuitively marked by the Codex Vaticanus and Stephen Langton. The following table illustrates this.[3]

---

[1] Morton 1980: 27-30: 'The constraints of codex and compilation'. G.H.C. Macgregor had introduced Morton to two classics on the subject of the book in antiquity, Wilhelm Schubart (1921) and Frederic G. Kenyon (1932).

[2] Morton 1980: ch. 5, esp. 76-77.

[3] I have allowed 450 characters to the page. This is a rough-and-ready procedure, and nothing much hangs on it. Whatever number of characters is chosen, the results will still display the ratio between each of the books and the total corpus. The Chester Beatty Papyrus of Paul, $\mathfrak{P}^{46}$, which contained Romans, Hebrew, 1 Corinthians, 2 Corinthians, Ephesians, Galatians, Philippians, Colossians, 1 Thessalonians, and 2 Thessalonians, was made up of 52 sheets folded once into one quire of 104 leaves. So there were 208 pages. The number of characters on each page varied, there being a larger number of characters to the page in the second part of the codex. The average number of characters to the page was about 840. See Junack *et al.* 1989: xl-xlvi. The text of the Bodmer Papyrus, $\mathfrak{P}^{66}$, contains 39 sheets of papyrus, folded to make 78 leaves and 156 pages. The

	No. of characters (WH)	No. of pp. (450 chars. per page)	No. of 4-page quires	Codex Vaticanus chapters	Modern chapters (Langton)
Romans	34,439	76:5	19:0	21	16
1 Corinthians	32,717	72:7	18:0	21	16
2 Corinthians	22,257	49:5	12:0	11	13
Galatians	11,080	24:6	6:0	6	6
Ephesians	11,979	26:6	6:6	6	6
Philippians	8,006	17:8	4:5	4	4
Colossians	7,865	17:5	4:4	6	4
1 Thess	7,390	16:4	4:0	4	5
2 Thess	4,035	9:0	2:0	3	3
1 Timothy	8,858	20:0	5:0	–	6
2 Timothy	6,526	14:5	3:6	–	4
Titus	3,722	8:3	2:0	–	3
Philemon	1,558	3:5	1:0	–	1

The following hypothesis presents itself for examination. Thirteen official letters from Paul to churches or to subordinates have been preserved in the canon. The letters would originally have been written on one side of a papyrus roll. The text would probably have been rolled up, tied with a fibre taken from one end of the roll, and sealed.[4]

The compilers of our present canonical epistles would have first to transcribe the beginning, middle, and end of the letter on to separate sheets of papyrus in order to add to those sheets the other sheets of traditional material to make a book.

Each official letter, if we can judge by other official letters, is unlikely to have contained text enough to fill more than twelve pages.[5]

---

number of lines per page runs from 14 to 25, and the number of characters in a line from 18 to 28. Page 34 of John 6:5-11 contains 20 lines of about 24 characters a line: about 480 characters to a page. See Finegan 1974: 90-94, 102-104. For my calculations, I have used the text of Westcott and Hort (WH), including all the words they have set in brackets. The number of characters for 1 Corinthians, for example, are 32,717 WH; 32,754 *UBSGNT* 1966 used by Morton; and 32,753 Thesaurus Linguae Graecae (TLG) kindly provided for me by Colin Brough in 1995. All three give 11,080 for Galatians. The number of characters in the Textus Receptus (TR) for 1 Corinthians is 33,174 and for Galatians, 11,188. The text of the TR and WH was The Online Bible, which proved easy to use for the calculation of the number of characters.

[4] Turner 1968: 5.
[5] Claudius to Alexander, *CPJ* II 153 (P.Lond. VI 1912), 4 November AD 41, contains approximately 4,830 characters. See White 1986: 131-37. Demetrius to the Jews, 1 Macc 10:25-45, is just under 3,000 characters.

Most were much shorter. Philemon, when transcribed from a scroll to sheets of papyrus, was probably four pages long.

The compilers inserted into the body of the letter related sacred texts, each insertion usually four pages long. The insertions were often more ancient than Paul, rather than written later, since the compilers would probably regard themselves as mainly supplying traditions which Paul himself would have held to be authoritative.

The basic form of sacred writing, as Ewald discerned, was the isolated saying spoken by a prophet or seer or wise teacher and written down by disciples.[6]

The sections inserted into Paul's letters are, then, likely to have been catenas of sayings.

E. Earle Ellis has recently published, as the fruit of long and faithful labour, a monograph which includes a substantial section on the making of the New Testament letters.[7] He draws attention to five types of what he calls 'pre-formed traditions' in the epistles: expositions of Old Testament texts, lists of vices and virtues, household regulations, congregational regulations, and hymns. He thinks of these traditions as having been previously composed by Paul and inserted by him into his epistle,[8] or composed by other apostles, prophets and teachers 'often reworked and adapted to the occasion of his letter'.[9] He also suggests that the secretary and the co-workers could have influenced the content of the letters.[10]

How does Ellis picture Paul at work on writing what he calls 'teaching pieces clothed in an adaptable letter-form'?[11] Paul sits in his office, surrounded by a little library of pre-formed midrashes on Old Testament texts; lists of virtues and vices; creeds, some perhaps gathered from the parallel missions under the leadership of James, Peter, and John; hymns, some of which came from these parallel missions; sayings of Jesus; old sermons written by himself or others; household regulations; congregational regulations; transcripts of

---

[6] Ewald 1849: 157; translated in O'Neill 1991a: 137-38. Cf. Alt 1964: 81-132.
[7] Ellis 1999: Part II, 49-142.
[8] Ellis 1999: 262.
[9] Ellis 1999: 262-63.
[10] Ellis 1999: 117.
[11] Ellis 1999: 116. For a summary of Ellis's picture of how Paul worked, see pp. 86-87, 430 *et passim*.

expositions used on previous occasions when a crisis had arisen in a church; and so on.

An amanuensis sits ready to take dictation, to incorporate one of the pre-formed documents and even to adapt it for the new context. One or two fellow-workers also sit ready to contribute to the work, either by suggesting words or by inserting one of the pre-formed traditions, perhaps from their own store, and adapting it for the current letter. For example, a 'gifted co-worker' composed an Old Testament exposition which Paul adapted (1 Cor 2:6-16).[12]

Paul would have directed that a copy of the letter be placed in his personal archive.[13] The church where he was working would have probably also kept a copy. The church that received the letter would send copies to neighbouring churches and some churches would already be making small local collections of Paul's letters.

Ellis argues from the multiplicity of copies that were immediately made of the original letter that it was impossible for any interpolation to be inserted into it because such an insertion would be made in only one of the copies so that the textual tradition would carry forward both longer and shorter texts. None of the pre-formed traditions is absent from any manuscript, so none of the pre-formed traditions was added to the original 'teaching pieces clothed in an adaptable letter-form'.[14]

The strength of Ellis's case is that Paul's letters (and the other New Testament epistles, bar the Johannine epistles) often give Old Testament citations accompanied by commentary applying the prophecies to current events. We now have many examples of the same sort among the Dead Sea Scrolls. The weakness of his case is that none of these commentaries occurs in a letter. The so-called Epistle to the

---

[12] Ellis 1999: 79.

[13] In 1 Cor 11:3-16, Ellis (1999: 84-87) notes that the pre-formed piece is somewhat roughly joined to its context and that late copyists tried to smooth the transitions (1 Cor 11:2, 17). He is sure that the passage could not be a post-Pauline addition because it is lacking in no extant manuscript. (See below for a discussion of this curious argument.) He accounts for the roughness of the seams by supposing that 'it may have been inserted...into an initial secretarial draft or into the completed roll or codex before Paul's retained copy was made and before the letter was sent to Corinth' (p. 86).

[14] Romans 16:25-27 is absent only from two ninth-century manuscripts and one fourteenth-century manuscript (Ellis 1999: 98-99). Ellis seems to think that late manuscripts always contain late readings. These manuscripts are F G 629. Neither Tertullian, Cyprian nor Irenaeus cited the doxology. Jerome knew manuscripts that lacked it.

Hebrews is only an apparent exception since it lacks an epistolary introduction and the only letter it contains is appended to the end in its entirety.

Ellis makes no attempt to find independent evidence outside of the circles that produced 1 and 2 Peter, James, *1 Clement*, the Epistles of Ignatius, Polycarp and *Barnabas* of someone like Paul composing official 'teaching pieces clothed in an adaptable letter-form' such as he supposes Paul's letters to be. He never asks himself why Marcion thought it at all plausible to publish short versions of some of Paul's letters on the assumption that Jewish editors, who misunderstood the radical nature of Paul's attack on the Jewish God, had added large sections to them. Marcion's excisions are not likely to have been based on exact knowledge of the process by which Paul's letters known to him were formed. But Marcion may have had accurate knowledge that the letters of Paul in the collections had been formed by supplementing Paul's actual letters with relevant Jewish material.

Ellis makes frequent appeal to the argument that no pre-formed tradition could have been added to the original letter because no extant manuscript lacks the supposed addition. He ignores the evidence that it was customary for sacred writings to be surcharged with other sacred writings by disciples and successors of the original compilers. If only one copy of the surcharged writing has survived, we naturally have no textual evidence for the additions. In the case of the book of the prophet Jeremiah we do possess two versions, the Masoretic text and the LXX. The LXX has two sections in different positions (Jer 46:1–51:64 cf. LXX 25:14–31:44; Jer 25:15–45:5 cf. LXX 32:1–51:35); the order of the oracles against the foreign nations is different; and the LXX lacks about one-eighth of the material in the Masoretic text, notably Jer 29:16-20; 33:14-26; and 39:4-13. The Chester Beatty Papyrus, $\mathfrak{P}^{46}$, breaks off at 1 Thess 5:28, and, if it contained 2 Thessalonians, there would not be room for the Pastoral Epistles. It is unlikely that the last five leaves of ten pages would have been left blank, since the scribe must have calculated, before he started, how many sheets folded one time each he required for the Pauline corpus. Henry A. Sanders suggested that 1 Timothy and 2 Timothy in shortened form would have been inscribed on these nine to ten pages.[15] Perhaps, then, there did exist shorter versions of the Pastorals. In the case of the Epistles of Ignatius, we possess the shorter Syriac

---

[15] Sanders 1935. See Junack *et al.* 1989: xli.

version, a medium-sized version in one Greek manuscript and fragments in Greek, Latin, Syriac, Armenian, Arabic, and Coptic (the version usually printed), and a longer version in Greek and Latin containing also six additional letters. The order of the epistles differs widely.

Ellis rightly assumes that small local collections of Paul's letters were made.[16] I think it most likely that Romans and the collection 1 and 2 Corinthians once stood separately alone, for Marcion and the Muratorian canon have them in the reverse order. Galatians probably stood alone since it occurs in different positions from the later standard position in each of $\mathfrak{P}^{46}$, Codex Claromontanus, Marcion, and the Muratorian canon. It is possible that Philippians and Philemon were collected early on, for they occur in that order in $\mathfrak{P}^{46}$, Codex Claromontanus, and Marcion. Ephesians and Colossians always come in that order and probably were a collection. 1 and 2 Thessalonians were probably another collection and 1 and 2 Timothy and Titus seems to belong in yet another collection.

The strength of Ellis's reconstruction of the processes by which Paul's letters came into existence is that he imagines scribes working in the setting of libraries containing ancient documents. The weakness of his reconstruction lies in his imaging Paul as the one commanding figure who not only wrote large parts of his 'teaching pieces clothed in an adaptable letter-form' but also masterminded the incorporation (and adaptation) of 'pre-formed traditions', setting his staff to work on them like a German professor with his *Assistenten*.

Ellis does not ask himself why Luke, the author of Luke–Acts, whom he believes to have been an occasional companion of Paul,[17] never depicts Paul as writing a letter, let alone carrying around an archive which he set up and staffed in every church from which he sent an official letter to others of his churches or to Timothy and Titus.

Nevertheless, Ellis has issued a challenge to those who argue that Paul's original letters had sacred collections loaded into them. If it is hard to imagine Paul himself doing this, is it not equally difficult to imagine libraries with the necessary resources to compile the sort of books we now have?

Since the discovery at Qumran of the monastic settlement containing a scriptorium near to caves in which were stored sacred

---

[16] Ellis 1999: 296-97, 430 *et passim*.
[17] Ellis 1999: 397-400.

writings of various types, we now have definite evidence that celibate communities housing scribes and libraries were possible in the centuries in which the present Pauline corpus was formed. It is pretty clear that small monastic communities were always a part of the church from the beginning, and at least some of them were bound to have libraries.[18] Since these monastic libraries preserved for posterity the bulk of the Jewish writings in Greek that we possess, it is likely that previously existing Jewish monastic communities came to believe that Jesus was the Messiah and brought over their libraries with them. The Epistle to the Hebrews, apart from the letter at the end that mentions the resurrection of Jesus, was, I would argue, a collection of Jewish sacred traditions about an earlier Messiah who was crucified on the Day of Atonement and who was believed to have entered the heavenly holy of holies, but was not believed to have risen from the dead.[19]

In these monastic communities it is possible to imagine the letters of Paul being surcharged with ancient traditional material supplemented by more recent collections of sayings and being turned into books. The weakest part of Ellis's case is his constant assertion—borrowed from forerunners who are obsessed with the myth of the creative author who felt free to change and adapt sacred traditions handed down to him—that the pre-formed traditions were somehow altered to suit their new context. These scholars never ask why the alterations were not more complete so that we would have no grounds for supposing that earlier material was being employed at all. The assumption that any Jewish or Christian scribe or compiler felt free to shorten, lengthen or change the sacred traditions they were passing on to their successors is wildly improbable.[20]

I have asserted so far that much of the material loaded in was written before Paul. How do I oppose the arguments of those who posit a massive development of thought in the church which was responsible for the distinctive theology of Ephesians and Colossians or the 'developed' church order of the Pastorals?

The Qumran writings and the related Damascus Document show all the features of the alleged 'developed' church order of the apostles, the overseer of the camps, the overseers of individual camps, presbyters, and deacons. Eusebius noted that the apostolic church order was described by Philo in *De Vita Contemplativa*; Eusebius

---

[18] O'Neill 1989; 1998.
[19] O'Neill 1999.
[20] O'Neill 1991b.

knew of a tradition that Philo spoke to Peter in Rome, and he thought the report not improbable, since the treatise composed later 'obviously contains the rules of the Church which are still observed in our own time' (Eusebius, *Hist eccl* 2.17.1; 2.17.23). We know that Philo was describing a Jewish monastic community, probably related to the Essenes, but Eusebius was right that church order was derived from their hierarchical order (Philo, *Contempl* 64-79; *Ebr* 98; *Her* 30; CD 9:18-20; 13:7-13; 14:8-13; 1QS 6:8-14; 1QM 13:1).

Similarly, the Qumran documents and the Syriac *Odes of Solomon* give us all the elements of ethical dualism and a high Christology that used to be thought part of a later developed Johannine theology, and the Dead Sea Scrolls and Philo give us the ingredients of the language typical of Ephesians and Colossians.

Another sign that the material is indeed early is the inclusion of traditional material that mentions the death of the Messiah and his ascension without mentioning the resurrection, as in the revelatory discourses of John, Phil 2:5-11, 1 Pet 3:18, and Hebrews (except for the letter in Heb 13:18-25).

Ellis's constant reference to the virtual absence of textual evidence for the omission of any of his pre-formed traditions as proof that none was added after Paul sent off the original letters is based on a misunderstanding of how ancient writings were copied and preserved. Episcopal libraries and libraries of schools were a late development possible only when Christianity was able to exist in public and be guarded from harm by the authorities. Even state libraries were likely to be destroyed by fire or civil disturbance—for example, the great library in Alexandria in 47 BC or the Capitol Library in Rome in AD 69 and in AD 363.[21] It was less likely that episcopal libraries or the libraries of Christian schools would be very safe. Clement of Alexandria was head of a school, yet only three of his works have survived, two in one manuscript and the third in another manuscript. Origen his successor, who worked in two great centres, wrote many books, but the original Greek of any of them has hardly survived at all. It was also unlikely that local churches had secure archives. I have argued that there always were libraries, but libraries in small communities and in remote and isolated places.[22]

---

[21] Preisendanz 1975: cols. 892-96.
[22] O'Neill 1989; 1998.

Ellis assumes that Paul was revered and his letters were treasured in flourishing churches from the beginning. He ignores the evidence from Justin Martyr that Paul was as good as forgotten in parts of the flourishing church. Justin never quotes Paul and never mentions his name.[23] Where Paul was known, he was not well known. Clement of Rome praises Paul as a great martyr (*1 Clem* 5.5-7) but he seemed to think that Paul wrote only one letter to the Corinthians (*1 Clem* 47.1) and he clearly refers to Paul's call for unity in the opening chapter and probably in ch. 3. He never cites from Paul: 1 Cor 2:9 in *1 Clem* 34.8 comes from a common source, the Apocalypse of Elijah, and he gives more of Ps 32:1-2 in *1 Clem* 50.6 than is found in Rom 4:7-9. He alludes to ideas also found in our collection of Paul's letters, but never in the same words (the resurrection 1 Cor 15:20; *1 Clem* 24.1; the body 1 Cor 12:21; *1 Clem* 37.5; the resurrection compared to a seed sprouting 1 Cor 15:36-37; *1 Clem* 24.5; love is patient 1 Cor 13:4-7; *1 Clem* 49.5; do not sin because you have grace Rom 6:1; *1 Clem* 33.1). The only cases of exact agreement in words are very short ('complete every good work' Titus 3:1; *1 Clem* 2.7; 33.1; 34.4; Jesus was a Jew 'according to the flesh' Rom 9:5; *1 Clem* 32.2) or are employed in a completely different sense ('each in his own order' 1 Cor 15:23; *1 Clem* 37.3; 41.1). Ignatius of Antioch mentions Paul by name as having been martyred and as having referred to the Ephesian Christians 'in every epistle' (Ignatius, *Eph* 12.2; cf. 1 Cor 15:32; 16:8; Eph 1:1; 1 Tim 1:3; 2 Tim 1:18; 4:12—so at most he knew 1 Corinthians and the two to Timothy, besides Ephesians itself). He also reminds the Romans that Peter and Paul gave orders to the churches there because of their apostolic status (Ignatius, *Rom* 4.3). But he never cites any letter of Paul, for the phrases that are sometimes taken to be echoes of Paul are simply common traditions ('the end is in love' 1 Tim 1:5; Ignatius, *Eph* 14.1; 'not inherit the kingdom of God' 1 Cor 6:9, 10; Ignatius, *Eph* 16.1; *Phld* 3.3; the cross is a scandal 1 Cor 1:23; Ignatius, *Eph* 18.1; 'where is the wise; where is the disputer?' 1 Cor 1:20; Ignatius, *Eph* 18.1; I was fighting wild beasts 1 Cor 15:32; Ignatius, *Rom* 5.1; I am last, a miscarriage 1 Cor 15:8-9; Ignatius, *Rom* 9.2).

The only epistles of Paul to survive were likely to be those preserved and gathered in monastic libraries. With the great renewal of interest in Paul's letters in the main church in the mid second

---

[23] O'Neill 1961: 26-27.

century, with Polycarp, Marcion, Irenaeus and Tertullian, it was these editions that were copied and circulated. And these editions would already have converted letters into books by loading into them the ancient and more recent collections to so many of which Ellis has again drawn our attention. There is nothing surprising in the virtual absence in the textual tradition of shorter versions of any of Paul's epistles. In any case, should a shorter manuscript survive, the church would prefer the longer version, on the grounds that it was dangerous for any scribe to subtract from any sacred writing; faced with the choice, it was safer to add (Deut 4:2; 13:1; Rev 22:18-19).

The likelihood of the survival of the original scroll of any of Paul's letters in the churches to which they were sent is almost nil. Only copies of these scrolls made on papyrus sheets and kept in secure remote libraries were at all likely to survive. But the very means of survival—the transcription on to sheets of papyrus—almost guaranteed that they would be supplemented by other ancient sacred traditions already in the libraries as sheets of papyrus folded once to make two leaves and four pages.

The official letters of Paul themselves called out for such additions. When Paul (Rom 1:17) said that the righteousness of God was revealed in the gospel from faith to faith according to Hab 2:4, the monastic librarians were bound to add collections of sayings about revelation, righteousness, and faith. When Paul said he would gladly lose his own chance of salvation if only his kinsmen according to the flesh could be saved (Rom 9:1-5), the librarians naturally bound in with that sheet a number of collections of teachings about the tragic split between Judaism and Judaism (to recall Henry St. John Hart's striking phrase). When Paul said that when he came again to the church in Corinth he would set in order the remaining features of common life (1 Cor 11:34b), the librarians were almost required to insert existing collections of sayings about church practice and Christian morals. When Paul reminded Timothy of Hymenaeus and Alexander who had made shipwreck of the faith (1 Tim 1:19-20) and told him to hold fast the form of sound words (1 Tim 6:3; 2 Tim 1:13) and told Titus to set in order the things that were wanting in church order (Titus 1:5), the librarians would know themselves required to bring out of their store collections of sayings about heresy, true doctrine and church order.

These ancient traditions were commonly collections of sacred sayings. The monasteries needed libraries of sacred sayings because the members of the community spent much time not only meditating on Scripture but also meditating on later sayings and hymns and psalms of seers and teachers and leaders of their order, going back to the prophets who founded them (Philo, *Contempl* 25-29). Ellis, here following a century's work on the various genres of writing to be found lodged in the Pauline corpus and elsewhere, has overlooked a common feature that binds together entities that scholars have labelled hymns, household tables, manuals of discipline, sections of paraenesis, lists of vices and virtues, tracts of wisdom literature, midrashes, creeds, catenas, testimonies and so on. All of these share one common feature. They are not compositions of an author. They are collections of the sacred sayings of prophets and seers and leaders of communities of the sons and daughters of the prophets and singers of God's praise. The fact that the canonical Psalms in the Hebrew Bible have resisted all but the loosest patterns of analysis should have alerted us sooner to this feature of Jewish sacred literature. It is likely that the acrostic pattern of Psalm 119 is the closest we get to a formal structure. Like Psalm 119, all the psalms seem to be collections of related strophes: laments, exclamations of praise, beatitudes, prayers, thanksgivings, curses and so on.

The common literary form of all these genres is the catena, and the vehicle of preservation of the traditions in the Greek-speaking Jewish world was the sheet of papyrus folded once to produce two leaves and four pages.

Ellis rightly notices the prevalence of catchword connections between sayings.[24] The presence of such catchword connections is widely underestimated. It is the most common way of ordering Jewish and Christian literature, from the Wisdom of Solomon to the Coptic *Gospel of Thomas*[25] to the Mishnah.[26] Isolated sayings were grouped by general theme and subject-matter, and were ordered by the simple device that a word in the first saying suggested to the collector the addition of a similar saying containing the same word or its opposite, and a word in the second saying suggested the addition of a third saying containing the same word or its opposite. And so on.[27]

---

[24] Ellis 1999: e.g. 97 and n. 227; 129 and n. 441.
[25] Fieger 1991: 5-6 *et passim*.
[26] Jeremias 1930.
[27] O'Neill 1975: 192-241 on Rom 12:1–15:13; 1994a on John 13:10 in its context; 1994b on Rom 5:12-21; 1995a: 182-85 on John 5; 1995b on Gal 5:17 in its context.

We should expect the individual sayings in the collections sometimes to show marked poetic structures, differing from the structures of the sayings on either side. To that end, I shall write down the Greek in sense lines, and expect to discern patterns by counting the syllables in each line. For example (and notice the two different senses of διώκω):

Rom 12:13   ταῖς χρείαις τῶν ἁγίων κοινωνοῦντες
            τὴν φιλοξενίαν διώκοντες

Rom 12:14   εὐλογεῖτε τοὺς διώκοντας [ὑμᾶς]
            εὐλογεῖτε καὶ μὴ καταρᾶσθε

Rom 12:15   χαίρειν μετὰ χαιρόντων
            κλαίειν μετὰ κλαιόντων

The syllable counts are: 12, 10; 9, 10; 7, 7. There are three different ways of expressing the imperative mood.

The following strategy for explaining Paul's letters and the other contemporary letters of the same kind (James, 1 and 2 Peter, 2 and 3 John, Jude, *1* and *2 Clement*, the letters of Ignatius, *Barnabas*, and Polycarp, *Ephesians*) suggests itself. Assume that the body of the letter will be made up of collections of traditional sayings. Look at the beginning, in the middle, and at the end for signs of an official letter of not more than 5,400 characters. This actual official letter will make a limited set of practical points. The collections in the body of the letter will normally form a 'chapter' of about 1,800 characters. They will separate themselves from their neighbours fairly easily by theme. Often we shall find distinctive religious terms dominating one chapter, and a greater or lesser degree of dependence on Greek religious ideas, particularly on Stoicism, affecting others. The two sections on Adam in the Pauline corpus obviously separate themselves off from the rest (Rom 5:12-21; 1 Cor 15:20-28). The old distinction first made by Hermann Lüdemann in *Die Anthropologie des Apostels Paulus* in 1872 and popularized by Alfred Loisy and exploited by Albert Schweitzer between the two conceptions of *flesh* in the Pauline corpus (denoting either natural frailty or a spiritual power that causes sin) is one more sign of the diverse nature of the collections.[28]

---

[28] Lüdemann's book is summmarized by Albert Schweitzer 1912: 28-32. Loisy 1935.

Part of the supposedly contradictory notions of the law in the Pauline corpus are due, not to Paul's muddled head, but to the variety of aphorisms on the law in the various collections.[29] Part of the trouble is also due to the tiny corruptions introduced into the text by scribes with Marcionite tendencies (e.g. in Eph 2:15 where D* reads καταρτίσας against 330* κατάρας and the rest καταργήσας, and D* is the original, for no scribe would convert an unfavourable mention of the law into a favourable one). And unless we recognize the collections we shall find it even harder to detect the scribal corruptions.

The collections of aphorisms was commonplace: Wisdom, Sirach, *1 Enoch, Testaments of the Twelve Patriarchs*, 1QH, 1QS, etc. It is likely that only genuine official letters from an apostle or a bishop would have precipitated the practice of using the letter as the bearer of collections. Pseudonymity became possible later on, but only when the official letter enlarged by traditional material to form a book had become well-known (as in the case of the presbyter reported by Tertullian, *Bapt* 17).

If we follow the strategy outlined above, it looks as though Romans and Galatians, for example, were based on genuine official letters containing about 5,000 characters and no more than 6,000. Romans 1:1-17; 9:1-5; 15:14-33; 16:1-24 contains 5,340 characters in the Westcott and Hort text. Galatians 1:1-10; 1:11–2:14; 4:12b-14; 5:2, 10-12; 6:11, 17, 18 contains about 3,760 characters. Of course, glosses were introduced even into the letter of Paul that formed the framework of Romans. For example, Ellis follows many scholars in recognizing a creed in Rom 1:3-4.[30] He thinks Paul himself inserted it at this point, but the over-loaded nature of the sentence indicates that it was a later addition.[31] Ellis does not notice that the manuscript G omits from ἀφωρισμένος in Rom 1:1 to πίστεως in v. 5 (though the words are present in F). The rest of the material in Romans and Galatians comes mainly from traditional Jewish collections, supplemented from sayings of more recent fathers, since the monastic houses where the collections were made had come to believe that Jesus was the Messiah whom God had raised from the dead.

2 Corinthians is widely recognized as a compendium of Paul's letters. H.D. Betz, for example, building on the work of Günther Bornkamm, detected five letters: The First Apology: 2 Cor 2:14–6:13;

---

[29] Räisänen 1983.
[30] Ellis 1999: 94-95.
[31] O'Neill 1975: 26-29.

7:2-4; The Second Apology: 2 Cor 10:1–13:10; The Letter of Reconciliation: 2 Cor 1:1–2:13; 7:5-16; 13:11-13; and Two Administrative Letters: 2 Corinthians 8 to Corinth, and 2 Corinthians 9 to Achaia.[32] I would suggest that our 2 Corinthians contains the bodies of six or perhaps seven letters from Paul, which attracted the usual addition of collections of sayings and traditional teachings. The letters of Paul are in 2 Cor 1:1–2:13; 7:2-16; 8:1-6, 16-24; 9:1-5; 10:1–11:33; 12:1-19; 12:20–13:14.

1 Corinthians is also a compendium of letters, perhaps containing the opening and closing of some important early letter on the unity of the congregation (1:1-17; 3:1-10; 16:1-24) and then the body of letters about specific matters of morality (5:1-13; 6:1-11; 7:1-40), how to deal with unbelievers and their practices (8:1-13; 9:1-27; 10:23-33), the conduct of worship (11:1-15, 16-22, 33-34) and Paul's claim to have seen the resurrected Lord (15:1-11). All these matters have attracted traditional collections of aphorisms on the same and related subjects.

Ephesians and Colossians each contain similar traditional material. Paul's original letters probably came to be lodged at first in different monasteries, but monasteries that were heir to the same sort of Jewish traditions of theology, spirituality and discipline. The supplementary traditions added to each are remarkably similar.

The letter of Paul to the Ephesians that provided the framework for our book probably consisted of Eph 1:1-2, 3-6; 1:15-19; 3:1-7, 8-20; 4:1-24; 6:18-23, about 4,859 characters. The original letter to the Colossians consisted of Col 1:1-9, 21-29; 2:1-5; 4:2-18, about 3,525 characters. Since first writing this, John Muddiman has published an outstanding commentary on Ephesians, in which he argues that an original letter of Paul to the Laodiceans lay behind our Ephesians. On his hypothesis, 'the writer of Ephesians is no mere scissors-and-paste editor. He has used this main source [Paul to the Laodiceans] and other traditions available in his community in a creative and effective way.' Muddiman's Laodiceans consists of our Eph 1:1-2, 15-19; 3:1-8, 12-14, 16-21; 4:1-3, 7, 13-15, 17-32; 5:3-12, 15-20, 22, 25; 6:1, 4, 5-9, 18-24, and he provides a 'tentative reconstruction' in his Appendix B.[33]

---

[32] Betz 1985.
[33] Muddiman 2001: 29-30; Appendix B, pp. 302-305.

The original letter to the Philippians perhaps consisted of Phil 1:1-30; 2:12-30; 4:2-3, 9, 10-23, about 5,121 characters.

Paul's first letter to the Thessalonians perhaps consisted of 1 Thess 1:1-2; 2:14-16, 17-20; 3:1-13; 5:14-28, about 2,792 characters; and the second to the Thessalonians of 2 Thess 1:1-12; 2:1-5, 13-17; 3:1-18, about 3,483 characters.

The Pastoral Epistles are widely regarded as constructed out of traditional creeds and tracts on the duties of ministers, the ordering of families, and the moral life. C.K. Barrett largely followed P.N. Harrison in ascribing Titus 3:12-15 and a few verses from 2 Timothy 1 and 3 and much of 2 Timothy 4 to Paul. Barrett persisted in ascribing the three epistles to an author, feeling able to 'say no more than that certain sentences in his Epistles were not composed but received by him'.[34] I. Howard Marshall argues that an authentic letter behind 2 Timothy gave the impulse to a group, which may have included Timothy and Titus themselves, to produce our three epistles.[35]

James D. Miller has now shown reason to believe that the Pastorals were composite documents: 'the letters appear...to be much more the work of a compiler than of an author'. He believes that we can extract a genuine 'core' of letters written by Paul: 1 Tim 1:1-7, 18-20; 3:14-15; 6:20-21; Titus 1:1-5; 3:9-15; 2 Timothy A = 1:1-2, (3-5?), 15-18; 4:6-8, 22a; 2 Timothy B = 4:9-21, 22b.[36] I am not sure that it is necessary to posit two letters for 2 Timothy, and would be happy with 2 Tim 1:1-6, 15-18; 4:9-22. Miller's genuine 1 Timothy would be about 1,988 characters, my 2 Timothy about 1,791 characters, and his Titus about 952 characters.

Some of these reconstructions of what Paul originally wrote are based on close and detailed study over many years—but some are little more than hasty guesses.

Much work remains to be done. The first task is to jettison all theories about how ancient traditions were rewritten by Paul and his collaborators. Is it likely that they would feel free to tamper with ancient traditions, and how would we know at what points they were supposed to have made alterations or additions? Then we should jettison all theories that try to explain the tortuous switches in argument to which scholars, wedded to the idea that we are reading the work of one author writing to one situation on one occasion,

---

[34] Harrison 1921; Barrett 1963: 10-12.
[35] Marshall 1999: 92.
[36] Miller 1997: 18 and 147-51.

constantly resort. The tell-tale sign of such theories is the introduction of imaginary opponents whose unusual doctrines explain the twists and turns of the alleged author's train of thought.[37]

Then the textual history of the letters needs close attention, for later scribes are bound to be influenced subconsciously by theories that held Paul to have made a decisive break with Judaism, for these scribes belonged to a church that was tragically forced to separate itself from its spiritual mother by the pressure of persecution and by a sharpening of differences on both sides.

Finally we have to learn to read the texts afresh, discerning the parts of the official letter, on the one hand, and the collections of sayings, on the other hand.

Official letters were turned into books in monasteries, as the letters were written on to papyrus sheets folded once. The collections of sayings in the library were bound in with the sheets containing the start, the middle and the end of the letter, or the body of several letters, to form a book.

WORKS CITED

Alt, A.
1966 'The Origins of Israelite Law', in his *Essays on Old Testament History and Religion* (ET of German original of 1934; Oxford: Blackwell, 1966): 81-132.

Barrett, C.K.
1963 *The Pastoral Epistles in the New English Bible* (The New Clarendon Bible [New Testament]; Oxford: Clarendon Press).

Betz, H.D.
1985 *2 Corinthians 8 and 9: A Commentary on Two Administrative Letters of the Apostle Paul* (Hermeneia; Philadelphia: Fortress Press).

---

[37] See the latest interesting attempt by van Spanje (1999) to answer Räisänen and to save the unity of the Pauline corpus of Romans, 1 and 2 Corinthians, Galatians, Philippians, Colossians, 1 and 2 Thessalonians by referring to Paul's strategy as Pastor, Rhetorician and Theologian. He does, however, notice (1999: 215-28) the fragmentary structure of Paul's letters (e.g. Romans 2; Rom 6:1-14; 6:15-23; 7:1-6; 7:7-12). On Rom 1:18–2:29, see Walker 1999. In a letter to me of 13 January 2000, William Walker says he is 'inclined to regard 1:18-32 and chapter 2 as two separate interpolations'.

Ellis, E.E.
1999 *The Making of the New Testament Documents* (BIS 39; Leiden: Brill).

Ewald, H.
1849 'Über die kürze des Bibelwortes', *Jahrbücher der Biblischen Wissenschaft* 1: 54-160.

Fieger, M.
1991 *Das Thomasevangelium. Einleitung Kommentar und Systematik* (NTAbh 22; Münster: Aschendorff).

Finegan, J.
1974 *Encountering New Testament Manuscripts: A Working Introduction to Textual Criticism* (Grand Rapids: Eerdmans).

Harrison, P.N.
1921 *The Problem of the Pastoral Epistles* (London: Oxford University Press/Humphrey Milford).

Jeremias, J.
1930 'Zur Hypothese einer schriftlichen Logienquelle Q', *ZNW* 29: 147-49 = *Abba: Studien zur neutestamentlichen Theologie und Zeitgeschichte* (Göttingen: Vandenhoeck & Ruprecht, 1966): 90-92.

Junack, K., et al.
1989 *Das Neue Testament auf Papyrus. II. Die Paulinischen Briefe. Teil 1: Röm., 1. Kor., 2. Kor.* (ANTF 12; Berlin: Walter de Gruyter).

Kenyon, F.G.
1932 *Books and Readers in Ancient Greece and Rome* (Oxford: Clarendon Press).

Loisy, A.
1935 *Remarques sur la littérature épistolaire du Nouveau Testament* (Paris: Nourry).

Marshall, I.H., with P.H. Towner
1999 *A Critical and Exegetical Commentary on the Pastoral Epistles* (ICC; Edinburgh: T. & T. Clark).

Miller, J.D.
1997 *The Pastoral Letters as Composite Documents* (SNTSMS 93; Cambridge: Cambridge University Press).

Morton, A.Q., and J. McLeman
1980 *The Genesis of John* (Edinburgh: St. Andrew).

Muddiman, J.
2001 *A Commentary on the Epistle to the Ephesians* (London: Continuum).

O'Neill, J.C.
1961 *The Theology of Acts in its Historical Setting* (London: SPCK, 2nd rev. and sup. edn, 1970).
1975 *Paul's Letter to the Romans* (Harmondsworth: Penguin).
1989 'The Origins of Monasticism', in R. Williams (ed.), *The Making of Orthodoxy: Essays in Honour of Henry Chadwick* (Cambridge: Cambridge University Press): 270-87.
1991a *The Bible's Authority: A Portrait Gallery of Thinkers from Lessing to Bultmann* (Edinburgh: T. & T. Clark).
1991b 'The Lost Written Records of Jesus' Words and Deeds behind our Records', *JTS* 42: 483-504.
1994a 'John 13:10 Again', *RB* 101: 67-74.
1994b 'Adam, Who Is the Figure of him That Was to Come: A Reading of Romans 5:12-21', in S.E. Porter, P. Joyce and D.E. Orton (eds.), *Crossing the Boundaries: Essays in Biblical Interpretation in Honour of Michael D. Goulder* (BIS 8; Leiden: Brill): 183-99.
1995a *Who Did Jesus Think He Was?* (BIS 11; Leiden: Brill).
1995b 'The Holy Spirit and the Human Spirit in Galatians: Gal 5,17', *ETL* 71: 101-20.
1998 'New Testament Monasteries', in J.V. Hills *et al.* (eds.), *Common Life in the Early Church: Essays Honoring Graydon F. Snyder* (Harrisville, PA: Trinity Press International): 118-32.
1999 '*Jesus* in Hebrews', *The Journal of Higher Criticism* 6.1: 64-82.

Preisendanz, K.
1975 'Bibliothek(en)', in *Der Kleine Pauly. Lexikon der Antike*. I (5 vols.; Munich: Alfred Drukenmüller/Artemis): cols. 892-96.

Sanders, H.A.
1935 *A Third Century Papyrus Codex of the Epistles of Paul* (University of Michigan Studies, Humanities Series 38; Ann Arbor: University of Michigan Press).

Schubart, W.
1921 *Das Buch bei den Griechen und Römern* (Handbüchern der Berliner Museen; Berlin: de Gruyter, 2nd edn [3rd posthumous edn ed. E. Paul; Heidelberg: Lambert Schneider, 1961]).

Schweitzer, A.
1912 *Paul and His Interpreters: A Critical History* (trans. W. Montgomery; London: A. & C. Black; ET of *Geschichte der Paulinischen Forschung von der Reformation bis auf die Gegenwart* [Tübingen: Mohr, 1911]).

van Spanje, T.E.
1999   *Inconsistency in Paul? A Critique of the Work of Heikki Räisänen* (WUNT 2.110; Tübingen: Mohr Siebeck).

Turner, E.G.
1968   *Greek Papyri: An Introduction* (Oxford: Clarendon Press).

Walker, W.O., Jr.
1999   'Romans 1:18–2:29: A Non-Pauline Interpolation?', *NTS* 45: 533-52.

White, J.L.
1986   *Light from Ancient Letters* (FFNT; Philadelphia: Fortress Press).

INTERPOLATIONS IN THE PAULINE LETTERS[1]

WILLIAM O. WALKER, JR.

Trinity University
San Antonio, Texas, USA

1. Introduction

Victor Paul Furnish notes that 'hypotheses about textual glosses and the presence of even longer interpolated units [in the Pauline letters] have long been a part of textual and literary criticism'.[2] Indeed, some have asserted that the letters as a whole have been heavily interpolated. First advanced in nineteenth-century Germany and particularly the Netherlands,[3] this view was revived in the 1920s and 1930s by such scholars as P.-L. Couchoud[4] and Alfred F. Loisy[5] and, in the United States in the 1940s, by Robert Martyr Hawkins.[6] More

---

[1] A later and expanded version of this paper has already appeared in my *Interpolations in the Pauline Letters* (JSNTSup 213; London: Sheffield Academic Press, 2001), 15-90. This version is being published with permission from T. & T. Clark International, which now includes Sheffield Academic Press.

[2] V.P. Furnish, 'Pauline Studies', in E.J. Epp and G.W. MacRae (eds.), *The New Testament and Its Modern Interpreters* (The Bible and Its Modern Interpreters 3; Philadelphia: Fortress; Atlanta: Scholars Press, 1989), 324.

[3] For a summary and critical evaluation, see C. Clemen, *Die Einheitlichkeit der paulinischen Briefe an der Hand der bisher mit bezug auf die aufgestellten Interpolations- und Compilations-hypothesen* (Göttingen: Vandenhoeck & Ruprecht, 1894).

[4] P.-L. Couchoud, 'Reconstitution et classement des Lettres de Saint Paul', *RHPR* 87 (1923), 8-31; and 'La première édition de Saint Paul', *RHR* 94 (1926), 242-63.

[5] A.F. Loisy, *Remarques sur la littérature épistolaire du Nouveau Testament* (Paris: Nourry, 1935), *passim*; and *The Origins of the New Testament* (Hyde Park, NY: University Books, 1962; French original, Paris: Nourry, 1936), *passim*.

[6] R.M. Hawkins, *The Recovery of the Historical Paul* (Nashville, TN:

recently, J.C. O'Neill has proposed that both Galatians and Romans contain numerous glosses and interpolations, some inadvertently included by copyists but many deliberately added,[7] and Winsome Munro has argued for an extensive stratum of 'Pastoral' interpolations in the Pauline corpus as a whole (and in 1 Peter).[8] Finally, Darrell J. Doughty has maintained that the letters 'can only be understood as complex redactional compositions, that may include appropriations of early Pauline material, but most certainly include an abundance of later material as well'; thus, in his view, the burden of proof rests with the claim that *any* of the material in the letters is authentically Pauline.[9]

Such 'radical' proposals, however, have gained little scholarly acceptance. Georg Strecker, for example, acknowledges that glosses and interpolations are 'to be expected' in the Pauline letters but insists that 'nineteenth century Netherlands conjectural criticism went beyond responsible limits'.[10] Similarly, Furnish accuses O'Neill of a 'wholesale resort to hypotheses', asserting that the latter's work intermixes 'highly subjective judgments about content and tone' with 'often-questionable generalizations about the apostle's style and vocabulary', resulting in 'a Paul created in the interpreter's own image'.[11] More peremptorily, Joseph A. Fitzmyer declares that 'short shrift...has to be given to the proposals of O'Neill' regarding interpolations and glosses in Romans.[12]

Nevertheless, the question of later additions to the Pauline letters

---

Vanderbilt University Press, 1943), 14-20, 291-92, *et passim*; see also his 'Romans: A Reinterpretation', *JBL* 60 (1941), 129-40.

[7] J.C. O'Neill, *The Recovery of Paul's Letter to the Galatians* (London: SPCK, 1972), 1-15, 73-87, *et passim*; and *Paul's Letter to the Romans* (Baltimore: Penguin, 1975), 11-22, 264-74, *et passim*.

[8] W. Munro, *Authority in Paul and Peter: The Identification of a Pastoral Stratum in the Pauline Corpus and 1 Peter* (SNTSMS 45; Cambridge: Cambridge University Press, 1983); cf. also D.R. MacDonald, *The Legend and the Apostle: The Battle for Paul in Story and Canon* (Philadelphia: Westminster Press, 1983), 86.

[9] D.J. Doughty, 'Pauline Paradigms and Pauline Authority', *Westar Institute Seminar Papers* (Spring 1995), 85-102 (quotation from p. 85).

[10] G. Strecker, *History of New Testament Literature* (Harrisburg, PA: Trinity Press International, 1997), 40.

[11] Furnish, 'Pauline Studies', 325.

[12] J.A. Fitzmyer, *Romans: A New Translation with Introduction and Commentary* (AB 33; New York: Doubleday, 1993), 65.

remains open. Indeed, as Furnish notes, 'several older hypotheses have attracted new supporters' in recent years, 'and some further passages have been added to the list of suspect texts'.[13] Thus, quite apart from the sweeping proposals of O'Neill and Munro, the roster of proposed interpolations in Romans alone now includes the following passages: 1:18–2:29;[14] 1:19–2:1;[15] 1:32;[16] 2:1;[17] 2:16;[18] 3:12-18;[19] 3:24-26;[20] 4:14;[21] 4:17;[22] 4:18-19;[23] 5:1;[24] 5:6-7;[25] 5:12-21;[26] 5:17;[27] 6:13, 19;[28] 6:17;[29] 7:6;[30] 7:25b;[31] 8:1;[32] 8:9-11;[33] 9:5;[34] 10:9;[35] 10:17;[36]

---

[13] Furnish, 'Pauline Studies', 324.
[14] W.O. Walker, Jr., 'Romans 1.18-2:29: A Non-Pauline Interpolation?', *NTS* 45 (1999), 533-52.
[15] P.N. Harrison, *Paulines and Pastorals* (London: Villiers, 1964), 79-85.
[16] Listed without documentation as a proposed 'secondary gloss' by Fitzmyer (*Romans*, 65).
[17] R. Bultmann, 'Glossen im Römerbrief', *TLZ* 7 (1947), 200.
[18] Bultmann, 'Glossen im Römerbrief', 200-201.
[19] J.C. O'Neill, 'Glosses and Interpolations in the Letters of St. Paul', *SE*. VII. *Papers Presented to the Fifth International Congress on Biblical Studies held at Oxford, 1973* (TU 126; Berlin: Akademie-Verlag, 1982), 383-84.
[20] C.H. Talbert, 'A Non-Pauline Fragment at Romans 3:24-26', *JBL* 85 (1966), 287-96.
[21] See n. 16 above.
[22] See n. 16 above.
[23] See n. 16 above.
[24] See n. 16 above.
[25] L.E. Keck, 'The Post-Pauline Interpretation of Jesus' Death in Rom 5,6-7', in C. Andresen and G. Klein (eds.), *Theologia Crucis—Signum Crucis: Festschrift für Erich Dinkler zum 70. Geburtstag* (Tübingen: Mohr Siebeck, 1979), 237-48.
[26] O'Neill, 'Glosses and Interpolations in the Letters of St. Paul', 384-85.
[27] See n. 16 above.
[28] W.H. Hagen, 'Two Deutero-Pauline Glosses in Romans 6', *ExpTim* 92 (1981), 364-67.
[29] Bultmann, 'Glossen im Römerbrief', 202.
[30] See n. 16 above.
[31] Bultmann, 'Glossen im Römerbrief', 198-99.
[32] Bultmann, 'Glossen im Römerbrief', 199.
[33] F. Refoulé, 'Unité de l'Épître aux Romains et histoire du salut', *RSPT* 71 (1987), 219-42.
[34] See n. 16 above.
[35] See n. 16 above.
[36] Bultmann, 'Glossen im Römerbrief', 199.

11:6;[37] 12:11;[38] 13:1-7;[39] 13:5;[40] 14:6;[41] 15:4;[42] 16;[43] 16:5;[44] and 16:25-27.[45] In the other letters,[46] serious arguments have been raised against the authenticity of such passages as 1 Cor 2:6-16;[47] 4:6c;[48]

---

[37] See n. 16 above.

[38] See n. 16 above.

[39] E.g., E. Barnikol, 'Römer 13. Der nichtpaulinische Ursprung der absoluten Obrigkeitsbejahrung von Römer 13,1-7', in Der Kommission für spätantike Religionsgeschichte (ed.), *Studien zum Neuen Testament und zur Patristik. Erich Klostermann zum 90. Geburtstag dargebracht* (TU 77; Berlin: Akademie-Verlag, 1961), 65-133; J. Kallas, 'Romans xiii.1-7: An Interpolation', *NTS* 11 (1965), 365-74; W. Schmithals, *Der Römerbrief als historisches Problem* (SNT 9; Gütersloh: Mohn, 1975), 185-97; and W. Munro, 'Romans 13:1-7: Apartheid's Last Biblical Refuge', *BTB* 20 (1990), 161-68.

[40] Bultmann, 'Glossen im Römerbrief', 200.

[41] See n. 16 above.

[42] L.E. Keck, 'Romans 15:4: An Interpolation?', in J.T. Carroll, C.H. Cosgrove, and E.E. Johnson (eds.), *Faith and History: Essays in Honor of Paul W. Meyer* (Scholars Press Homage Series; Atlanta: Scholars Press, 1990), 125-36.

[43] J. Knox ('The Epistle to the Romans: Introduction and Exegesis', *IB* 9.654) regards the interpolation theory as 'the least difficult' of the possibilities 'and therefore the most likely to be true'; see the entire discussion, pp. 365-68.

[44] See n. 16 above.

[45] Romans 16:25-27 is widely regarded as an interpolation; for the evidence, see, e.g., E. Käsemann, *Commentary on Romans* (Grand Rapids: Eerdmans, 1980), 421-28 and Fitzmyer, *Romans*, 48, 753-56. For more extensive interpolation hypotheses regarding Romans, see, e.g., Schmithals, *Der Römerbrief als historisches Problem*; and M. Widmann, 'Der Israelit Paulus und sein antijüdischer Redaktor. Eine literarkritische Studie zu Rom. 9-11', in E.L. Ehrlich and B. Klappert with U. Ast (eds.), *'Wie gut sind deine Zelte, Jaakow...' Festschrift zum 60. Geburtstag von Reinhold Mayer* (Gerlingen: Bleicher, 1986), 150-58.

[46] On 1 and 2 Corinthians, see, e.g., Schmithals, *Der Römerbrief als historisches Problem*, 202-209; and W. Schenk, 'Korintherbriefe', *TRE* 19.621-22. On 1 Corinthians, see, e.g., W. Schenk, 'Der Erste Korintherbrief als Briefsammlung', *ZNW* 60 (1969), 219-44; and J. Murphy-O'Connor, 'Interpolations in 1 Corinthians', *CBQ* 48 (1986), 81-94.

[47] M. Widmann, '1 Kor 2.6-16: Ein Einspruch gegen Paulus', *ZNW* 70 (1979), 44-53; and W.O. Walker, Jr., '1 Corinthians 2.6-16: A Non-Pauline Interpolation?', *JSNT* 47 (1992), 75-94.

[48] Only the words τὸ μὴ ὑπὲρ ἃ γέγραπται; J. Strugnell, 'A Plea for Conjectural Emendation in the New Testament, with A Coda on 1 Cor 4:6', *CBQ* 36 (1974), 555-58.

6:14;[49] 7:29-31;[50] 10:1-22;[51] 11:2-16 (or, more likely, only vv. 3-16);[52] 11:23-25;[53] 12:31b–14:1a;[54] 14:34-35 (or perhaps vv. 33b-36);[55] 15:3-11;[56] 15:21-22;[57] 15:31c;[58] 15:44b-48;[59] 15:56;[60] 2 Cor 6:14–7:1;[61] Gal 2:7b-8;[62] Phil 1:1c;[63] 2:6-7;[64] 1 Thess 2:13-16;[65] 4:1-8; 4:10b-12; 4:18;

---

[49] U. Schnelle, '1 Kor 6:14—Eine nachpaulinische Glosse', *NovT* 25 (1983), 217-19.

[50] O'Neill, 'Glosses and Interpolations in the Letters of St Paul', 381-83.

[51] L. Cope, 'First Corinthians 8–10: Continuity or Contradiction?', *ATRSup* Sup 11 (1990), 114-23.

[52] W.O. Walker, Jr., '1 Corinthians 11:2-16 and Paul's Views regarding Women', *JBL* 94 (1975), 94-110; L. Cope, '1 Cor 11:2-16: One Step Further', *JBL* 97 (1978), 435-36; G.W. Trompf, 'On Attitudes toward Women in Paul and Paulinist Literature: 1 Corinthians 11:3-16 and Its Context', *CBQ* 42 (1980), 196-215; W.O. Walker, Jr., 'The Vocabulary of 1 Corinthians 11.3-16: Pauline or Non-Pauline?', *JSNT* 35 (1989), 75-88.

[53] J. Magne, 'Les paroles sur la coupe', in J. Delobel (ed.), *Logia: Les paroles de Jésus—The Sayings of Jesus: Mémorial Joseph Coppens* (BETL 59; Leuven: Peeters/Leuven University Press, 1982), 485-90; *From Christianity to Gnosis and From Gnosis to Christianity: An Itinerary through the Texts to and from the Tree of Paradise* (BJS 286; Atlanta: Scholars Press, 1993), 33; and 'A Summary History of the Eucharist' (unpublished paper, 1999) 3.

[54] E.L. Titus, 'Did Paul Write I Corinthians 13?', *JBR* 27 (1959), 299-302; and W.O. Walker, Jr., 'Is First Corinthians 13 a Non-Pauline Interpolation?', *CBQ* 60 (1998), 484-99.

[55] E.g., G. Fitzer, *Das Weib schweige in der Gemeinde. Über den unpaulinischen Charakter der mulier-taceat Verse in 1. Korinther 14* (Theologische Existenz Heute n.s. 110; Munich: Kaiser, 1963); J. Murphy-O'Connor, 'Interpolations in 1 Corinthians', *CBQ* 48 (1986), 90-92; and G.D. Fee, *The First Epistle to the Corinthians* (NICNT; Grand Rapids: Eerdmans, 1987), 699-708.

[56] R.M. Price, 'Apocryphal Apparitions: 1 Corinthians 15:3-11 as a Post-Pauline Interpolation', *The Journal of Higher Criticism* 2 (1995), 69-99.

[57] O'Neill, 'Glosses and Interpolations in the Letters of St. Paul', 384-85.

[58] D.R. MacDonald, 'A Conjectural Emendation of 1 Cor 15:31-32: Or the Case of the Misplaced Lion Fight', *HTR* 73 (1980), 265-76.

[59] Widmann, '1 Kor 2.6-16', 47-48.

[60] F.W. Horn, '1 Korinther 15,56—Ein exegetischer Stachel', *ZNW* 82 (1991), 88-105.

[61] E.g., W.K.M. Grossouw, 'Over de echtheid van 2 Cor 6:14-7:1', *Studia Catholica* 26 (1951), 203-206; J.A. Fitzmyer, 'Qumran and the Interpolated Paragraph in 2 Cor. 6:14-7:1', *CBQ* 23 (1961), 271-80; J. Gnilka, '2 Cor 6:14-7:1 in the Light of the Qumran Texts and the Testaments of the Twelve Patriarchs', in J. Murphy-O'Connor (ed.), *Paul and Qumran* (London: Chapman, 1968), 48-68; H.D. Betz, '2 Cor 6:14-7:1: An Anti-Pauline Fragment?', *JBL* 92 (1973), 88-108.

[62] E. Barnikol, 'The Non-Pauline Origin of the Parallelism of the Apostles

5:1-11;[66] 5:12-22; and 5:27.[67]

At the same time, however, 'there has been no general scholarly agreement on the probability, or even the plausibility, of any of these hypotheses about glosses and interpolations'.[68] Indeed, as Winsome Munro notes, 'no particular passage, not even the benediction in Romans 16:25-27, has gained undisputed interpolation status'.[69] Interpolation theories 'are not generally presupposed by Pauline scholarship'; further, as Doughty observes, they actually 'encounter fierce resistance in some quarters'.[70] According to Munro, scholars are more inclined to view entire epistles as pseudonymous than to agree that 'short pockets of material' are non-Pauline additions. In part, she

---

Peter and Paul. Galatians 2:7-8', *The Journal of Higher Criticism* 5 (1998), 285-300 (German original 1931).

[63] W. Schenk, *Der Philipperbrief des Paulus. Kommentar* (Stuttgart: Kohlhammer, 1984), 78-82, 334.

[64] E. Barnikol, *Philipper 2. Der marcionistische Ursprung des Mythos-Satzes Phil. 2,6-7* (Prolegomena zur neutestamentlichen Dogmengeschichte 2; Forschungen zur Entstehung des Urchristentums des Neuen Testament und der Kirche 7; Kiel: Mühlau, 1932).

[65] E.g., B.A. Pearson, '1 Thessalonians 2:13-16: A Deutero-Pauline Interpolation', *HTR* 64 (1971), 79-94; D. Schmidt, '1 Thess 2:13-16: Linguistic Evidence for an Interpolation', *JBL* 102 (1983), 269-79.

[66] G. Friedrich, '1. Thessalonischer 5,1-11, der apologetische Einschub eines Späteren', *ZTK* 70 (1973), 288-315.

[67] On 1 Thess 2:13-16; 4:1-8; 4:10b-12; 4:18; 5:12-22; and 5:27, K.-G. Eckart, 'Der zweite echte Brief des Apostels Paulus an die Thessalonischer', *ZTK* 58 (1961), 30-44.

[68] Furnish, 'Pauline Studies', 325.

[69] W. Munro, 'A Paradigmatic Shift in Pauline Studies?' (unpublished paper presented at the 1983 Annual Meeting of the Society of Biblical Literature in Dallas, Texas), 4.

[70] Doughty, 'Pauline Paradigms and Pauline Authenticity', 95-96. See, e.g., Fee, *The First Epistle to the Corinthians*, 626 n. 6, for the characterization of Titus's interpolation hypothesis regarding 1 Corinthians 13 as 'criticism run amok'; Fitzmyer, *Romans*, 65, for the dismissive assertion that 'short shrift' should be given to J.C. O'Neill's argument for numerous interpolations and glosses in Romans; and F.W. Wisse, 'Textual Limits to Redactional Theory in the Pauline Corpus', in J.E. Goehring, C.W. Hedrick, and J.T. Sanders with H.D. Betz (eds.), *Gospel Origins & Christian Beginnings: In Honor of James M. Robinson* (Forum Fascicles 1; Sonomo, CA: Polebridge, 1990), 167-78, for the argument that 'redactional theory [including interpolation hypotheses] that steps outside the bounds of textual evidence and minimizes the burden of proof is counter-productive and a hindrance to Pauline studies' (quotation from p. 178).

suggests, this is because it is more difficult to establish 'the alien character of relatively small blocks of writing' than of 'complete compositions'.[71] This is surely true, but a major problem, in my own judgment, is the fact that most of the debate regarding glosses and interpolations has focused directly upon individual passages, with little or no systematic attention to such important preliminary questions as the *a priori* likelihood of interpolations in the Pauline letters and what specific types of data would count as evidence for interpolation. What is now needed, if the discussion is to proceed in a fruitful manner, is a consideration of these preliminary questions.

Before proceeding to such matters, however, certain terminological distinctions are necessary. First, it is important to distinguish between 'gloss' and 'interpolation'. A *gloss* is an explanatory note or comment, originally written generally in the margin or occasionally between the lines of a manuscript by a reader, scribe, or possibly even the author of the document in which it now appears.[72] Apparently not intended as an addition to the text, a gloss was designed merely to clarify, explain, or comment regarding an item in the text. Numerous examples could be cited.[73] An *interpolation*, however, is foreign

---

[71] Munro, 'A Paradigmatic Shift in Pauline Studies?', 4-5.

[72] For a distinction among 'glosses' ('brief explanations of difficult words or phrases'), 'scholia' ('random 'interpretive remarks' intended 'to instruct the reader'), 'commentaries' ('systematically developed' comments intended 'to elucidate' an entire passage), 'catenae' ('chains' of comments extracted from older ecclesiastical writers), and 'onomastica' ('philological aids' purporting 'to give the meaning and etymology of proper names'), see B.M. Metzger, *The Text of the New Testament: Its Transmission, Corruption, and Restoration* (New York and Oxford: Oxford University Press, 3rd edn, 1992), 27-28. In this study, however, 'gloss' refers to any type of explanatory note or comment originally written in the margin or between the lines of a manuscript.

[73] E.g., Metzger (*The Text of the New Testament*, 194) suggests that that the clause μὴ κατὰ σάρκα περιπατοῦσιν ἀλλὰ κατὰ πνεῦμα ('who walk not according to the flesh but according to the spirit') found in some manuscripts at Rom 8:1 'was originally an explanatory note (perhaps derived from vs. 4) defining "those who are in Christ Jesus"'. As an example of an absurdity resulting from 'heedlessness that passes comprehension', Metzger cites 2 Cor 8:4: '...after εἰς τοὺς ἁγίους a good many minuscule manuscripts have added the gloss δέξασθαι ἡμᾶς. It appears that a scribe of one of these manuscripts wrote in the margin beside δέξασθαι ἡμᾶς the comment ἐν τολλοῖς τῶν ἀντιγράφων οὕτως εὕρηται ("it is found thus in many of the copies"). Then the scribe of a subsequent manuscript...incorporated this comment on the gloss directly in his text as though it were part of the apostle Paul's instructions to the Corinthians!'

material inserted deliberately and directly into the text of a document. In many instances, of course, a gloss might be copied by a scribe into the body of a manuscript, be reproduced in later transcriptions, and thus now appear in some or perhaps even all of the surviving texts. In such cases, the distinction between gloss and interpolation becomes problematic. Thus, as Leander E. Keck notes, 'it is not always possible to differentiate precisely what is gloss and what is interpolation'.[74] In the present study, the term 'interpolation' will be applied to any secondary addition to the text of one of the Pauline letters, with no attempt to determine whether the passage in question originated as a gloss or as an interpolation *per se*.

A distinction is also to be noted between 'interpolation' and 'redaction'. Because an *interpolation* is a discrete body of material inserted deliberately and directly into the text of a document, it can often be identified and removed without disrupting the logical and/or linguistic flow of the material immediately preceding and following. *Redaction*, however, is the rewriting of a text in such a way as to incorporate new material; here, any separation of the new from the old becomes problematic. As in the case of interpolations and glosses, 'it is often impossible to distinguish between an interpolation and a redaction', for 'an apparent interpolation might be a passage in which the redactor has failed to achieve the usual integration, transition or flow of thought', and 'interpolations are often made to documents which are redactional in character'.[75] In principle, however, the distinction is clear. The present study will deal with redaction only insofar as it relates to the presence of interpolations.

Finally, it should be noted that the present study will employ the term 'interpolation' in a somewhat restricted sense, referring only to material that is non-Pauline in the double sense of non-Pauline authorship and non-Pauline insertion at its present location in one of the Pauline letters. Material composed by Paul for some other occasion but secondarily inserted at its present location, either by Paul or by someone else, will not be regarded as an interpolation, nor will material composed by someone other than Paul but secondarily inserted at its present location by Paul. In short, the present study is

---

[74] L.E. Keck, *Paul and His Letters* (Proclamation Commentaries; Philadelphia: Fortress Press, 2nd edn, 1988), 18.

[75] J.H. Charlesworth, 'Reflections on the SNTS Pseudepigrapha Seminar at Duke on the Testaments of the Twelve Patriarchs', *NTS* 23 (1977), 303.

concerned only with non-Pauline material that has been added to the text of a Pauline letter by someone other than Paul.

In the remaining sections of the study, I shall: (1) argue that it is reasonable, simply on *a priori* grounds, to expect non-Pauline interpolations in the Pauline letters; (2) contend that direct text-critical evidence is not an essential prerequisite for the identification of non-Pauline interpolations; (3) discuss various types of evidence that might be cited in support of interpolation hypotheses; and (4) illustrate the use of such evidence with reference to one particular passage.

2. A Priori Considerations

It is generally agreed that individual passages in letters judged otherwise authentically Pauline are themselves to be regarded as Pauline unless compelling arguments to the contrary can be adduced. In short, the burden of proof rests with the argument for interpolation. Munro has complained, however, that the weight of this burden is unreasonably heavy: 'scholars advancing theories of interpolation' are confronted with 'an insurmountable obstacle which no amount of evidence or argument is allowed to overcome', for theirs is the task 'of proving beyond any doubt that a passage does not owe its presence to the author of the whole'.[76] Thus, Munro appeals for 'scholarly openness, both to the concept of later expansion of the text, and to the probability that particular passages or sets of passages are later additions or rewritten versions, even if the evidence falls short of "proof" in an absolute sense'.[77]

It is in the spirit of such 'scholarly openness' that the question must be raised: Is it reasonable to assume, simply on *a priori* grounds, that the Pauline letters, as we now have them, are likely to contain non-Pauline interpolations?[78] If so, the burden of proof in the case of

---

[76] Munro, 'A Paradigmatic Shift in Pauline Studies?', 7.

[77] W. Munro, 'Interpolation in the Epistles: Weighing Probability', *NTS* 36 (1990), 432.

[78] See, e.g., F.W. Wisse, 'The Nature and Purpose of Redactional Changes in Early Christian Texts: The Canonical Gospels', in W.L. Petersen (ed.), *Gospel Traditions in the Second Century: Origins, Recensions, Text, and Transmission* (Notre Dame and London: University of Notre Dame Press, 1989), 41: 'Before we can argue for a specific interpolation we must first establish the probability that early Christian texts were extensively redacted.'

individual passages may be somewhat lighter than has generally been assumed: no longer will the question be simply 'Is this passage an interpolation?'; rather, it will become 'Is this passage one of the interpolations that are likely to be found in the Pauline letters?'. Although the difference is subtle, it is important—not least in terms of its psychological impact upon the exegete.[79] Further, once the non-Pauline character of *any* passage is established beyond reasonable doubt, the authenticity of *every* passage is thereby called into question. If there is one non-Pauline interpolation in a letter, there may well be more!

In what follows, therefore, I shall: (a) call attention to the almost certain presence of interpolations in other ancient literature, including early Christian writings; (b) consider relevant aspects of the literary history of the Pauline corpus; and (c) note the undoubted presence of actual textual alteration in the Pauline letters, including numerous short additions to the text. The conclusion will be that it is indeed reasonable, simply on *a priori* grounds, to assume that the Pauline letters, as we now have them, are likely to contain non-Pauline interpolations.

a. *Interpolations in Other Ancient Literature*

Eugene Harrison Lovering has noted that interpolations almost certainly 'made their way into the widest diversity of materials in the ancient world', that 'the ancients were fully aware of this', and that 'literary critics occupied themselves with sorting out the secondary elements'.[80] In the case of Homer, for example, Karl Maurer asserts that 'the fact [of interpolation] is notorious',[81] and George Melville Bolling, among others, has identified numerous interpolations in both the *Iliad* and the *Odyssey*.[82] Interpolations have also been detected in the works of such authors as Orpheus, Musaeus, Hippocrates,

---

[79] See, e.g., Wisse, 'Textual Limits to Redactional Theory in the Pauline Corpus', 173: 'Although certainty about the reality of redactional changes in the Pauline letters has no obvious bearing on the burden of proof in individual cases, still it will inevitably influence the researcher's attitude towards the text.'

[80] E.H. Lovering, Jr., *The Collection, Redaction, and Early Circulation of the Corpus Paulinum* (unpublished Ph.D. dissertation; Southern Methodist University, 1988), 109.

[81] K. Maurer, *Interpolation in Thucydides* (Mnemosyne: Biblica Classica Batava 150; Leiden: Brill, 1995), 181.

[82] G.M. Bolling, *The External Evidence for Interpolation in Homer* (Oxford: Clarendon Press, 1925).

Aristophanes, Euripedes, and Thucydides.[83] Regarding Thucydides, Maurer, though generally conservative in his conclusions regarding particular passages, concludes that 'a somewhat crude insertion of glosses and other notes into the text of Thuc[ydides] is not a nineteenth-century mirage, but a historical fact for which there is abundant evidence'.[84]

Of direct relevance to the present study is the almost certain presence of interpolations in precisely the genre of ancient literature most closely akin to the Pauline letters: the letters of philosophers (e.g., Plato, Aristotle, Epicurus, and Seneca), and particularly those 'letters of exhortation in which teachers seek to guide and mold the characters of disciples'.[85] Like parts of the Pauline corpus, many of these letters are pseudonymous;[86] more to the point, however, is the fact that the Epicurean correspondence, for example, 'has been very heavily edited (redacted) by Epicurus's followers who amplified the master's teachings and adapted them to later situations'.[87] This may well provide a precedent for the presence of interpolations in the letters of Paul, which also can be seen as 'letters of exhortation in which [a teacher] seek[s] to guide and mold the characters of disciples'.

Additionally, there is ample evidence that early Christians themselves introduced interpolations into Jewish writings that they regarded as in some manner deficient, defective, or less 'Christian' than might be desired. It is widely agreed, for example, that material was added to the Greek text of Flavius Josephus in order to create a non-Christian testimony to the messiahship and resurrection of Jesus[88]

---

[83] Regarding Orpheus, Musaeus, and Hippocrates, see, e.g., R.M. Grant, *Heresy and Criticism: The Search for Authenticity in Early Christian Literature* (Louisville: Westminster/John Knox, 1993), 21-22, 61-66; regarding Aristophanes and Euripedes, see, e.g., Maurer, *Interpolation in Thucydides*, 181.

[84] Maurer, *Interpolation in Thucydides*, xi; for a review of the evidence, see the entire book.

[85] S.K. Stowers, 'Greek and Latin Letters', *ABD* 4 (1992), 292.

[86] According to Stowers ('Greek and Latin Letters', 292), these 'show marked similarities to pseudonymous Christian letters such as the Pastoral Epistles (1 Timothy, 2 Timothy, Titus)'.

[87] Stowers, 'Greek and Latin Letters', 292.

[88] Josephus, *Ant* 18.3.3. For judicious reviews of the evidence, see, e.g., L.H. Feldman, 'Josephus', *ABD* 3 (1992), 990-91; and J.P. Meier, *A Marginal Jew: Rethinking the Historical Jesu. I. The Roots of the Problem and the Person* (ABRL; New York: Doubleday, 1991), 56-88; for a treatment of the matter by a classicist, see, e.g., E.M. Sanford, 'Propaganda and Censorship in the

(indeed, some scholars attribute this material to Eusebius, fourth-century Bishop of Caesarea and eminent church historian).[89] Similarly, it appears clear that early Christians rewrote and expanded certain of the Jewish pseudepigraphical texts such as the *Sibylline Oracles*, the Hellenistic Synagogal Prayers, the *Testaments of the Twelve Patriarchs*, the *Martyrdom and Ascension of Isaiah*, and the *Fourth Book of Ezra*.[90] Even the Septuagint, the Greek translation of the Hebrew Scriptures, was not exempt from Christian interpolation.[91]

The possibility of Christian interpolation was not confined, however, to Jewish documents. For example, Dionysius, Bishop of Corinth (ca. 160 CE), claimed that 'heretics' had both added materials to and deleted materials from his letters.[92] Similarly, Irenaeus (late second century) 'express[ed] the greatest apprehension that his writings against heretics would be altered—naturally, by the heretics'.[93] Likewise, the late-fourth-century writer Rufinus claimed 'that many Greek patristic writings had been interpolated'.[94] In the second century, Marcion removed numerous alleged interpolations from the Gospel of Luke and the letters of Paul,[95] and, according to Robert M.

Transmission of Josephus', *TAPA* 66 (1935), 127-45.

[89] E.g., S. Zeitlin, 'The Christ Passage in Josephus', *JQR* 18 (1927–1928), 237-40. For a contrary view, see, e.g., D.S. Wallace-Hadrill, 'Eusebius of Caesaria and the *Testimonium Flavianum* (Josephus, Antiquities, XVIII, 63f.)', *JEH* 25 (1974), 361. In the most recent contribution to the debate, K.A. Olson ('Eusebius and the *Testimonium Flavianum*', *CBQ* 61 [1999], 305-22) concludes: 'Complete certainty is unattainable, but we have very good reasons to suppose that Eusebius wrote the *Testimonium*.'

[90] See, e.g., J.H. Charlesworth, 'Christian and Jewish Self-Definition in Light of the Christian Additions to the Apocryphal Writings', in E.P. Sanders with A.I. Baumgarten and A. Mendelson (eds.), *Jewish and Christian Self-Definition*. II. *Aspects of Judaism in the Greco-Roman Period* (Philadelphia: Fortress Press, 1981), 27-55.

[91] See, e.g., M.K.H. Peters, 'Septuagint', *ABD* 5 (1992), 1097; H.B. Swete, *An Introduction to the Old Testament in Greek* (rev. R.R. Ottley; Cambridge: Cambridge University Press, 1914), 423-24; and O'Neill, 'Glosses and Interpolations in the Letters of St. Paul', 384.

[92] Grant, *Heresy and Criticism*, 12.

[93] W. Bauer, *Orthodoxy and Heresy in Earliest Christianity* (ed. R.A. Kraft and G. Krodel; Philadelphia: Fortress Press, 1971), 166.

[94] Grant, *Heresy and Criticism*, 111.

[95] See, e.g., Grant, *Heresy and Criticism*, 33-47; and R.M. Grant, 'Marcion and the Critical Method', in P. Richardson and J.C. Hurd (eds.), *From Jesus to Paul: Studies in Honour of Francis Wright Beare* (Waterloo: Wilfrid Laurier

Grant, his 'insistence that both *Gospel* and *Apostle* had been interpolated suggests that he knew current theories about interpolated religious documents, as well as the editorial procedures of the great Hellenistic textual critics'.[96] Indeed, Munro maintains that 'redactional expansion of earlier documents [including Christian documents] was commonplace in the early church'.[97]

Various types of textual expansion can be detected even in the writings that now comprise the Hebrew Scriptures and the Christian New Testament. Munro observes that both the Pentateuch and the New Testament Gospels are widely viewed as consisting of multiple strata of earlier and later material,[98] and O'Neill asserts that 'outside the New Testament epistles, we should all agree that every book of the Bible is either a compilation of various pieces, or a basic document to which additions have been made'.[99] In addition, the 'adulterous woman' pericope in most manuscripts of the Fourth Gospel (John 7:53–8:11) is almost certainly an interpolation,[100] and the same is probably true regarding the 'longer ending' of Mark.[101] Further, the so-called 'Western Text' of the Gospels, Acts, and (to a lesser extent) the Pauline letters contains a number of passages not found in other manuscripts (generally regarded as Western interpolations), but it also omits certain materials (often referred to as 'Western Non-Interpolations').[102] These variant readings make it clear that materials

---

University Press, 1984), 207-15.

[96] Grant, *Heresy and Criticism*, 34; cf. Grant, 'Marcion and the Critical Method'.

[97] Munro, 'Interpolation in the Epistles', 432.

[98] Munro, 'A Paradigmatic Shift in Pauline Studies?', 2-3.

[99] O'Neill, 'Glosses and Interpolations in the Letters of St. Paul', 379-80.

[100] For a summary of the evidence, see, e.g., C.K. Barrett, *The Gospel According to John: An Introduction with Commentary and Notes on the Greek Text* (Philadelphia: Westminster Press, 2nd edn, 1978), 589-90.

[101] For a summary of the evidence and the conclusion that the verses represent a later addition to the text, see, e.g., C.S. Mann, *Mark: A New Translation with Introduction and Commentary* (AB 27; Garden City, NY: Doubleday, 1986), 672-76. For an extensive review followed by the cautious conclusion that the verses are likely original, see W.R. Farmer, *The Last Twelve Verses of Mark* (SNTSMS 25; Cambridge: Cambridge University Press, 1974). For the conclusion that the question is 'still open and perhaps "insoluble at present"', see K.W. Clark, 'The Theological Relevance of Textual Variation in Current Criticism of the Greek New Testament', *JBL* 85 (1966), 9-10.

[102] See, e.g., E.J. Epp, 'Western Text', *ABD* 6 (1992), 909-12.

were sometimes added to and/or deleted from manuscripts of the New Testament writings.[103] Finally, Munro cites Rev 22:18-19 as testimony to the practices of both redactional expansion and editorial excision in the early church.[104]

Although debate continues regarding specific details, the basic point made by Munro and O'Neill appears incontrovertible: both Jewish and early Christian writings (including those that eventually attained the status of 'Scripture') were subject to various types of textual expansion including interpolation. But what about the letters of Paul? Were they exempt from such treatment? Both Munro and O'Neill suggest that they were not.[105] Responding to the objection that the Pauline letters represent a distinctive literary genre and thus may not have been subject to the same literary processes as the other biblical writings, O'Neill agrees that the letters are 'a distinct literary form', but he also observes that 'they are odd as letters anyway'. Noting that 'no ancient letters, except letters modelled on Paul's, are so long or so like treatises in parts', O'Neill suggests 'that the oddness of Paul's letters is partly due to their having been glossed and interpolated'; thus, 'they may be distinct as letters because they are letters that have been treated in exactly the same way as the rest of the sacred books contained in the Old and New Testament canons'.[106]

Is it the case, however, that the Pauline letters are 'odd as letters'? The Hellenistic letter-writing tradition has been preserved in two quite distinct forms, which John L. White terms respectively 'the documentary tradition' (papyri and ostraca) and 'the literary tradition' (the classical and later writers).[107] White observes that, with few exceptions, letters in the New Testament are significantly longer and 'more literary' than the former,[108] and William Doty notes that 'the Pauline

---

[103] H. Eshbaugh (*Theological Variants in the Western Text of the Pauline Corpus* [unpublished Ph.D. dissertation: Case Western Reserve University, 1975], 202) suggests that what he terms 'theological variants' in the Western text of the Pauline letters 'show the fluidity of the text in the early church'.

[104] Munro, 'Interpolation in the Epistles', 432.

[105] Munro, 'Interpolation in the Epistles', 432; and O'Neill, 'Glosses and Interpolations in the Letters of St. Paul', 380.

[106] O'Neill, 'Glosses and Interpolations in the Letters of St. Paul', 380.

[107] J.L. White, *Light from Ancient Letters* (FFNT; Philadelphia: Fortress Press, 1986), 19.

[108] J.L. White, 'Letter', *HCBD*, 601; cf. White, *Light from Ancient Letters*, 18-19.

letters are briefer' than the latter.[109] Doty goes on to say that 'the letter form which developed in the Pauline letters was richer than either the brief private letters or the more developed letter-essays of Hellenism'.[110] Similarly, Stanley K. Stowers states that the New Testament letters 'resemble neither the common papyri from the very lowest levels of culture and education nor the works of those with the highest levels of rhetorical training'; rather, 'they fall somewhere in between'.[111] In short, the Pauline letters differ in significant respects both from 'the brief private letters' and from 'the more developed letter-essays of Hellenism'. Thus, although his specific reference to length and treatise-like features applies not to 'the literary tradition' but only to 'the documentary letter tradition', the basic thrust of O'Neill's point regarding the 'oddness' of Paul's letters would appear to be valid.

In short, there is no reason to assume that the Pauline letters would have been less subject to textual expansion than were other documents that now comprise the Hebrew Scriptures and the Christian New Testament. Moreover, as a possible precedent, the presence of interpolations has already been noted in the Hellenistic literary genre most closely resembling the Pauline corpus: the letters of philosophers and moralists to their disciples.

By way of summary and conclusion: the presence of interpolations in other ancient literature—Classical, Hellenistic, Jewish, and Christian—would lead us to expect, simply on *a priori* grounds, that the Pauline letters, as we now have them, are likely to contain non-Pauline interpolations.[112]

b. *The Literary History of the Pauline Corpus*
This expectation is strengthened, however, by a consideration of the literary history of the Pauline corpus. Indeed, Daryl Schmidt suggests that 'the better we understand the...process that formed the Pauline

---

[109] W.G. Doty, *Letters in Primitive Christianity* (GBS; Philadelphia: Fortress Press, 1973), 42.
[110] Doty, *Letters in Primitive Christianity*, 42.
[111] S.K. Stowers, *Letter Writing in Greco-Roman Antiquity* (LEC; Philadelphia: Westminster Press, 1986), 25.
[112] Indeed, in recent private conversations with me, two of my colleagues in the Trinity University Department of Classical Studies, Professors Colin M. Wells and Joan B. Burton, have independently stated that they would be very surprised if there were no interpolations in the letters of Paul.

corpus and shaped it into a part of the emerging Christian canon, the clearer it becomes that the final canonical text reflects evidence of both editing and textual revision'. Indeed, it is Schmidt's view that 'the...process that produced a corpus of published letters...went through several stages at which "interpolations" to the original letters were added for their published recension'.[113]

Unfortunately, we know considerably less about the early history of the Pauline corpus than we might wish,[114] and it is obviously beyond the scope of the present study to attempt a comprehensive reconstruction. There are, however, two relatively clear points regarding this history that are directly relevant to the question of interpolations in the Pauline letters.

1. *The individual Pauline letters are available to us not as separate documents but only as parts of a collection that was assembled, preserved, and transmitted by the early church under the name of Paul*. It remains unclear whether this collection came into being through a gradual and informal process of the sharing of individual letters among the churches, by the conscious and deliberate work of one or more collectors, or by some combination of the two.[115] Also uncertain is exactly what materials would have been available to any collector of Paul's letters or, indeed, what the physical condition of these materials might have been. Early Christians who preserved letters from Paul very likely also preserved other writings, some of them

---

[113] D. Schmidt, 'Identifying Seams in Authentic Pauline Letters: Evidence for Letter Fragments and Interpolations' (unpublished paper prepared for the Paul Seminar of the Westar Institute, 1998), 2.

[114] To my knowledge, the most comprehensive survey is Lovering's Ph.D. dissertation, *The Collection, Redaction, and Early Circulation of the Corpus Paulinum*.

[115] See, e.g., J. Murphy-O'Connor, *Paul the Letter-Writer: His World, His Options, His Skills* (GNS; Collegeville, MN: Liturgical, 1995), 41 114-18, for a discussion of 'The Evolutionary Theory' and 'The Big Bang Theory'; for a somewhat similar but more detailed discussion of 'theories of sudden collection' and 'theories of gradual growth', see Lovering, *The Collection, Redaction, and Early Circulation of the Corpus Paulinum*, 283-345. For a more elaborate taxonomy that categorizes the various hypotheses 'according to the distance they posit between the career of the Apostle Paul and the collection of his letters', see R.M. Price, 'The Evolution of the Pauline Canon' (unpublished paper prepared for the Spring 1995 Meeting of the Paul Seminar of the Westar Institute). See also, e.g., H.Y. Gamble, 'The Canon of the New Testament', in Epp and MacRae (eds.), *The New Testament and Its Modern Interpreters*, 205-208.

perhaps of unknown origin. Prolonged use of such writings—whether Pauline or non-Pauline—would have resulted in physical deterioration and perhaps fragmentation of the scrolls or codices. What was available to a collector, then, may have been a more-or-less miscellaneous assortments of written materials, in various stages of deterioration, fragmentation, and perhaps combination, with no clear distinction between Pauline and non-Pauline texts. If the goal of a collector was to include all available Pauline writings, as seems at least plausible, the tendency almost inevitably would have been to err on the side of inclusion, not exclusion. Thus, non-Pauline materials may well have been introduced into the Pauline corpus quite unintentionally, perhaps on more than one occasion and by more than one hand.

2. *This collection of materials assembled, preserved, and transmitted by the early church under the name of Paul represents not only 'an expanded Paul' and 'an abbreviated Paul', but also 'an edited Paul'.*[116] Indeed, the collection can be termed 'the letters of Paul' only with serious qualifications. It surely omits some authentically Pauline letters,[117] it includes one or more letters that are non-Pauline in origin,[118] and, most significantly for purposes of the present study, at least some of the letters almost certainly have been subject to various forms of editing. Indeed, as Keck observes, 'what we have are those forms of Paul's letters that were prepared for church use long after Paul himself wrote them'.[119] There is, of course, considerable debate regarding the exact nature and extent of the editing, as well as just when in the history of the corpus it would have occurred. Never-

---

[116] L.E. Keck and V.P. Furnish, *The Pauline Letters* (Interpreting Biblical Texts; Nashville: Abingdon, 1984), 50.

[117] One could assume *a priori* that some of Paul's letters almost certainly would not have survived. In addition, there are apparent references in 1 Cor 5:9; 2 Cor 2:4; 7:8; 10:10 to letters that are no longer extant, at least in their entirety and as separate documents (note also the reference in Col 4:16 to 'the letter from Laodicea').

[118] All of the earliest extant manuscripts—$\mathfrak{P}^{46}$ (late second or early third century), ℵ and B (fourth century), and A and C (fifth century)—originally included not only the seven letters now generally regarded as authentically Pauline (Philemon is missing from $\mathfrak{P}^{46}$) but also the letters whose Pauline authorship is disputed: 2 Thessalonians, Colossians, Ephesians, and Hebrews. For discussion of the authorship of the latter four, see, e.g., R.F. Collins, *Letters That Paul Did Not Write: The Epistle to the Hebrews and the Pauline Pseudepigrapha* (GNS 28; Wilmington, DE: Glazier, 1988).

[119] Keck, *Paul and His Letters*, 18.

theless, it is now widely held that what we know as 2 Corinthians is a 'composite' letter, comprising parts of at least two originally separate Pauline letters,[120] and 'partition' hypotheses have also been advanced regarding Philippians,[121] 1 Corinthians,[122] and Romans.[123] Indeed, Keck asserts that, 'of the seven undoubtedly genuine letters, only in the case of Philemon can we be certain that what we have is virtually identical with what Paul wrote'.[124]

In short, it is now generally agreed that the Pauline letters were assembled, preserved, and transmitted by the early church only as parts of an edited collection—what today would be termed an edited 'anthology'. Further, most scholars would grant, at least in principle, that the editing of the letters would almost certainly have included some editorial additions. Indeed, Helmut Koester asserts that 'if the letters of Paul are...not preserved as direct copies of the original autographs, but as later editions, it is not surprising that they also contain a number of editorial additions'.[125] Finally, it is my own judgment that Munro is correct in her assertion that 'it strains credulity to assume that [these editorial additions] would have been confined to brief connections and minor improvements'.[126]

c. *Actual Textual Alterations in the Pauline Letters*

Furthering strengthening the *a priori* assumption that the Pauline letters are likely to contain interpolations is the fact that the surviving manuscripts of these letters provide abundant evidence of actual textual alteration including numerous short additions to the text. The extant manuscripts contain countless variant readings.[127] Most of the

---

[120] For a summary of the evidence, see, e.g., V.P. Furnish, *II Corinthians: Translated with Introduction, Notes, and Commentary* (AB 32A; Garden City, NY: Doubleday, 1984), 30-32, 35-41. As Furnish notes (pp. 32-33), however, other scholars have argued for as many as six original letters.

[121] See, e.g., F.W. Beare, *A Commentary on the Epistle to the Philippians* (HNTC; San Francisco: Harper & Row, 1959), 1-5.

[122] For discussion, see, e.g., R.F. Collins, *First Corinthians* (SP 7; Collegeville, MN: Liturgical, 1999), 10-14.

[123] For discussion, see, e.g., Fitzmyer, *Romans*, 55-67.

[124] Keck, *Paul and His Letters*, 17.

[125] H. Koester, *History and Literature of Early Christianity*. I. *Introduction to the New Testament* (Hermeneia: Foundations and Facets; Philadelphia: Fortress Press; Berlin and New York: de Gruyter, 1982), 54.

[126] Munro, *Authority in Paul and Peter*, 19.

[127] For a distinction between a 'reading' ('any textual difference or any

variants represent simply inadvertent errors on the part of copyists: obvious misspellings, transpositions, omissions, repetitions, and the like. Others, however, appear to be intentional, intended to correct, clarify, or even amplify the text.[128] Among these latter are numerous glosses (marginal or interlinear comments that were later copied into the text). In principle, one of the purposes of critical texts is the elimination of such glosses.[129] Lloyd Gaston asserts, however, that 'many who argue in principle against the whole concept [of interpolations] nevertheless continue to use a Greek text which is full of short interpolations [or glosses]'. In his view, 'the new Textus Receptus',[130] as he terms it, 'fearing to lose even a single Pauline word, has surely erred on the side of inclusion', for 'the longer reading seems always to have been preferred'.[131] As an example, Gaston cites Gal 3:19a, where virtually all translators and commentators follow the longer reading but Gaston argues for serious consideration of the shorter.[132] Although a judgment regarding the accuracy of the 'always' in Gaston's assertion would require a comprehensive survey of the text, a random check of a few passages suggests that the longer reading is at least *often* preferred. Indeed, in 1 Thessalonians alone, Koester notes five passages in which Nestle–Aland[26] adds in brackets words that were omitted in the previous edition; regarding the bracketed words in each passage, Koester concludes: 'it can be said with great certainty that

---

varying text formulation in a ms found by comparison with the same passage in any other ms') and a 'variant' (a textual difference that is '"significant" or meaningful in the major tasks of NT textual criticism' such as 'determining ms relationships, locating mss within NT textual history and transmission, and in establishing the original or earliest possible NT text'), see E.J. Epp, 'Textual Criticism: New Testament', *ABD* 6 (1992), 413-14.

[128] For a discussion of the various types of alterations, see Metzger, *The Text of the New Testament*, 186-206.

[129] See, e.g., O'Neill, 'Glosses and Interpolations in the Letters of St. Paul', 379: 'We all accept that Paul's letters have been glossed, for we all use an edition of the New Testament [i.e., 'Nestle or one of its derivatives'] in which, in effect, a systematic attempt has been made to eliminate glosses' (i.e., either by suppressing or by moving to the foot of the page 'the numerous glosses...which appeared in the Textus Receptus').

[130] United Bible Societies[3] = Nestle-Aland[26].

[131] Lloyd Gaston, Letter to W.O. Walker, Jr. (September 6, 1985).

[132] L. Gaston, 'Angels and Gentiles in early Judaism and in Paul', *SR* 11 (1982), p. 74 n. 43; see also H. Eshbaugh, 'Textual Variants and Theology: A Study of the Galatians Text of Papyrus 46', *JSNT* 3 (1979), 62-63.

these words are not part of the original text'.[133] Moreover, in the case of the Gospels, Schmidt asserts that the 'new Textus Receptus' appears to be 'definitely inclined toward the longer Byzantine text' and that 'the most consistent canon applied...seems to be "when in doubt, insert"'.[134] Perhaps related to this apparent tendency toward inclusion of disputed variants is Kent D. Clarke's conclusion that the most recent (4th) edition of the United Bible Societies text is overly optimistic in presenting 'a much more confident and much more certain text than any of the earlier *UBSGNT* editions'.[135]

The relevance of such observations for the question of possible interpolations in the Pauline letters is obvious: a predisposition to follow the longer reading of disputed texts may blind the interpreter to the presence of numerous glosses and/or short interpolations, and this, in turn, may create a presumption against the presence of longer additions to the text. Conversely, recognition of such glosses and/or short interpolations may open the exegete to the possibility of more substantial insertions. In any case, there can be no question regarding the presence of numerous short additions to the text in the surviving manuscripts of the Pauline letters. This leads O'Neill to ask, 'If St. Paul's letters as we have them almost certainly contain glosses, is it also likely that they contain interpolations?'. O'Neill's answer is a *probable* 'Yes'.[136] Particularly in light of the other *a priori* considerations discussed above, however, my own response to O'Neill's question would be, '*Almost certainly* yes!'.

Conclusion
The widespread presence of interpolations in other ancient literature—Classical, Hellenistic, Jewish, and Christian—is virtually certain. The Pauline letters were assembled, preserved, and transmitted by the early church only as parts of an 'expanded', 'abbreviated', and

---

[133] H. Koester, 'The Text of 1 Thessalonians', in D.E. Groh and R. Jewett (eds.), *The Living Text: Essays in Honor of Ernest W. Saunders* (Lanham: University Press of America, 1985), 220-22 (quotation from p. 227).

[134] D. Schmidt, 'Response' to G.D. Kilpatrick, 'A Textus Receptus Redivivus?', *Protocol of the Colloquy of the Center for Hermeneutical Studies in Hellenistic and Modern Culture* 32 (1978), 26.

[135] K.D. Clarke, *Textual Optimisn: A Critique of the United Bible Societies' Greek New Testament* (JSNTSup 138; Sheffield: Sheffield Academic Press, 1997), quotation from p. 183.

[136] O'Neill, 'Glosses and Interpolations in the Letters of St. Paul', 379.

'edited' anthology. The surviving manuscripts of these letters bear witness to actual textual alterations including numerous short additions to the text. In my judgments, these considerations alone lead to the virtually inescapable conclusion, simply on *a priori* grounds, that the Pauline letters, as we now have them, are likely to contain non-Pauline interpolations. Indeed, as Munro asserts, 'it strains credulity to assume that interpolation did not take place'.[137]

3. THE ABSENCE OF TEXTUAL EVIDENCE FOR INTERPOLATION

Despite the *a priori* likelihood of interpolations in the Pauline letters, however, the actual identification of such interpolations faces a potentially serious problem. Assuming that, 'when textual revisions have taken place they have left their marks in the [manuscript] evidence',[138] some scholars have insisted that no passage can confidently be identified as an interpolation unless it is absent from or more of the early witnesses to the text.[139] In the Pauline letters, however, this is true only of Rom 16:25-27.[140] In every other case of proposed interpolation, the passage in question appears in all of the extant early manuscripts.[141]

This raises the crucial question: Is it possible that a passage appearing in all of the surviving manuscripts might nevertheless be a non-Pauline interpolation? In other words, is direct textual evidence—the absence of a passage from one or more of the early witnesses—an indispensable prerequisite for the confident identification of

---

[137] Munro, 'Interpolation in the Epistles', 431:

[138] H.Y. Gamble, 'The Redaction of the Pauline Letters and the Formation of the Pauline Corpus', *JBL* 92 (1975), 418; cf., e.g., K. Aland and B. Aland, *The Text of the New Testament* (Grand Rapids: Eerdmans, 1981; 2nd edn, 1989), 295.

[139] See, e.g., Wisse, 'Textual Limits to Redactional Theory in the Pauline Corpus'; E.E. Ellis, 'The Silenced Wives of Corinth (I Cor. 14:34-5)', in E.J. Epp and G.D. Fee (eds.), *New Testament Textual Criticism: Its Significance for Exegesis: Essays in Honour of Bruce M. Metzger* (Oxford: Clarendon Press, 1981), 220; and E.E. Ellis, 'Traditions in I Corinthians', *NTS* 32 (1986), 488 and 498 n. 58.

[140] The verses are missing from a few witnesses; in others, they appear variously after 14:23, after 15:33, after 16:23(24), after both 14:23 and 15:33, and after both 14:23 and 16:23(24).

[141] 1 Corinthians 14:34-35, however, is located after v. 40 in the texts of the 'Western' tradition.

interpolations? As a preliminary response, I suggest that the absence of textual evidence for interpolation should be seen as precisely what it is: the *absence* of evidence. It means only that any presumed interpolations must have been introduced into the letters prior to the date of the oldest surviving manuscript. In the face of otherwise compelling evidence for interpolation, this absence of evidence should not be allowed to decide the issue. Beyond this, I propose to address two interrelated questions: (a) Is it reasonable to assume that interpolations were in fact introduced into the Pauline letters prior to the date of the oldest surviving manuscript? (b) If so, why have manuscripts not containing such interpolations not survived?

a. *Interpolations before the End of the Second Century?*
As C.K. Barrett has observed, 'the evidence of the [manuscripts] can tell us nothing about the state of the Pauline...literature before its publication' (presumably late in the first century).[142] Barrett's observation can be pushed a bit further, however: the evidence of the manuscripts can provide no certain information regarding the state of the Pauline literature prior to the date of the oldest surviving manuscript of the letters[143] (near the end of the second century).[144] Despite the conscientious and skilled efforts of generations of textual critics, we can make only educated guesses regarding the text of the Pauline letters during the first century and more of their existence. As regards possible interpolations, we can be certain only that a particular passage appeared at its present location in the Pauline corpus near the

---

[142] C.K. Barrett, *A Commentary on the First Epistle to the Corinthians* (HNTC; New York and Evanston: Harper & Row, 1968), 14; see also, e.g., Aland and Aland, *The Text of the New Testament*, 297.

[143] To be sure, citations in second-century Christian writers can sometimes shed light on the early text of the letters, but this would be of little direct help in identifying possible interpolations.

[144] Various dates have been suggested for the oldest extant manuscript, $\mathfrak{P}^{46}$, ranging from late first century to the first half of the third century; for discussion, see, e.g., P.W. Comfort and D.P. Barrett (eds.), *The Complete Text of the Earliest New Testament Manuscripts* (Grand Rapids: Baker, 1999), 18 and 194-97. Although Comfort and Barrett (p. 196) suggest a date 'sometime after 125', most scholars have settled on a date of approximately 200 CE; see, e.g., Aland and Aland, *The Text of the New Testament*, 87; and Metzger, *The Text of the New Testament*, 37. Both Codex Vaticanus (B) and Codex Sinaiticus (ℵ) date from the fourth century, and Codex Alexandrinus (A) and Codex Ephraemi (C) from the fifth century.

end of the second century. Whether it was included earlier and, if so, how much earlier, simply cannot be decided on the basis of direct textual evidence. Thus, it is at least possible that passages now appearing in all of the surviving manuscripts might nevertheless be interpolations that were introduced prior to the latter part of the second century. It is possible, but is it likely?

In a remarkable study of what he terms 'The Orthodox Corruption of Scripture', Bart D. Ehrman notes that 'Christianity in the second and third centuries was in a remarkable state of flux' and, more specifically, that 'this was an age of competing interpretations of Christianity'.[145] He then argues cogently that 'the scribes of the second and third centuries in fact altered their texts of Scripture at significant points in order to make them more orthodox on the one hand and less susceptible to heretical construal on the other'—in short, 'to make them "say" what they were already thought to "mean"'.[146] Ehrman also concludes that 'the vast majority of all textual variants originated during...the second and third centuries'.[147]

Although Ehrman focuses his attention on the second and third centuries, what he says is almost certainly relevant also to the latter years of the first century. Indeed, he cites the view of 'a wide-range of eminent textual specialists who are otherwise not known for embracing compatible views' that 'the period of relative creativity was early, that of strict reproduction late'.[148] Kurt and Barbara Aland agree. Noting that the text of the New Testament writings 'was a "living text" in the Greek literary tradition, unlike the text of the Hebrew Old Testament, which was subject to strict controls because (in the oriental tradition) the consonantal text was holy', they acknowledge that 'until the beginning of the fourth century the text of the New Testament developed freely'. Significantly, they go on to say that 'this was all the more true of the early period, when the text had not yet attained canonical status, *especially in the earliest period when Christians considered themselves filled with the Spirit* [emphasis added]'.[149] Similarly, Kenneth W. Clark asserts that '*the earliest stage*

---

[145] B.D. Ehrman, *The Orthodox Corruption of Scripture: The Effect of Early Christological Controversies on the Text of the New Testament* (New York and Oxford: Oxford University Press, 1993), 3, 24.
[146] Ehrman, *The Orthodox Corruption of Scripture*, 25, 26.
[147] Ehrman, *The Orthodox Corruption of Scripture*, 29.
[148] Ehrman, *The Orthodox Corruption of Scripture*, 44 n. 112, 28.
[149] Aland and Aland, *The Text of the New Testament*, 68.

of transmission was marked by an attitude of freedom in theological interpretation [emphasis added]'.[150] This 'earliest period when the Christians considered themselves filled with the Spirit', which was also 'the earliest stage of transmission', must surely include the time between Paul (mid-first century) and the date of the oldest surviving manuscript (late second century). Thus, if the Alands and Clark are correct, it can only be assumed that alterations of the text were even more numerous and significant before the end of the second century than we know them to have been later. This, in turn, clearly increases the likelihood that interpolations were introduced during this early period.

Speaking of the Gospels in terms that would be equally applicable to the Pauline letters, Koester makes explicit what appears to be implicit in the words of the Alands and Clark. Koester declares that 'the problems for the reconstruction of the textual history of the canonical Gospels in *the first century of transmission* are immense [emphasis added]'. Asserting that 'textual critics of the New Testament writings have been surprisingly naïve in this respect', Koester goes on to note that 'textual critics of classical texts know that *the first century of their transmission* is the period in which the most serious corruptions occur [emphasis added]'. Koester also observes that 'the Gospels [and the same could be said regarding the Pauline letters], from the very beginning, were not archival materials but used texts'; this, in his judgment, 'is the worst thing that could happen to any textual tradition' because 'a text, not protected by canonical status, but used in liturgy, apologetics, polemics, homiletics, and instruction of catechumens is most like to be copied frequently and is thus subject to frequent modifications and alterations'.[151] Thus, according to Koester, 'whatever evidence there is indicates that not only minor, but also substantial revisions of the original texts have occurred [during the first century of their transmission]'.[152] Indeed, Clark even asks whether 'there really was a stable text at the beginning'. Noting that 'the earliest witnesses to the NT text even from the first century already show such variety and freedom that we may well wonder if the text remained stable long enough to hold a

---

[150] Clark, 'The Theological Relevance of Textual Variation in Current Criticism of the Greek New Testament', 7.

[151] H. Koester, 'The Text of the Synoptic Gospels in the Second Century', in Petersen (ed.), *Gospel Traditions in the Second Century*, 19-20.

[152] Koester, 'The Text of the Synoptic Gospels in the Second Century', 37.

priority', he concludes: 'it may be doubted that there is evidence of one original text to be recovered'.[153] Thus, it may well be the case that 'editorial revision' of the Pauline texts (including interpolation) began almost as soon as the letters appeared.

In short, it would appear that the period between the actual composition of Paul's letters (mid-first century) and the date of the earliest extant manuscript of the these letters (late second century at best) was precisely the time at which the letters would have been most susceptible to alteration, including interpolation.[154] Indeed, the circumstances of the time provided ample motivation, opportunity, and the means for the introduction of such interpolations. All of this, in my judgment, makes it reasonable to assume that interpolations are almost certain to have been introduced into the Pauline letters prior to the date of the earliest surviving manuscript—some, no doubt, accidental and inadvertent; others, however, almost certainly intentional.

b. *What Became of the Manuscripts?*

If interpolations were in fact introduced into the Pauline letters prior to the date of the oldest surviving manuscript, what became of the earlier manuscripts that presumably did not contain these interpolations? Why have they not survived?

My initial response is to note that precisely the same questions could be raised regarding (1) early manuscripts of individual Pauline letters, (2) manuscripts of presumed earlier collections of Pauline letters, and (3) manuscripts not reflecting other types of editorial revision widely assumed to have been applied to the Pauline letters. Not a single early manuscript of an individual Pauline letter has survived. Even if the individual letters first circulated only as parts of a

---

[153] Clark, 'The Theological Relevance of Textual Variation in Current Criticism of the Greek New Testament', 16.

[154] Even Wisse ('Textual Limits to Redactional Theory in the Pauline Corpus', 175) agrees that 'the strongest argument in favour of setting the early history of transmission of the text apart from the later periods is the fact that it took some time for the Pauline corpus to gain full canonical status'; thus, 'Christian scribes would have been very reluctant to tamper with the text of a canonical writing but would have felt free to introduce changes before a text was recognized as apostolic and authoritative'. For a discussion of this issue as it relates to the Gospels and more particularly to the Synoptic Problem, see W.O. Walker, Jr., 'An Unexamined Presupposition in Studies of the Synoptic Problem', *Religion in Life* (1979), 41-52.

collection, and this appears unlikely,[155] they must first have existed as separate documents. Nevertheless, no early manuscripts of individual letters have survived. Why? Similarly, no manuscripts have survived of earlier collections of the Pauline letters. That such earlier collections once existed is virtually certain. It is clear, for example, that Clement of Rome, Ignatius, Polycarp, and the author of 2 Peter were acquainted with more than one of the letters. Moreover, the early appearance of pseudo-Pauline letters suggests that Paul's writings were known outside the particular communities to which they were addressed. Indeed, Gamble believes that there is evidence for the early existence of two forms of a ten-letter collection (not including the Pastorals or Hebrews).[156] In whatever form these earlier collections may have existed, however, not a single manuscript of any such collection has survived. Why? Finally, as has already been noted, 2 Corinthians is widely regarded as a 'composite' letter, and compilation theories have also been proposed for various others of the letters. If manuscripts of earlier forms of these letters ever existed, however, they have not survived. Why?

In short, early manuscripts of individual letters have not survived, manuscripts of earlier collections of letters have not survived, and (if they existed) manuscripts not reflecting other types of editorial revision have not survived. Why, then, should it be assumed that manuscripts not containing presumed interpolations, if such manuscripts existed, would have survived?

It is impossible, of course, to know the fate either of the autographs or of any copies of the Pauline letters that were made prior to the latter part of the second century. The manuscripts may simply have deteriorated and disintegrated from constant use (or from neglect), or they may have perished during the Roman persecutions of the period.[157]

---

[155] See, e.g., L. Mowry, 'The Early Circulation of Paul's Letters', *JBL* 63 (1944), 73-86.

[156] Gamble, 'The Canon of the New Testament', 205-208; and H.Y. Gamble, 'Canon: New Testament', *ABD* 1 (1992), 853-54.

[157] See, e.g., Metzger, *The Text of the New Testament,* p. 201 n. 1: 'Their early loss is not surprising, for during persecutions the toll taken by imperial edicts aiming to destroy all copies of the sacred books of Christians must have been heavy. Furthermore, simply the ordinary wear and tear of the fragile papyrus, on which at least the shorter Epistles of the New Testament had been written..., would account for their early dissolution. It is not difficult to imagine what would happen in the course of time to one much-handled manuscript, passing from reader to reader, perhaps from church to church (see Col. iv.16), and

There are, however, other possible scenarios. The disappearance of earlier versions of the letters may in some way have been related to the appearance of the final edited collection. It is possible that the collection simply rendered earlier versions superfluous and that they gradually disappeared. It is surely also possible, however, that once the final edited collection appeared, earlier versions of the letters were deliberately suppressed by Christians themselves.

We know that Paul and his letters were the subject of considerable controversy in the second century and later.[158] At one extreme were groups of Jewish Christians who rejected Paul because of his views regarding justification and the Jewish Law. At the opposite extreme, Marcion was convinced that all of the apostles except Paul had misunderstood Jesus and that Paul was the only true apostle. In something of a mediating position were the precursors of 'Catholic' Christianity, who accepted the apostleship and the letters of Paul but only after, in various ways, 'domesticating' or 'taming' the more radical features of the apostle's thought.[159]

It is also clear that at least two significantly different versions of the Pauline corpus circulated in the second century: that accepted by Marcion (no longer extant)[160] and that recognized by his opponents (the only surviving version). Marcion's enemies accused him of excising materials from the letters; he accused them of adding these materials. There may well have been an element of truth in both accusations. In any case, we cannot simply assume that Marcion's opponents made no additions to the text.[161] All we can know with

---

suffering damage from the fingers of eager if devout readers as well as from climatic changes.'

[158] See, e.g., W.A. Meeks (ed.), *The Writings of St. Paul: Annotated Text, Criticism* (Norton Critical Edition; New York: Norton, 1972), 149-213, and, for a short summary, 149-50.

[159] See, e.g., M.F. Wiles, *The Divine Apostle: The Interpretation of St. Paul's Epistles in the Early Church* (Cambridge: Cambridge University Press, 1967), esp. the 'Epilogue'.

[160] On the difficulties involved in reconstructing Marcion's text of the Pauline letters, see J. Knox, *Marcion and the New Testament: An Essay in the Early History of the Canon* (Chicago: University of Chicago Press, 1942), 46-53.

[161] See, e.g., H. Detering, 'The Dutch Radical Approach to the Pauline Epistles', *The Journal of Higher Criticism* 3 (1966), 177: 'There is no excuse in an unprejudiced investigation for excluding from the outset the possibility of the Marcionite edition of the *Paulina* being older and more original than the canonical, even if only for methodological reasons... It would seem that the

certainty is that the surviving text of the Pauline letters is the one promoted (and perhaps in part produced) by the historical winners in the theological and ecclesiastical struggles of the second and third centuries. Marcion's text simply disappeared—another example, no doubt, of the well-documented practice of suppressing and even destroying what some Christians regarded as deficient, deviant, or dangerous texts.[162] Other versions of the Pauline letters than Marcion's may well have met the same fate. That such suppression and destruction of texts could occur, even as late as the fifth century, is well illustrated by the fate of Tatian's Diatessaron ('harmony' of the four Gospels): as F.W. Beare notes, 'The Syrian episcopate...made a determined and successful effort to end the use of the Diatessaron', which 'was so thoroughly suppressed that no copy of it has ever been discovered, apart from a single leaf of vellum containing a fragment of the Greek text of it'.[163]

In short, it is at least possible that the emerging 'Catholic' leadership of the churches 'standardized' the text of the Pauline corpus in the light of 'orthodox' views and practices,[164] suppressing and even destroying all deviant texts and manuscripts. What Wisse refers to, therefore, as 'a remarkably unified text without a hint of major editing'[165] may well point not to a uniform transmission of the text from the very beginning but rather to such a deliberate standardizing of the text at some point(s) in its transmission.[166] This would

---

general opinion still is that only Marcion could have had a *Tendenz*. It seems to remain inconceivable that the Catholic Church, too, which, like the Marcionite Church, constituted itself in the second century, might have had a strong interest in finding its theological interests already represented in the documents of the apostolic time. But the possibility that the Catholic Church of the second century introduced its theological tendency into the Pauline Epistles cannot be a priori precluded.'

[162] See, e.g., M. Smith, *Jesus the Magician* (New York: Harper & Row, 1978), 1-2; E. Pagels, *The Gnostic Gospels* (New York: Random House, 1979), xvii-xix; and A. Vööbus, 'Syriac Versions', *IDBSup* 851.

[163] Beare, 'Canon of the NT', *IDB* 1.532.

[164] See, e.g., Bauer, *Orthodoxy and Heresy in Earliest Christianity,* 147-94 and esp. 160-67.

[165] Wisse, 'Textual Limits to Redactional Theory in the Pauline Corpus', 174.

[166] See, e.g., O'Neill, *Paul's Letter to the Romans,* 14: 'Admittedly it is hard to see how various additions made to different manuscripts at different times should have produced such a uniformly attested text. How do a paragraph added in one manuscript and an explanatory note added in another come together in the

explain why it is that we have no manuscripts dating from earlier than the latter part of the second century, why it is that all of the extant manuscripts are remarkably similar in most of their significant features, and why it is that the manuscript evidence can tell us nothing about the state of the Pauline literature prior to the latter part of the second century.[167]

What the earlier text of Paul's letters may have been remains, probably forever, shrouded in the mists of obscurity. Suppression and destruction of earlier manuscripts (if it occurred) would suggest, however, that these manuscripts may have differed in significant ways from the standardized text that survived (surely, this was the case with Marcion's version!); otherwise, it is difficult to understand why they would have disappeared so completely. We know that the surviving version of the Pauline letters includes passages not found in the Marcionite version; it may well also include passages not found in other earlier versions either of the collected letters or of individual letters. Thus, the surviving version may well contain interpolations for which no direct and explicit textual evidence exists.

If, however, one were unwilling to accept what Wisse terms such a 'conspiracy theory' regarding the disappearance of earlier manuscripts,[168] another plausible scenario is possible. Robert M. Price suggests that 'scribes comparing longer with shorter versions of the same epistle [i.e., versions with and without interpolations] would harmonize the two, always following the longer reading'; in other words, 'scribes would on the whole prefer to transcribe the longest text, being unwilling to lose anything precious'.[169] Thus, interpolations (if they existed) would be copied into new manuscripts. Once the longer texts appeared, they almost certainly would have been preferred and thus preserved by the early church. Shorter manuscripts, not containing the added material, would be regarded as incomplete or

---

one recognized text? The answer must be that at various stages in the transmission of the text powerful editors collected together as many manuscripts as possible and made a standard edition which became the one uniformly copied thereafter in that part of the church.'

[167] See, e.g., Price, 'The Evolution of the Pauline Canon', 20: 'interpolations were made and then gradually permeated the text tradition of each letter until final canonization of the Pauline edition (and concurrent burning of its rivals) put a stop to that'.

[168] Wisse, 'Textual Limits to Redactional Theory in the Pauline Corpus', 177.

[169] Assuming, to be sure, that the longer readings were not judged to be heretical or otherwise unacceptable.

defective and would be either destroyed or allowed to fall into disuse and thus disrepair and eventual disintegration.[170] Thus, it would by no means be surprising that interpolations might appear in all of the surviving manuscripts of the Pauline letters. The fact that the surviving manuscripts betray so little evidence of interpolation, or indeed of any type of editing, suggests merely that such editing had virtually come to an end by the close of the second century (that is, once the text of the letters had been standardized), at least within 'Catholic' circles.

Conclusion

I have suggested that the absence of textual evidence for interpolation must be seen as precisely what is: the *absence* of evidence, which, in the face of other compelling evidence for interpolation, should not be allowed to decide the issue. Further, I have argued that the Pauline letters would have been most susceptible to textual alteration including interpolation precisely during the period prior to the date of the oldest surviving manuscript. Finally, I have proposed plausible answers to the question of why no manuscripts not containing presumed interpolations have survived. I submit, therefore, that the presence of a passage in all of the extant manuscripts should not be viewed as persuasive evidence against interpolation. In short, the absence of textual evidence for interpolation does not negate the conclusion drawn earlier in this study: It is reasonable to assume, simply on *a priori* grounds, that the Pauline letters, as we now have them, are likely to contain non-Pauline interpolations.

This means that the pertinent question regarding particular passages suspected of being interpolations is no longer simply 'Is this passage a non-Pauline interpolation?'; rather, it becomes 'Is this passage one of the non-Pauline interpolations that are likely to be found in the Pauline letters?'. We cannot simply assume that any passage is authentically Pauline. It may be, or it may not be. The problem becomes that of determining, if possible, which of the materials are Pauline and which are not. Everything is 'up for grabs'. Moreover, Doughty may well be correct when he observes, 'Once one grants the probability of secondary interpolations, the roller coaster is already

---

[170] Price, 'The Evolution of the Pauline Canon', 19; cf. e.g., Mowry, 'The Early Circulation of Paul's Letters', p. 86 n. 28: the 'textual additions' in various early copies of Paul's letters 'survived', but 'their omissions tended to disappear'.

plunging down the first drop, and the ride will be furious'.[171] Who knows where the ride will finally end?

To be sure, the burden of proof still rests with the argument that any particular passage is a non-Pauline interpolation, but the weight of this burden is significantly lighter than has generally been supposed. The task now at hand, therefore, is that of identifying the various types of data that might count as evidence for interpolation in the case of particular passages in the Pauline letters.

4. Types of Evidence for Interpolation

Some years ago, Furnish lamented the fact 'that so far no firm and convincing techniques or criteria [had] been developed to aid in the identification of glosses and interpolations' in the Pauline letters. As evidence, he cited what he viewed as 'the wholesale resort to hypotheses', the 'highly subjective judgments about content and tone', and the 'often-questionable generalizations about the apostle's style and vocabulary' that characterized the work of O'Neill. Indeed, in Furnish's judgment, what O'Neill had produced was 'a Paul created in the interpreter's (i.e., O'Neill's) own image'.[172]

Furnish is surely correct that, insofar as possible, attempts to identify interpolations in the Pauline letters should avoid both 'subjective judgments about content and tone' and 'questionable generalizations about the apostle's style and vocabulary'. Further, they should by no means produce 'a Paul created in the interpreter's own image'. It should be noted, however, that 'subjective judgments' and 'generalizations' are to some extent inevitable when one attempts to distinguish between possible earlier and later materials in the same document. Thus, with regard to the work of Thucydides, Maurer observes: 'It is obvious that in the matter of interpolation as in everything else an editor must trust in part to his [sic] mere intuition; for the [manuscripts] themselves, made not by machines but persons, embody centuries of concrete historical reality; and for reasons invisible to us, any particular case may defy a general pattern'. Thus, in the case of particular passages, subjective judgments (including what Maurer terms 'mere intuition') will inevitably result in differing conclusions

---

[171] Doughty, 'Pauline Paradigms and Pauline Authority', 102.
[172] Furnish, 'Pauline Studies', 325.

regarding the actual presence or absence of interpolation.

Maurer asserts, however, that 'there are patterns' that can aid in the recognition of interpolations,[173] thereby suggesting that it is possible, at least in principle, to identify these patterns. More explicitly, Munro insists that it is 'possible to apply criteria to direct attention to the kind of elements in the text that can point to interpolation'. Indeed, in her view, agreement regarding criteria for the identification of interpolations 'is essential, not only to establish what is not original to a given writer, but also to confirm that the rest can be assumed to be "genuine"'. Otherwise, 'every part of every epistle should be suspect, for there is no way to determine which passages may properly be called into question, or judged to be secondary additions.[174]

Characteristically, criteria for identifying interpolations have been invoked, if at all, on a more-or-less *ad hoc* (and sometimes highly subjective) basis. In the 1940s, Hawkins offered some helpful suggestions regarding criteria, but his comments were far too sketchy and programmatic to be persuasive to most readers.[175] In his treatment of Galatians and Romans, O'Neill mentions and makes use of a variety of criteria, but he provides no comprehensive and systematic discussion of these criteria.[176] In a separate article, however, appealing to the practice of scholars of the Hebrew Bible, O'Neill lists 'contradictions' and 'changes in style' as the relevant criteria for the identification of interpolations.[177] Lovering provides a comprehensive list of criteria employed by advocates of 'partition' theories, and this list applies rather well, *mutatis mutandis*, to the identification of interpolations.[178]

To my knowledge, however, Munro is the first to attempt a systematic and more-or-less comprehensive treatment of the question of criteria for the identification of interpolations.[179] She identifies nine

---

[173] Maurer, *Interpolations in Thucydides*, 187.

[174] Munro, 'Interpolation in the Epistles', 433.

[175] Hawkins, *The Recovery of the Historical Paul*; see also his 'Romans: A Reinterpretation', *JBL* 60 (1941), 129-40.

[176] O'Neill, *The Recovery of Paul's Letter to the Galatians* and *Paul's Letter to the Romans*.

[177] O'Neill, 'Glosses and Interpolations in the Letters of St. Paul', 380.

[178] Lovering, *The Collection, Redaction, and Early Circulation of the Corpus Paulinum*, 66-81.

[179] Munro, *Authority in Paul and Peter*, 21-25; 'Interpolation in the Epistles', 431-43; and 'Criteria for Determining the Authenticity of Pauline Letters: A Modest Proposal', *Westar Institute Program 2-6 March 1994*, 78-80, esp. 79-80.

types of criteria for such identification. The first five, which she labels 'initial indicators', are direct textual, ideological, stylistic/linguistic, and contextual criteria, and the criterion of literary dependence. The last four, which she calls 'confirming factors', are literary/historical coherence, omission in external attestation, contextual plausibility, and historical plausibility; these latter 'generally only carry weight if there are other good reasons [i.e., initial indicators] to think a passage may be interpolated'.[180]

For the most part, I am in agreement with Munro regarding the appropriate criteria for the identification of interpolations. I have chosen not to include 'literary dependence', however, both because I regard such dependence as virtually impossible to establish and because any evidence of literary dependence might also serve as evidence of common authorship. In addition, I shall not treat 'omission in external attestation' as a separate category but rather subsume it under the rubric of text-critical evidence. Finally, I shall speak of 'types of evidence for interpolation' rather than 'criteria for the identification of interpolations'. In part, this is because 'criteria' might imply a greater degree of certainty than is actually warranted (*if* a passage satisfies certain specified criteria, it *is* a non-Pauline interpolation). More importantly, however, 'criteria' tends to focus one's attention on the more theoretical aspects of the debate regarding interpolation, not on the actual *evidence* that must be examined when one attempts to determine whether a particular passage is in fact an interpolation. Thus, I propose to discuss eight types of evidence that might indicate the presence of an interpolation. Following Munro's lead, I regard the first four (text-critical, contextual, linguistic, and ideational evidence) as 'initial indicators' of possible interpolation, and the last four (situational, comparative, motivational, and locational evidence) as possible 'confirming factors'.

It is essential to keep in mind, as Munro points out, that no one type of evidence for interpolation 'can stand by itself'. Different kinds of 'analyses can correct and complement each other'. In the final analysis, 'the judgment as to whether any passage is interpolated depends on a variety of factors and depends on no one infallible criterion'; rather, it is a matter of taking into account the cumulative effect of

---

[180] Munro, 'Interpolation in the Epistles', 440. For the most part, my list of types of evidence for interpolation corresponds to Munro's list of 'criteria' for the identification of interpolations.

converging lines of evidence'.[181] The strongest possible argument for interpolation would, of course, appeal to all eight types of evidence, but in most cases this is not possible.

a. *Text-Critical Evidence for Interpolation*

Text-critical evidence for interpolation would be data suggesting that a passage at one time may not have appeared at its present location in one of the Pauline letters. Such evidence might include one or more of the following phenomena: (1) the passage is missing from one or more of the 'best' surviving witnesses to the text; (2) it is present in all of the 'best' witnesses, but it is missing from one or more of the other surviving witnesses and the principle of 'transcriptional probability'[182] suggests the likelihood that it was added to rather than deleted from the text; (3) it appears at different locations in various of the surviving witnesses, and 'transcriptional probability' suggests the greater likelihood that it was added to the text than that it was originally a part of the text but was moved from one location to another; and (4) it is not cited by one or more early Christian writers who, because of demonstrable familiarity with the letter in which it now appears and congruence of subject matter, would have been expected to refer to it if it had been a part of their text of the letter in which it now appears (text-critical evidence of this last type, however, is at best indirect and based upon an argument from silence).

At most, text-critical evidence can only indicate that a passage did not originally appear at its present location in one of the Pauline letters. Such evidence cannot show that the passage is non-Pauline in origin, for it may have been composed by Paul for some other purpose but secondarily inserted at its present location. Moreover, such evidence cannot show conclusively that the passage was inserted at its present location by someone other than Paul.[183] Thus, text-critical evidence alone forms an inadequate basis for concluding that a passage is a non-Pauline interpolation as defined for purposes of the present study. For this, support is needed from other types of evidence.

---

[181] Munro, *Authority in Paul and Peter*, 21, 23, 24-25.

[182] This principle has to do with what a copyist is 'likely' to have done.

[183] In the case of 1 Cor 14:34-35, E.E. Ellis ('The Silenced Wives of Corinth', 213-20) suggests that the passage was originally a marginal gloss inserted either by Paul himself or at his direction and later copied into the text; see also, e.g., E.E. Ellis, 'Paul's Sense of Place: An Anthropological Approach to Community Formation in Corinth', *NTS* 32 (1986), 229-30.

b. *Contextual Evidence for Interpolation*

Contextual evidence for interpolation would be data suggesting that a passage may not 'fit' at its present location in one of the Pauline letters. There are within the Pauline corpus a number of passages that exhibit little or no apparent conceptual, stylistic and/or 'tonal'[184] relation to their immediate contexts. Indeed, they appear to 'interrupt' these contexts and, in some cases, even to contradict them conceptually. When such passages are removed, there often results a smooth conceptual, stylistic, and/or 'tonal' connection between what immediately precedes and what immediately follows;[185] indeed, as Charlesworth notes, 'when the passage is removed, the flow of thought is often clarified or improved'.[186] In addition, the passages themselves can often stand alone as independent, self-contained units. Finally, two other phenomena sometimes accompany such contextual features: (1) the presence—immediately preceding, near the beginning, near the end, and/or immediately following the passage in question—of one or more apparently insignificant textual variants that could be interpreted as attempts to improve an otherwise rough transition between the passage and its immediate context; and (2) the repetition—near the end of the passage in question or in the verse immediately following—of a significant word or phrase from the verse immediately preceding the passage (this, too, might be seen as an attempt to improve the connection between the passage and its immediate context).

As in the case of text-critical evidence, however, contextual evidence alone cannot show that a passage is non-Pauline in origin or that it was included at its present location by someone other than Paul. At most, such evidence can indicate only that the passage may represent a secondary addition to the text. Thus, neither text-critical nor

---

[184] By 'tone' is meant the emotional or atmospheric quality of the discourse (e.g., 'a happy tone of voice', 'a sad tone of voice', or 'an angry tone of voice'; 'the tone of the debate was hostile', 'the tone of the statement was threatening', or 'the tone of the question was friendly').

[185] In some cases, however, an interpolator or a later copyist, seeking to smooth out an otherwise rough transition between the passage in question and its immediate context, may have made slight modifications in the material immediately preceding and/or following the passage; in such cases, the removal of the passage in question might result in a less smooth transition from the material preceding to that immediately following the passage.

[186] Charlesworth, 'Christian and Jewish Self-Definition in Light of the Christian Additions to the Apocryphal Writings', 30.

contextual evidence—either alone or in combination—constitutes a sufficient basis for concluding that a passage is a non-Pauline interpolation as defined for purposes of the present study. For this, support is needed from other types of evidence.

c. *Linguistic Evidence for Interpolation*

Linguistic evidence for interpolation would be data suggesting that significant features of the vocabulary and/or literary style of a passage are not characteristically Pauline. Unlike text-critical and contextual evidence, linguistic evidence may indeed point to non-Pauline authorship of a passage. When the vocabulary (both actual choice of words and/or phrases and specific meanings attached thereunto) and/or literary style (genre, grammar and syntax, various types of rhetorical and artistic devices, and the like) of a passage appear to be significantly different from those appearing elsewhere in the authentically Pauline writings, this may be an indication that the passage was composed by someone other than Paul. It does not necessarily mean, however, that it was someone other than Paul who included the passage at its present location: Paul may well have used material written by someone else for his own purposes. Moreover, as Munro warns, extreme caution is necessary in the use of linguistic evidence for the identification of possible interpolations. On the one hand, there is the very real danger of circular argumentation: 'to determine which stylistic characteristics [including vocabulary] do or do not pertain to a certain writer, a prior judgment is required as to what he [*sic*] has written'. On the other hand, the same author may exhibit different linguistic features, depending upon the intended audience, subject matter, situation, purpose, or even which section of a letter is under consideration; moreover, an author's linguistic usage may change with the passing of time.[187] Nevertheless, as Munro concludes, 'stylistic unity tends to confirm authenticity [or common authorship], while stylistic diversity strengthens the possibility that more than one hand has been at work in the text'.[188]

d. *Ideational Evidence for Interpolation*

Ideational evidence for interpolation would be data suggesting that significant features of the substantive content of a passage are not

---

[187] Munro, *Authority in Paul and Peter*, 22.
[188] Munro, *Authority in Paul and Peter*, 22.

characteristically Pauline or, in some cases, perhaps that they are even anti-Pauline. If the ideas are simply *non*-Pauline, the passage may have been composed by someone other than Paul but included by Paul at its present location in one of his letters. If, however, it can be shown that the ideas are antithetical to Pauline thought as seen elsewhere in his letters, the most reasonable assumption would be that the passage was neither composed by Paul nor included by him in the letter. Here, then, for the first time, is a type of evidence that may point to interpolations that are non-Pauline in the double sense of non-Pauline composition and non-Pauline inclusion in one of the Pauline letters.

As in the case of linguistic evidence, however, extreme caution is required in the use of ideational evidence for interpolation. In the first place, the same author may (and Paul certainly sometimes does) express different ideas, depending upon the intended audience, subject matter, situation, purpose, or even which section of a letter is under consideration; moreover, an author's ideas, like his/her vocabulary and literary style, may change with the passing of time. In the second place, as already noted, significant conceptual differences may simply be an indication that the author is incorporating alien material into his/her own work.

e. *Situational Evidence for Interpolation*
Situational evidence for interpolation would be data suggesting that a passage reflects a situation, occasion, or set of circumstances different from that reflected in the remainder of the letter in which the passage appears, and perhaps even from that known or believed to have prevailed during Paul's lifetime. Great caution must be exercised, however, in the use of such evidence. Reconstruction of the situation presupposed by a text is generally highly speculative. Moreover, a situation presupposed by a particular passage may in fact have prevailed during Paul's own lifetime despite the absence of other evidence to this effect; thus, arguments for interpolation based upon situational evidence are necessarily arguments from silence. For these reasons, unless one can be certain that the situation presupposed by a passage existed only after the time of Paul, situational evidence for interpolation can serve only a corroborative function in the case of passages suspected on other grounds of being interpolations.

f. *Comparative Evidence for Interpolation*
Comparative evidence for interpolation would be data suggesting that

significant features of a passage—linguistic, ideational, and/or situational—are more closely akin to those of known non-Pauline (and particularly pseudo-Pauline) writings than to those of the authentically Pauline letters. Munro refers to this phenomenon as 'literary or historical coherence'. As she states it, 'The case for dissociation [from Paul] is considerably strengthened if it can be argued that an alleged interpolation coheres with material belonging to another milieu'.[189] Thus, comparative evidence for interpolation can often be seen as the 'flip-side' of linguistic, ideational, and/or situational evidence: the latter 'dissociate' a passage from Paul, while the former 'associates' it with someone other than Paul. When a passage can thus be both 'dissociated' from Paul and 'associated' with someone other than Paul, this may serve as compelling evidence that the passage was neither composed by Paul nor inserted by him at its present location in one of the Pauline letters.

g. *Motivational Evidence for Interpolation*
Motivational evidence for interpolation would be data suggesting plausible reasons why a particular passage might have been added to one of the Pauline letters. For the most part, such evidence would involve considerations of the ideational content of a possible interpolation. The question would be, 'Why would someone wish to attribute this material to Paul?' Conceivably, however, the primary consideration might be linguistic in nature. In the case of 1 Cor 12:31b–14:1a, for example, an interpolator might simply wish to give Paul credit for the magnificent encomium on love; in this case, both ideational and linguistic factors might be involved.

Motivational evidence for interpolation, however, is inevitably highly speculative in nature. Moreover, plausible reasons for the addition of a passage to a Pauline letter might also constitute evidence that the passage was included by Paul himself. Thus, like situational and comparative evidence, motivational evidence is of value only in the case of passages already suspected on other grounds of being non-Pauline interpolations.

h. *Locational Evidence for Interpolation*
Locational evidence for interpolation would be data suggesting reasons why a passage might have been inserted specifically at its

---

[189] Munro, *Authority in Paul and Peter*, 24.

present location in one of the Pauline letters. Such evidence might involve items of either an ideational or a linguistic nature. In the former case, it would be the content of the passage that led to its insertion at its present location; in the latter, some feature(s) of vocabulary and/or literary style. Like motivational evidence for interpolation, however, locational evidence is inevitably highly speculative in nature and is of value only in the case of passages already suspected on other grounds of being non-Pauline interpolations.

Conclusion
In principle, any or all of the following conclusions might be drawn on the basis of text-critical, contextual, linguistic, ideational, comparative, situational, motivational, and/or locational evidence: (1) a particular passage at one time did not appear at its present location in one of the Pauline letters, (2) it does not 'fit' at this location, (3) significant features of its vocabulary and/or literary style are non-Pauline, (4) certain of its ideas are non-Pauline or even anti-Pauline, (5) it reflects a situation not otherwise known to have prevailed during the lifetime of Paul; (6) it is more closely akin to non-Pauline and particularly pseudo-Pauline materials than to the authentically Pauline writings, (7) there are plausible reasons why it might have been added to one of the Pauline letters, and (8) there are plausible reasons why it might have been inserted specifically at its present location in one of the letters. If all of these conclusions were to be reached regarding any passage, it would almost inevitably follow that the passage is a non-Pauline interpolation. As a matter of fact, however, there is no such passage in the Pauline letters. In particular, direct text-critical evidence for interpolation can be cited in only two cases: Rom 16:25-27 and 1 Cor 14:34-35. Elsewhere, there is only contextual, linguistic, ideational, situational, comparative, motivational, locational, and/or perhaps *indirect* textual evidence.

Another important consideration, however, must not be overlooked. It has already been noted that a passage might appear in all of the surviving witnesses to the text—and indeed at the same location in all of the witnesses—and nevertheless be a non-Pauline interpolation. Analogous observations can be made, however, regarding contextual, linguistic, ideational, situational, comparative, motivational, and locational evidence. A passage might appear to 'fit' perfectly within its context and nevertheless be a non-Pauline interpolation. In such case, the interpolator would simply have composed or adapted the passage in such a way as to make it 'fit'. Similarly, an interpolator might deliberately imitate Paul's vocabulary and/or literary style, thereby producing an interpolation with linguistic features remarkably similar to those of Paul himself. Further, a passage might express ideas that are in agreement, or at least not in conflict, with those of Paul himself and nevertheless be a non-Pauline interpolation. Additionally, a passage might both reflect a situation known to have existed during Paul's lifetime and appear more closely akin to the authentically Pauline letters than to non-Pauline (including pseudo-Pauline) writings and nevertheless be a non-Pauline interpolation. Finally, there might be no apparent reasons for the secondary insertion of a passage into one of the Pauline letters, either at its present location or elsewhere, and the passage might nevertheless be a non-Pauline interpolation. Thus, as has already been noted in the case of text-critical evidence, the absence of evidence for interpolation—whether text-critical, contextual, linguistic, ideational, situational, comparative, motivational, or locational—must be seen as precisely what it is: the *absence* of evidence. In the face of otherwise compelling evidence for interpolation, this absence of evidence should not be allowed to decide the issue. Moreover, it must be acknowledged that the Pauline letters may well contain non-Pauline interpolations that, because of such absence of evidence, will never be identified.

In short, the attempt to identify non-Pauline interpolations in the Pauline letters must be satisfied with probabilities not certainties. The most that can be said with confidence is that the letters are likely to contain such interpolations and that certain individual passages probably are in fact interpolations.

5. A Test Case 1 Corinthians 14:34-35

An excellent example of a passage exhibiting all eight of the possible types of evidence for interpolation is 1 Cor 14:34-35.[190]

a. *Text-Critical Evidence for Interpolation*
Although 1 Cor 14:34-35 is present in all of the extant manuscripts, it

---

[190] For full discussion of evidence that this passage is a non-Pauline interpolation, see, e.g., Fitzer, *Das Weib schweige in der Gemeinde*; for a summary, see, e.g., Fee, *The First Epistle to the Corinthians*, 699-708.

is treated as a separate paragraph by the earliest,[191] located by a few after v. 40,[192] and marked in Codex Vaticanus (fourth century) by a siglum interpreted by some experts as indicating awareness of a textual variant.[193] According to Fee, such evidence suggests three possible scenarios: (1) the verses originally appeared after v. 33 but were subsequently moved to a position after v. 40; (2) they originally appeared after v. 40 but were moved forward so as to follow v. 33; or (3) they were originally a marginal gloss, not a part of the text, and were added to the text at two different locations. On the basis of 'Bengel's first principle' of text criticism ('That form of the text is more likely the original which best explains the emergence of all the others'), Fee argues persuasively for the third scenario.[194]

In addition, Philip B. Payne notes that, although Clement of Alexandria (died ca. 215) demonstrates clear knowledge of 1 Corinthians including parts of ch. 14 and 'discusses the behaviour of women in church', he nevertheless 'calls both men and women without distinction to silence in church'. To Payne, this suggests 'that 1 Cor 14.34-5 was not in [Clement's] text of 1 Corinthians'. Further, as Payne observes, 'none of the Apostolic Fathers or the next generation of church fathers gives any indication of awareness of 1 Cor 14.34-5', and 'the eareliest extant citation of 1 Cor 14.34-5 appears to be by Tertullian (AD 160–240)'.[195]

Thus, there is both direct and indirect text-critical evidence suggesting that 1 Cor 14:34-35 at one time may not have appeared at its present location in 1 Corinthians—in short, that it may represent a secondary addition to the text.

---

[191] 𝔓46 (late second or early third century), B (fourth century), ℵ (fourth century), A (fifth century), D (sixth century), etc.

[192] Including D (sixth century) and 'the Western tradition' generally.

[193] See P.B. Payne, 'Fuldensis, Sigla for Variants in Vaticanus, and 1 Cor 14.34-5', *NTS* 41 (1995), 240-62; and 'MS. 88 as Evidence for a Text without 1 Cor. 14.34-5', *NTS* 44 (1998), 152-58. For an opposing view, however, see C. Niccum, 'The Voice of the Manuscripts on the Silence of Women: The External Evidence', *NTS* 43 (1997), 242-55.

[194] Fee, *The First Epistle to the Corinthians*, 699. Ellis ('The Silenced Wives of Corinth') suggests, however, that the gloss was added to the autograph of 1 Corinthians either by Paul himself or at his instruction.

[195] Payne, 'MS. 88 as Evidence for a Text without 1 Cor 14.34-5', 155-56; and 'Fuldensis, Sigla for Variants in Vaticanus and 1 Cor 14.34-5', 247-48.

b. *Contextual Evidence for Interpolation*

Regarding 1 Cor 14:34-35, Fee observes that 'one can make much better sense of the structure of Paul's argument without these intruding sentences', which have little, if anything, to do with the subject matter of the surrounding material. Indeed, 'these two verses simply lack any genuine correspondence with either the overall argument of chaps. 12–14 or the immediate argument of vv. 26-40'. With vv. 34-35 removed, v. 33b completes the sentence begun in 33a ('For God is not a God of confusion but of peace, as in all the churches of the saints'), which constitutes the conclusion to Paul's 'balanced guidelines for tongues with interpretation and prophecy with discernment'. Verses 36-38 then represent 'an *ad hominem* argument against those in the community who in the name of being *pneumatikos* ("spiritual") are leading [the Corinthian] church is another direction'.[196] Verses 34-35, however, represent a complete, self-contained unit of material that is in no way dependent upon its present context. Such contextual evidence suggests that 1 Cor 14:34-35 may represent a secondary addition to the text.

c. *Linguistic Evidence for Interpolation*

At several points, the vocabulary of 1 Cor 14:34-35 appears not to be characteristically Pauline: (1) The verb σιγάω (v. 34) appears elsewhere in the undisputed Pauline letters only at Rom 16:25 (part of a passage regarded by most scholars as a non-Pauline interpolation) and 1 Cor 14:28, 30 (the passage immediately preceding 14:34-35). (2) The verb ἐπιτρέπω (v. 34), is found elsewhere in the undisputed letters only at 1 Cor 16:7, where it is in the active voice (not passive as in 14:34) and refers not to some regulation regarding human conduct (as in 14:34) but simply to the Lord 'permitting' Paul to visit the Corinthians.[197] (3) The verb ὑποτάσσειν (v. 34) appears frequently in the Pauline letters, but in all except three cases it refers to submission either to God,[198] to Christ,[199] to God's law,[200] to God's

---

[196] Fee, *The First Epistle to the Corinthians*, 701-702.
[197] For the same idea and the same verb as in 1 Cor 14:34, however, see the pseudo-Pauline 1 Tim 2:12.
[198] 1 Cor 15:28.
[199] 1 Cor 15:27, 28; Phil 3:21.
[200] Rom 8:7.

righteousness,[201] or to 'futility'.[202] Apart from 1 Cor 14:34, the verb refers to submission to humans at only three places, the first of which is regarded by some as part of a non-Pauline interpolation: Rom 13:1, 5 (governing authorities), 1 Cor 14:32 (prophets), and 1 Cor 16:16 (Christian leaders).[203] (4) The verb ἐπερωτάω (v. 35) appears elsewhere in the undisputed letters only at Rom 10:20, in a quotation from Isa 65:1. (5) The adjective αἰσχρός (v. 35) is found elsewhere in the undisputed letters only at 1 Cor 11:16, which is part of another suspected non-Pauline interpolation.[204] (6) The phrase 'just as even the law says' (καθὼς καὶ ὁ λόγος λέγει), as it stands in v. 34, appears also not to be characteristically Pauline. As Raymond F. Collins notes, 'Paul generally expresses a somewhat negative view of the law' (cf. 1 Cor 15:56), and 'when he wants to develop a scriptural argument he cites the pertinent passage of Scripture (cf. 9:9; 14:21), rather than making a merely general reference under the rubric of "the law"'.[205]

Although there do appear to be certain linguistic links between 1 Cor 14:34-35 and the remainder of ch. 14 (e.g., 'speaking', 'silence', 'submission'), Fee suggests that these 'are used in such completely different ways as to make them suspect'. As an example, he observes that 'there is not a single absolute use of the verb "to speak" in its other 21 occurrences in this chapter, yet it is twice so used here'.[206] Thus, the linguistic evidence appears to suggest non-Pauline authorship of 1 Cor 14:34-35.

d. *Ideational Evidence for Interpolation*

It has already been noted that the ideational content of 1 Cor 14:34-35 has no apparent relation to that of its context. More to the point, it is often noted that 'these verses stand in obvious contradiction to 11:2-16, where it is assumed without reproof that women pray and

---

[201] Rom 10:3.
[202] Rom 8:20.
[203] In the Pseudo-Pauline writings, however, the verb almost always refers to submission to humans: husbands (Eph 5:24; Col 3:18; Titus 2:5; cf. 1 Pet 3:1, 5), masters (Titus 2:9; cf. 1 Pet 2:18), and governing authorities (Titus 3:1; cf. 1 Pet 2:13). The only exception is Eph 1:22, where it refers to Christ.
[204] See also, however, the pseudo-Pauline Titus 1:11.
[205] Collins, *First Corinthians*, 515 (note, however, that Collins regards 1 Cor 14:34-35 as Pauline). To be sure, 1 Cor 9:8 reads, ἢ καὶ ὁ λόγος λέγει ('does not even the law say...?'), but Paul then cites the appropriate scriptural passage.
[206] Fee, *The First Epistle to the Corinthians*, 702.

prophesy in the assembly'.[207] It should be noted, however, that 11:3-16 is also regarded by some as a non-Pauline interpolation. Thus, the contradiction indicates no more than that Paul could not have been the author of both passages. If 11:3-16 is in fact non-Pauline, then 14:34-35 might have been written by Paul.

There is, however, ideational evidence suggesting that 14:34-35 is non-Pauline. Even the immediate context in ch. 14 appears to assume that women are included among those who speak in church (note the 'all' in vv. 5, 18, 23, 24, and 31 and the 'each one' of v. 26). More importantly, 1 Cor 14:34-35 appears to contradict Paul's avowed egalitarianism as articulated in Gal 3:27-28 (i.e., in Christ 'there is neither Jew nor Greek, there is neither slave nor free, there is neither male nor female; for you are all one in Christ Jesus'); his surprisingly even-handed discussion of sex, marriage, and divorce in 1 Corinthians 7; and the very positive and non-discriminatory manner in which he speaks of women with whom he has been associated in the work of the church.[208] Indeed, it stretches the imagination to think that this Paul might also have written (or approved) the sentiments expressed in 1 Cor 14:34-35!

Thus, the ideational evidence appears to suggest that 1 Cor 14:34-35 is non-Pauline in the double sense of non-Pauline authorship and non-Pauline insertion in Paul's letter to the Corinthians.

e. *Situational Evidence for Interpolation*

The situational evidence for regarding 1 Cor 14:34-35 as a non-Pauline interpolation is largely inferential. Apart from this passage and perhaps 1 Cor 11:3-16 (which, as has already been noted, is also regarded by some as a non-Pauline interpolation), there is nothing whatsover in the undisputed letters to suggest that the activity of women in the church was regarded as a problem by Paul or during Paul's lifetime. This suggests that the passage may not have been composed until a later date.

f. *Comparative Evidence for Interpolation*

As has already been suggested, the comparative evidence for regarding 1 Cor 14:34-35 as non-Pauline is, to some extent, the 'flip-side' of the linguistic, ideational, and situational evidence. Some of

---

[207] Fee, *The First Epistle to the Corinthians*, 702.
[208] E.g., 1 Cor 16:19; Rom 16:1-2, 3-5, 6, 7, 12, 13, 15; Phil 4:2-3; Phlm 1.

the linguistic and ideational features of the passage that appear non-Pauline are found in certain of the pseudo-Pauline writings. In particular, 1 Cor 14:34-35 bears a close resemblance to the pseudo-Pauline 1 Tim 2:11-12. Both passages employ the verb ἐπιτρέπειν to enjoin silence on the part of women; both require that women be 'submissive' (using the same linguistic root: ὑποτάσσειν in 1 Cor 14:34 and ὑποταγή in 1 Tim 2:11), presumably to men, an idea that is also present elsewhere in the pseudo-Pauline writings;[209] and both suggest that men should be the teachers of women, not *vice versa*. In addition, the use of the adjective αἰσχρός in 1 Cor 14:35 is similar to that in 1 Cor 11:16, which is also regarded by some as a non-Pauline interpolation.[210] Moreover, although it is not elsewhere suggested in the authentically Pauline writings that the role and status of women was regarded as a problem during Paul's lifetime, there is ample evidence of this in the pseudo-Pauline writings, which contain strong restrictions regarding the status and role of women.[211] Such evidence suggests that 1 Cor 14:34-35 may have been written (and added to Paul's Corinthian letter) sometime after the death of the apostle.

g. *Motivational Evidence for Interpolation*
The motivational evidence for regarding 1 Cor 14:34-35 as a non-Pauline interpolation is closely related to the situational evidence. After the time of Paul, the status and role of women in the church apparently came to be regarded as something of a problem. Thus, it may have appeared desirable to have the apostle say something to address the problem. Hence, the addition of a passage such as 1 Cor 14:34-35 to one of the authentically Pauline letters.

h. *Locational Evidence for Interpolation*
If 1 Cor 14:34-35 was in fact a later addition, why was it inserted precisely at its present location and not elswehere?[212] In a general sense, of course, vv. 34-35, like all of ch. 14 and indeed both chs. 12

---

[209] Col 3:18; Eph 5:24; Titus 2:5; cf. also 1 Pet 3:1, 5 (all using the verb ὑποτάσσειν).

[210] Elsewhere in the Pauline corpus (and indeed in the entire New Testament), αἰσχρός appears only at the pseudo-Pauline Eph 5:12 and Titus 1:11.

[211] Col. 3:18; Eph. 5:22-33; 1 Tim 2:9-15; Titus 2:3-5; cf. also 1 Pet 3:1-6.

[212] As already noted, some manuscripts place vv. 34-35 at the end of ch. 14, not after v. 33. This, however, does not significantly affect the locational evidence for interpolation.

and 14, have to do with public worship. There are, however, more specific linguistic and ideational features that appear to link these verses to their immediate context: (1) Chapter 14 as a whole deals with 'speaking' in church, a theme that also characterizes vv. 34-35. (2) Verse 28 speaks of 'keeping silent in church', a notion that is picked up in v. 34. (3) Verse 32 speaks of 'being subject', an idea that reappears at v. 34 (using the same verb, ὑποτάσσεσθαι). (4) Verse 33 includes the phrase 'in all of the churches', and this reappears almost *verbatim* in v. 34 ('in the churches'). In short, it may simply have been the common themes of 'speech', 'silence', and 'submission', together with the setting of public worship 'in the churches', that led to the insertion of 14:34-35 precisely at its present location in 1 Corinthians.

One might argue, of course, that such commonalties point to Pauline authorship of the verses in question. As Fee notes, however, what appear to be common themes are treated so differently in vv. 34-35 as to make suspect any such argument.[213] For example, ch. 14 as a whole is concerned with the speech of *prophets and speakers in 'tongues'*, while vv. 34-35 addresses the speech of *women*. Similarly, in v. 28 it is *speakers in 'tongues'* who are to keep silent *unless an interpreter is available*, while in v. 34 it is *all women* who are to keep silent. Further, in v. 32 it is *'the spirits of prophets'* that are subject *to a particular class of people* (prophets), while in v. 34 it is *women* who are to be subject *to men*. In short, the exclusive focus on women in vv. 34-35 distinguishes these verses from the remainder of ch. 14.

Combining what I have termed 'comparative', 'motivational', and 'locational' evidence for interpolation, Dennis Ronald MacDonald has suggested a plausible reason for the insertion of 1 Cor 14:34-35 precisely at its present location in Paul's letter to the Corinthians:

> Some scribe apparently feared that others might interpret the egalitarian treatment of spiritual gifts in 1 Corinthians 14 to mean that Paul included women in the prophetic office. But the scribe knew better, for he had read (pseudo-)Paul's comment in 1 Timothy that women must remain silent; therefore, he added vv 33b-36[214] in order to clarify what he understood to have been Paul's position on the matter.[215]

---

[213] Fee, *The First Epistle to the Corinthians*, 702.

[214] Murphy-O'Connor ('Interpolations in 1 Corinthians', 90) has argued convincingly that the interpolation does not include vv. 33b and 36.

[215] MacDonald, 'A Conjectural Emendation', 267.

Conclusion

The text-critical and contextual evidence suggest that 1 Cor 14:34-35 may represent a secondary addition to the text of Paul's letter to the Corinthians. The linguistic and ideational evidence point to non-Pauline authorship of the passage, and indeed the latter suggests that it was someone other than Paul who inserted the verses in the Pauline letter. The situational and comparative evidence point to composition of the passage after the time of Paul and suggest both non-Pauline authorship and non-Pauline insertion. The motivational and locational evidence provide plausible reasons why someone other than Paul might both have composed the passage and inserted it at precisely its present location in Paul's Corinthian letter. Thus, the cumulative weight of the evidence appears to support the view that 1 Cor 14:34-35 is a non-Pauline interpolation.

In the case of other proposed interpolations, the evidence is less clearcut. As has already been noted, there is direct text-critical evidence for interpolation only in the cases of 1 Cor 14:34-35 and Rom 16:25-27. In the case of Rom 16:25-27, there appears to be little if any contextual evidence for interpolation; nevertheless, it is regarded as an interpolation by most scholars. Thus, any case for interpolation must be based upon the convergence of different lines of evidence, and conclusions must be qualified in light of the consistency and strength of the evidence. It is my own judgment, however, that a careful analysis of the evidence can at times lead to the reasonably confident conclusion that a passage is a non-Pauline interpolation. At this point, I myself am prepared to argue that the following passages are indeed such interpolations: Rom 1:18–2:29;[216] 13:1-7;[217] 16:25-27;[218] 1 Cor 2:6-16;[219] 10:1-22;[220] 11:3-16;[221] 12:31b–14:1a;[222] 2 Cor 6:14–7:1;[223] and 1 Thess 2:14-16.[224]

---

[216] Walker, 'Romans 1.18–2.29'.
[217] I have not written regarding this passage but have been convinced by the arguments of others.
[218] See n. 217 above.
[219] Walker, '1 Corinthians 2.6-16'.
[220] See n. 217 above.
[221] Walker, '1 Corinthians 11:2-16 and Paul's Views Regarding Women'.
[222] Walker, 'Is First Corinthians 13 a Non-Pauline Interpolation?'.
[223] See n. 217 above.
[224] See n. 217 above.

INDEX OF ANCIENT SOURCES

OLD TESTAMENT

Deut 4:2	179	Jer 25:15–45:15	174
Deut 13:1	179	Jer 29:16-20	174
		Jer 32:1–51:35 LXX	174
Ps 32:1-2	178	Jer 33:14-26	174
Psalm 119	180	Jer 39:4-13	174
		Jer 46:1–51:64	174
Isa 65:1	231		
		Hab 2:4	179
Jer 25:14–31:44 LXX	174		

NEW TESTAMENT

Matt 28:19-20	40	Rom 1:1	182
		Rom 1:3-4	182
Luke 1:1-4	126	Rom 1:3	131
		Rom 1:5	182
John 5	180	Rom 1:8-17	64, 83
John 7:53–8:11	152, 201	Rom 1:15	64
John 13:10	180	Rom 1:17	179
John 21	152	Rom 1:18–11:36	83, 84
		Rom 1:18-32	185
Acts 1:4-5	126	Rom 1:18–2:29	96, 185, 191, 235
Acts 1:7-8	126		
Acts 15:23-29	71	Rom 1:19–2:1	191
Acts 15:23	72	Rom 1:32	191
Acts 20:23-25	84	Romans 2	185
Acts 21:27-40	84	Rom 2:1	191
Acts 23:26	72	Rom 2:16	191
Acts 26:18	53	Rom 3:12-18	191
Acts 26:20	53	Rom 3:19	160
Acts 28:16-31	84	Rom 3:24-26	191
		Rom 4:1-24	23
Romans 1–15	150	Rom 4:7-9	178
Rom 1:1-17	182	Rom 4:14	191
Rom 1:1-7	83	Rom 4:17	191
Rom 1:1-5	154	Rom 4:18-19	191

Rom 5:1	191	Romans 14	150
Rom 5:6-7	191	Rom 14:6	192
Rom 5:12-21	180, 181, 191	Rom 14:23	150
Rom 5:17	191	Romans 15	150
Rom 6:1-14	185	Rom 15:4	192
Rom 6:1-11	13	Rom 15:14–16:23	84
Rom 6:1	178	Rom 15:14-33	182
Rom 6:3-5	54	Rom 15:23-24	160
Rom 6:5	159	Rom 15:24	81
Rom 6:8	159	Rom 15:28	160
Rom 6:13	191	Romans 16	46, 104, 120, 150, 192
Rom 6:15-23	185		
Rom 6:17	191	Rom 16:1-24	182
Rom 6:19	191	Rom 16:1-2	232
Rom 7:1-6	185	Rom 16:1	39
Rom 7:6	191	Rom 16:3-5	232
Rom 7:7-25	160	Rom 16:5	129, 192
Rom 7:7-12	185	Rom 16:6	232
Rom 7:16	160	Rom 16:7	232
Rom 7:25b	191	Rom 16:12	232
Rom 8:1	191, 195	Rom 16:13	232
Rom 8:7	230	Rom 16:15	232
Rom 8:9-11	191	Rom 16:17-20	40
Rom 8:17	160	Rom 16:22	120, 169
Rom 8:18-25	157	Rom 16:25	230
Rom 8:20	231	Rom 16:25-27	96, 108, 150, 173, 192, 194, 209, 227, 235
Romans 9–11	46, 151		
Rom 9:1-5	179, 182		
Rom 9:5	178, 191		
Rom 9:30–10:4	23	1 Cor 1:1–4:21	78
Rom 10:3	231	1 Cor 1:1-17	183
Rom 10:4	160	1 Cor 1:1-3	78
Rom 10:9	191	1 Cor 1:1	169
Rom 10:17	191	1 Cor 1:2	129
Rom 10:20	231	1 Cor 1:2b	108
Rom 11:6	192	1 Cor 1:4-9	78
Rom 12:1–15:13	83, 84, 180	1 Cor 1:8-15:58	78
Rom 12:1	44	1 Cor 1:10–16:12	78
Rom 12:11	192	1 Cor 1:10–4:21	64
Rom 12:13	181	1 Cor 1:10	78
Rom 12:14	181	1 Cor 1:11-17	78
Rom 12:15	181	1 Cor 1:11-13	131
Rom 13:1-7	192, 235	1 Cor 1:18–4:21	78
Rom 13:1	231	1 Cor 1:18-31	69
Rom 13:5	192	1 Cor 1:23	178
Rom 13:11-14	154	1 Cor 2:6-16	173, 192, 235

1 Cor 2:9	178	1 Cor 14:5	232
1 Cor 2:13	42	1 Cor 14:18	232
1 Cor 3:1-10	183	1 Cor 14:21	231
1 Cor 4:6c	192	1 Cor 14:23	209, 232
1 Corinthians 5–11	78	1 Cor 14:24	232
1 Cor 5:1-13	78, 183	1 Cor 14:26-40	230
1 Cor 5:3	59	1 Cor 14:28	230, 234
1 Cor 5:9	129, 205	1 Cor 14:30	230
1 Cor 5:19ff.	117	1 Cor 14:31	232
1 Cor 6:1-20	78	1 Cor 14:32	231, 234
1 Cor 6:1-11	183	1 Cor 14:33-36	151
1 Cor 6:9	178	1 Cor 14:33	229, 233, 234
1 Cor 6:10	178	1 Cor 14:33a	230
1 Cor 6:14	193	1 Cor 14:33b-36	158, 193, 234
1 Cor 7:1-40	78, 183	1 Cor 14:33b	234
1 Cor 7:17	100	1 Cor 14:34-35	151, 193, 209, 222, 227-35
1 Cor 7:29-31	193		
1 Cor 7:29	154	1 Cor 14:34	230, 231, 233, 234
1 Cor 8:1–11:1	78		
1 Cor 8:1-13	183	1 Cor 14:35	231, 233
1 Cor 9:1-27	183	1 Cor 14:36-38	230
1 Cor 9:8	231	1 Cor 14:36	234
1 Cor 9:9	231	1 Cor 14:40	209, 229
1 Cor 10:1-22	193, 235	1 Corinthians 15	78
1 Cor 10:11	154	1 Cor 15:1-58	78
1 Cor 10:23-33	183	1 Cor 15:1-11	183
1 Cor 11:1-15	183	1 Cor 15:3-11	193
1 Cor 11:2-34	78	1 Cor 15:3	143
1 Cor 11:2-16	193, 231	1 Cor 15:8-9	178
1 Cor 11:2	173	1 Cor 15:20-28	181
1 Cor 11:3-16	173, 193, 232, 235	1 Cor 15:20	178
		1 Cor 15:21-22	193
1 Cor 11:3	158	1 Cor 15:23	178
1 Cor 11:16-22	183	1 Cor 15:27	230
1 Cor 11:16	231, 233	1 Cor 15:28	230
1 Cor 11:17	173	1 Cor 15:31c	193
1 Cor 11:23-25	193	1 Cor 15:32	129, 178
1 Cor 11:33-34	183	1 Cor 15:33	209
1 Cor 11:34b	179	1 Cor 15:36-37	178
1 Corinthians 12–14	78, 161, 230	1 Cor 15:44b-48	193
1 Cor 12:1–14:40	78	1 Cor 15:51	154
1 Corinthians 12	233	1 Cor 15:56	193, 231
1 Cor 12:21	178	1 Cor 16:1-24	78, 183
1 Cor 12:31b–14:1a	193, 226. 235	1 Cor 16:1-18	78
1 Cor 13:4-7	178	1 Cor 16:5-12	78
1 Corinthians 14	229, 231-34	1 Cor 16:7	230

1 Cor 16:8	129, 178	2 Corinthians 9	76, 183
1 Cor 16:13-24	78	2 Cor 9:1-15	151
1 Cor 16:13-19	78	2 Cor 9:1-5	183
1 Cor 16:16	231	2 Cor 9:8	44
1 Cor 16:19-24	78	2 Corinthians 10–13	69, 75, 76, 150
1 Cor 16:19	129, 232	2 Cor 10:1–13:13	151
1 Cor 16:20	78	2 Cor 10:1–13:10	76, 77, 183
1 Cor 16:21	169	2 Cor 10:1–11:33	183
1 Cor 16:23	209	2 Cor 10:1	69
1 Cor 16:24	209	2 Cor 10:9-11	69
		2 Cor 10:9	100
2 Corinthians 1–9	150, 151	2 Cor 10:10	100, 205
2 Cor 1:1–6:14	75, 76	2 Cor 12:1-19	183
2 Cor 1:1–6:13	151	2 Cor 12:20–13:14	183
2 Cor 1:1–3:3	77	2 Cor 13:11-13	76, 77, 183
2 Cor 1:1–2:13	183	2 Cor 13:11	77
2 Cor 1:1-2	76	2 Cor 13:12	78
2 Cor 1:1	169		
2 Cor 1:3-11	76	Gal 1:1-10	182
2 Cor 1:8	129	Gal 1:1-5	83
2 Cor 1:12–9:15	76	Gal 1:1	143
2 Cor 1:12–3:3	64	Gal 1:2	169
2 Cor 1:12–2:13	76, 77	Gal 1:6-11	64, 83
2 Cor 1:20	154	Gal 1:11–2:14	182
2 Cor 2:4	76, 129, 151, 205	Gal 1:12–2:14	83
		Gal 1:12	143
2 Cor 2:14–6:13	182	Gal 2:7b-8	193
2 Cor 2:14-17	76	Gal 2:11-12	40
2 Cor 2:14-16	77	Gal 2:15-21	83
2 Cor 3:1-3	76, 77, 83	Gal 3:1–4:31	83, 84
2 Cor 3:1	100	Gal 3:1-5	64
2 Cor 3:4–6:13	76	Gal 3:19-25	23
2 Cor 5:20	39	Gal 3:19	23
2 Cor 6:14–7:1	76, 151, 193, 235	Gal 3:19a	207
		Gal 3:27-28	232
2 Cor 7:2-16	75, 76, 151, 183	Gal 3:28	158
		Gal 4:12b-14	182
2 Cor 7:2-4	183	Gal 5:1–6:10	83
2 Cor 7:5-16	183	Gal 5:2	182
2 Cor 7:8	129, 151, 205	Gal 5:10-12	182
2 Corinthians 8	76, 183	Gal 5:17	180
2 Cor 8:1–9:15	77	Gal 5:20	167
2 Cor 8:1-24	151	Gal 6:1-10	38
2 Cor 8:1-6	183	Gal 6:11-18	83
2 Cor 8:4	195	Gal 6:11	169, 182
2 Cor 8:16-24	183	Gal 6:17	182

INDEX OF ANCIENT SOURCES   241

Gal 6:18	182	Eph 6:18-23	183
		Eph 6:21-24	85
Eph 1:1-2	61, 85, 183		
Eph 1:1	178	Phil 1:1–3:1a	79
Eph 1:3-23	85	Phil 1:1-30	184
Eph 1:3-6	183	Phil 1:1-2	79, 80
Eph 1:15-19	183	Phil 1:1	39, 169
Eph 1:22-23	157	Phil 1:1c	193
Eph 2:1–3:21	85	Phil 1:3-26	80
Eph 2:4-6	160	Phil 1:3-11	12, 47, 79, 80
Eph 2:5-6	158-60	Phil 1:3-5	12
Eph 2:5	158	Phil 1:4	47
Eph 2:8-11	23	Phil 1:7	12
Eph 2:8-10	44	Phil 1:12-30	12
Eph 2:11-22	156, 157	Phil 1:12-26	80
Eph 2:15	182	Phil 1:12-18a	79
Eph 3:1-8	183	Phil 1:12-14	12
Eph 3:1-7	183	Phil 1:18b–3:21	79
Eph 3:3	156	Phil 1:18b–2:11	79
Eph 3:6	157	Phil 1:18b–2:4	64
Eph 3:7-13	157	Phil 1:18b-26	80
Eph 3:8-20	183	Phil 1:22-23	12
Eph 3:8-9	156	Phil 1:27-37	80
Eph 3:9-10	157	Phil 1:27	13
Eph 3:9	156	Phil 2:1–3:21	80
Eph 3:12-14	183	Phil 2:1	80
Eph 3:16-21	183	Phil 2:5-11	80, 177
Eph 4:1-24	183	Phil 2:6-7	193
Eph 4:1–6:20	85	Phil 2:12-30	79, 80, 184
Eph 4:1-3	183	Phil 2:17	12, 13
Eph 4:7	183	Phil 3:1	130, 151
Eph 4:13-15	183	Phil 3:1a	79
Eph 4:17-32	183	Phil 3:1b–4:1	79
Eph 5:3-12	183	Phil 3:2–4:3	80
Eph 5:12	233	Phil 3:2–4:1	151
Eph 5:15-20	183	Phil 3:2-21	80
Eph 5:22–6:9	158	Phil 3:2-11	12
Eph 5:22-33	233	Phil 3:2-3	79
Eph 5:22	183	Phil 3:4-16	12
Eph 5:24	231, 233	Phil 3:4-11	79
Eph 5:25	183	Phil 3:8	12
Eph 5:31	157	Phil 3:12-21	79
Eph 6:1	183	Phil 3:17-21	12
Eph 6:4	183	Phil 3:17-19	12
Eph 6:5-9	183	Phil 3:20	13, 20
Eph 6:18-24	183	Phil 3:21	80, 230

Phil 4:1-20	79, 80	Col 1:24–2:5	84
Phil 4:1-3	79	Col 1:24-29	48
Phil 4:1	80	Col 1:24	48
Phil 4:2-7	79	Col 1:25	48, 49
Phil 4:2-3	184, 232	Col 1:27-28	48-50
Phil 4:5	136	Col 1:27	49
Phil 4:8-9	79	Col 1:28	49, 51
Phil 4:9	184	Col 1:28a	49
Phil 4:10-23	79, 184	Col 1:28b	49
Phil 4:10-20	12	Col 1:29	48
Phil 4:15-20	12	Col 2:1-5	183
Phil 4:21-23	79, 80	Col 2:1	49, 53, 56
		Col 2:2-3	49, 50
Col 1:1-9	183	Col 2:2	48, 49, 53, 54
Col 1:1-2	84	Col 2:3	49, 54, 159
Col 1:1	84, 169	Col 2:6-23	84
Col 1:3-23	84	Col 2:6-7	46, 48
Col 1:3-6	46, 47	Col 2:7a	48
Col 1:3	46	Col 2:8	54-56
Col 1:3b-4a	47	Col 2:9-10	55
Col 1:4	46	Col 2:9	50, 51, 54
Col 1:5-6	50	Col 2:10	54
Col 1:5	46, 48	Col 2:11	54-56
Col 1:5b-6a	47	Col 2:12-13	159, 160
Col 1:6	46-48	Col 2:12	48, 53-55, 160
Col 1:6c	47	Col 2:20-23	55, 56
Col 1:9-11	47, 53	Col 2:20	54
Col 1:9-10	46, 47	Col 2:21	54
Col 1:9	46, 47, 52	Col 2:22	54
Col 1:9b-10	47	Col 2:23	54, 55
Col 1:10-12	48	Col 3:1–4:6	84
Col 1:10	46-48, 52, 53	Col 3:1-4	159
Col 1:11	48, 52, 53	Col 3:1-3	160
Col 1:12-14	53	Col 3:1	160
Col 1:12	48, 52, 56	Col 3:5	50
Col 1:13	52, 53	Col 3:8-9	50
Col 1:14	52, 53	Col 3:8	50, 55
Col 1:15-20	50, 51	Col 3:9	50, 55
Col 1:19-20	50, 55	Col 3:10	50, 55
Col 1:19	51	Col 3:11	55
Col 1:20	51	Col 3:12	50
Col 1:21-29	183	Col 3:15	55
Col 1:21-23	53, 84	Col 3:16	48-50, 55, 56
Col 1:21	49, 52, 53	Col 3:17	50
Col 1:22	48-54	Col 3:18–4:1	158
Col 1:23	47-50, 52, 129	Col 3:18	231, 233

Col 3:23	50, 56	1 Thess 4:1–5:11	74
Col 3:24	56	1 Thess 4:1–5:5	73
Col 3:25	56	1 Thess 4:1-8	193
Col 4:2-18	183	1 Thess 4:10b-12	193
Col 4:7-18	84	1 Thess 4:13–5:11	159
Col 4:7-9	56	1 Thess 4:13-18	74
Col 4:7	56	1 Thess 4:17	154
Col 4:8	56	1 Thess 4:18	193
Col 4:9	56	1 Thess 5:1-11	74, 194
Col 4:14	125	1 Thess 5:4-11	73
Col 4:16	45, 46, 51, 104, 111, 138, 205, 214	1 Thess 5:4	159
		1 Thess 5:12-25	73
		1 Thess 5:12-22	73, 74, 194
Col 4:18	169	1 Thess 5:14-28	184
		1 Thess 5:23-28	72, 73
1 Thess 1:1–3:13	72	1 Thess 5:23	73
1 Thess 1:1-10	73	1 Thess 5:27	61, 70, 111, 194
1 Thess 1:1-5	72		
1 Thess 1:1-2	184	1 Thess 5:28	174
1 Thess 1:1	72-74, 169		
1 Thess 1:2–3:13	73	2 Thess 1:1-12	75, 184
1 Thess 1:2–3:10	64	2 Thess 1:1-2	75
1 Thess 1:2-10	72, 74	2 Thess 1:1	169
1 Thess 1:2-3	47, 73, 74	2 Thess 1:3-12	75
1 Thess 1:4-10	73	2 Thess 1:7-9	169
1 Thess 1:5	73, 169	2 Thess 2:1-12	159
1 Thess 1:6–3:13	72	2 Thess 2:1-5	184
1 Thess 1:6-7	73	2 Thess 2:1-2	75
1 Thess 1:8-10	72	2 Thess 2:2	100, 145, 168
1 Thess 1:8-9a	74	2 Thess 2:3–3:5	75
1 Thess 1:8	129	2 Thess 2:8	22
1 Thess 1:9b-10	74	2 Thess 2:13-17	184
1 Thess 2:1–5:22	74	2 Thess 3:1-18	184
1 Thess 2:1–5:11	73	2 Thess 3:6-15	75
1 Thess 2:1–3:13	72, 73	2 Thess 3:6-13	75
1 Thess 2:1–3:10	73	2 Thess 3:14-18	75
1 Thess 2:1-12	74	2 Thess 3:14-15	75
1 Thess 2:13–3:13	74	2 Thess 3:16-18	75
1 Thess 2:13-16	73, 151, 193	2 Thess 3:17	100, 169
1 Thess 2:14-16	151, 184, 235		
1 Thess 2:14	151	1 Tim 1:1-7	184
1 Thess 2:17-20	184	1 Tim 1:1-2	85
1 Thess 3:1-13	184	1 Tim 1:1	21
1 Thess 3:1-5	74	1 Tim 1:3-20	85
1 Thess 3:11-13	73	1 Tim 1:3-7	12
1 Thess 4:1–5:22	72	1 Tim 1:3	18, 19, 178

1 Tim 1:4	13, 23	1 Tim 3:16	17, 40, 43
1 Tim 1:5	178	1 Tim 4:1-5	9
1 Tim 1:6-7	9	1 Tim 4:1-3	12
1 Tim 1:7	23	1 Tim 4:3-5	161
1 Tim 1:8-11	43, 160	1 Tim 4:6	19
1 Tim 1:8-10	12, 23	1 Tim 4:7	24, 43
1 Tim 1:8-9	9	1 Tim 4:8	43
1 Tim 1:12	20	1 Tim 4:10	21, 40
1 Tim 1:14	17, 21	1 Tim 4:11	19
1 Tim 1:15-17	40	1 Tim 4:13	18, 19, 25
1 Tim 1:15	21	1 Tim 4:14	20, 41
1 Tim 1:18-20	12, 184	1 Tim 4:16	19
1 Tim 1:18	19	1 Tim 5:5	17
1 Tim 1:19-20	179	1 Tim 5:10	43
1 Tim 1:20	18	1 Tim 5:17	20
1 Tim 2:1–6:2	85	1 Tim 5:18-19	17
1 Tim 2:1-15	39	1 Tim 5:21	19
1 Tim 2:1-2	39	1 Tim 5:22	20
1 Tim 2:2	17, 43	1 Tim 5:25	43
1 Tim 2:3-6	40	1 Tim 6:3-19	85
1 Tim 2:3-4	39	1 Tim 6:3	43, 179
1 Tim 2:3	21	1 Tim 6:5	43
1 Tim 2:4	21	1 Tim 6:6	43
1 Tim 2:5-7a	39	1 Tim 6:7	17
1 Tim 2:5-6	17	1 Tim 6:11-19	12
1 Tim 2:7	20	1 Tim 6:11	43
1 Tim 2:7a	39	1 Tim 6:14-16	40
1 Tim 2:8	17	1 Tim 6:14	22
1 Tim 2:8-15	39	1 Tim 6:18	43
1 Tim 2:9-15	233	1 Tim 6:20-21	85, 184
1 Tim 2:10	43	1 Tim 6:20	19, 161
1 Tim 2:11-13	151		
1 Tim 2:11-12	233	2 Timothy 1	184
1 Tim 2:11	233	2 Tim 1:1-6	184
1 Tim 2:12	230	2 Tim 1:1-2	85, 184
1 Tim 2:13-14	17	2 Tim 1:1	17
1 Tim 2:13	21	2 Tim 1:2	8
1 Tim 2:15	161	2 Tim 1:3-7	12, 18
1 Tim 3:1-8	20	2 Tim 1:3-5	85, 184
1 Tim 3:1	43	2 Tim 1:3	18
1 Tim 3:6	21	2 Tim 1:5	18
1 Tim 3:7b	39	2 Tim 1:6–4:8	85
1 Tim 3:13	17	2 Tim 1:6–3:17	85
1 Tim 3:14-15	184	2 Tim 1:6	18, 20, 41
1 Tim 3:14	18, 19	2 Tim 1:7	42
1 Tim 3:15	13, 39, 41, 161	2 Tim 1:8	12, 13

2 Tim 1:9-10	40	2 Tim 4:1	22
2 Tim 1:9	17, 21	2 Tim 4:5	12, 13
2 Tim 1:10	21, 22	2 Tim 4:6-22	18
2 Tim 1:11	18	2 Tim 4:6-8	12, 184
2 Tim 1:12	12, 18, 19, 161	2 Tim 4:6	13
2 Tim 1:13	17, 18, 179	2 Tim 4:8	22
2 Tim 1:14	18, 19	2 Tim 4:9-22	85, 184
2 Tim 1:15-18	18, 184	2 Tim 4:9-21	184
2 Tim 1:15	12	2 Tim 4:9-11	12
2 Tim 1:18	178	2 Tim 4:11	125
2 Tim 2:1-26	12	2 Tim 4:12	178
2 Tim 2:1	17	2 Tim 4:13	116, 117
2 Tim 2:2	18, 42, 146, 147, 160, 161	2 Tim 4:17	17
		2 Tim 4:18	21
2 Tim 2:3	12, 13	2 Tim 4:22a	184
2 Tim 2:8-13	40	2 Tim 4:22b	184
2 Tim 2:9	12		
2 Tim 2:10	17	Titus 1:1-5	184
2 Tim 2:11-13	17	Titus 1:1-4	86
2 Tim 2:11	13	Titus 1:1	43
2 Tim 2:14-26	41	Titus 1:3	8, 20, 21
2 Tim 2:14-21	41	Titus 1:4	12
2 Tim 2:15	18	Titus 1:5-9	12, 20
2 Tim 2:17-18	160	Titus 1:5	18, 86, 179
2 Tim 2:18	13	Titus 1:6–3:7	86
2 Tim 2:19	17	Titus 1:9-11	40
2 Tim 2:21	43	Titus 1:9	41
2 Tim 2:22-26	12	Titus 1:10-16	12, 23
2 Tim 3:1-13	12	Titus 1:10	9
2 Tim 3:1-5	13	Titus 1:11	10, 231, 233
2 Tim 3:5	43	Titus 1:12	40
2 Tim 3:8	17	Titus 1:14	9, 10, 23
2 Tim 3:10-11	12, 18	Titus 2:1-10	41
2 Tim 3:10	18	Titus 2:1	20
2 Tim 3:11	12, 13	Titus 2:3-5	233
2 Tim 3:12	17	Titus 2:4-5	41
2 Tim 3:14-16	25	Titus 2:5	231, 233
2 Tim 3:14	18	Titus 2:7	43
2 Tim 3:15-17	25	Titus 2:9	231
2 Tim 3:15	17, 18	Titus 2:10	8, 21
2 Tim 3:16b	29	Titus 2:11-14	40
2 Tim 3:17	43	Titus 2:11	8, 17, 22
2 Timothy 4	184	Titus 2:13	22
2 Tim 4:1-16	12	Titus 2:14	17, 43
2 Tim 4:1-8	85	Titus 3:1	43, 231, 178
2 Tim 4:1-2	18	Titus 3:4-7	40

Titus 3:4	8, 21, 22	Heb 1:1-4	86
Titus 3:5-7	17	Heb 1:5–2:18	86
Titus 3:5	8, 10, 21, 23, 161	Heb 2:17-18	86
		Heb 2:18	86
Titus 3:8-11	86	Heb 3:1–10:18	86
Titus 3:8	43	Heb 4:13	86
Titus 3:9-15	184	Heb 4:14–10:18	86
Titus 3:9	10	Heb 10:19–13:25	87
Titus 3:10	167	Heb 10:19–13:21	86
Titus 3:11	167	Heb 13:18-25	177
Titus 3:12-15	8, 18, 86, 184	Heb 13:22-25	86
Titus 3:14	43	Heb 13:23	135
Titus 3:15	8		
		1 Pet 2:13	231
Phlm 1-3	81	1 Pet 2:18–3:7	158
Phlm 1-2	81	1 Pet 2:18	231
Phlm 1	169	1 Pet 3:1-6	233
Phlm 4-7	81	1 Pet 3:1	231, 233
Phlm 4-5	47	1 Pet 3:5	231, 233
Phlm 8-20	64	1 Pet 3:18	177
Phlm 8-17	83		
Phlm 8-16	81	2 Peter 3	31
Phlm 12	232	2 Pet 3:2	21
Phlm 13-20	82	2 Pet 3:15-16	25, 26, 70
Phlm 17-22	81	2 Pet 3:16	30, 130
Phlm 19	169		
Phlm 23-25	81	Revelation 1–3	104
Phlm 24	125	Revelation 1–2	133
		Rev 22:18-19	145, 179, 202

QUMRAN DOCUMENTS

1QM 13:1	177	CD 9:18-20	177
		CD 13:7-13	177
1QS 6:8-14	177	CD 14:8-13	177

APOCRYPHA, PSEUDEPIGRAPHA AND OTHER EARLY JEWISH AND CHRISTIAN LITERATURE

1 Macc 10:25-45	171	*1 Clem* 2.7	178
		1 Clem 5.2	84
2 Macc 1:10	72	*1 Clem* 5.5-7	111, 178
		1 Clem 17.1	136
Wis 7:1-22a	165	*1 Clem* 17.5	136
Wis 8:17-18	165	*1 Clem* 19.2	136

INDEX OF ANCIENT SOURCES

1 Clem 21.9	136	Epiphanius,	
1 Clem 24.1	178	*Panarion* 42.9.3-4	132
1 Clem 24.5	178	Epiphanius,	
1 Clem 27.1	136	*Panarion* 42.9.4	132
1 Clem 27.2	136		
1 Clem 32.2	178	*Epistle of the*	
1 Clem 33.1	178	*Apostles* 29	145
1 Clem 34.4	178	*Epistle of the*	
1 Clem 34.8	178	*Apostles* 31	146
1 Clem 36.1	136		
1 Clem 36.2-5	135	Eusebius, *Hist eccl*	
1 Clem 37.3	178	2.17.1	177
1 Clem 37.5	178	Eusebius, *Hist eccl*	
1 Clem 41.1	178	2.17.23	177
1 Clem 47.1-3	129, 131	Eusebius, *Hist eccl*	
1 Clem 49.5	178	3.25	137, 140
1 Clem 50.6	178	Eusebius, *Hist eccl*	
1 Clem 56.4	136	3.25.4	140
		Eusebius, *Hist eccl*	
3 Cor 3.3	142, 145	3.38.1	135
3 Cor 3.4	147	Eusebius, *Hist eccl*	
3 Cor 3.36	142	3.38.2-3	134
3 Cor 3.37	160	Eusebius, *Hist eccl*	
		3.39.15-16	135
Acts of Paul 3.41	141	Eusebius, *Hist eccl*	
Acts of Paul 3.43	141	6.12.3	148
		Eusebius, *Hist eccl*	
Apos Con 6.16	145, 147, 148	6.14.2	134
		Eusebius, *Hist eccl*	
Athenagoras,		6.14.4	134
A Plea for the		Eusebius, *Hist eccl*	
Christians 37	131	6.14.6	135
		Eusebius, *Hist eccl*	
Augustine,		6.20	134
Ep 153.14	143	Eusebius, *Hist eccl*	
		6.25.11-14	134
Clement of Alexandria,		Eusebius, *Hist eccl*	
Protreptikos		6.25.13	135
90.87.19-21	136		
		Hippolytus, *Comm*	
Clement of Alexandria,		*Daniel* 3.29	140
Stromateis 7.17	147, 167		
Clement of Alexandria,		Ignatius, *Eph* 12.2	104, 129, 178
Stromateis 7.53	149	Ignatius, *Eph* 14.1	178
		Ignatius, *Eph* 16.1	178
		Ignatius, *Eph* 18.1	178

Ignatius, *Eph* 18.2	131	Polycarp, *Phil* 3.2	130
Ignatius, *Eph* 20.2	131	Polycarp, *Phil* 11.3	129
Ignatius, *Rom* 4.3	178	Ps.-Clementine,	
Ignatius, *Rom* 5.1	178	*Contestatio* 5.2	145
Ignatius, *Rom* 9.2	178		
		Tertullian, *Bapt* 17	182
Ignatius, *Phld* 3.3	178		
		Tertullian, *Haer* 36	108, 120
Irenaeus, *Haer* 1.23.1	126	Tertullian, *Marc* 4.2	135
Irenaeus, *Haer* 3.1.1	135	Tertullian, *Marc* 4.5	108, 120, 135, 149
Irenaeus, *Haer* 3.10.1	126	Tertullian, *Marc* 5.11	132
		Tertullian, *Marc* 5.17	132
Irenaeus, *Haer* 3.14.1	126	Tertullian, *Marc* 5.21	133
Irenaeus, *Haer* 4.41.4	167	Tertullian, *Praescr* 5-6	167
		Tertullian, *Praescr* 6	167
Jerome, *Vir* 12	143	Tertullian, *Praescr* 13	146
Lactantius, *Institutes* 6.24.13-14	143	Tertullian, *Praescr* 20-22	146
Muratorian canon ll. 6-61	134	Tertullian, *Praescr* 24	146
Muratorian canon ll. 59-63	133	Tertullian, *Praescr* 25	146
Muratorian canon ll. 62-63	134	Theophilus, *Letter to Autolycus* 3.14	131
Muratorian canon l. 70	134, 148, 165	*Treatise on the Resurrection* 45	167
Origen, *Comm Joh* 20.12	140	*Treatise on the Resurrection* 45.23	160
Origen, *Contra Celsum* 4.19	149	*Treatise on the Resurrection* 45.25	160
Origen, *Principiis* 1.2.3	140		

OTHER ANCIENT SOURCES

Aristotle, *Poetics* 6–22	64	Aristotle, *Poetics* 23–26	64
Aristotle, *Poetics* 6	66		

INDEX OF ANCIENT SOURCES

Aristotle, *Rhet*	
1.3.1-3 1358ab	67
Aristotle, *Rhet*	
1.3.1 1358ab	61
Aristotle, *Rhet* 3.13-19	
1414a-1420b	67
Aristotle, *Rhet*	
3.13 1414a	73
Aristotle, *Rhet* 3.16	
1416b-17b	67, 73
Cicero, *Att* 8.14.1	60
Cicero, *Att* 9.10.1	60
Cicero, *Att* 13.6.3	119
Cicero, *Att* 16.5.5	117
Cicero, *Att* 16.7.1	117
Cicero, *Fam* 2.4.1	59, 62
Cicero, *Fam* 7.18.1	119
Cicero, *Fam* 9.26.1	119
Cicero, *Fam* Bk 13	117, 118
Demetrius 223–235	59
Demetrius 223	60
Demetrius 224	60
Josephus, *Ant* 18.3.3	199
P.Lond. VI 1912	171
Philo, *Contempl*	
25-29	180
Philo, *Contempl*	
64-79	177
Philo, *Ebr* 98	177
Philo, *Her* 30	177
Plato, *Republic*	
2.376E–383C	149
Plato, *Republic*	
3.389B	149
Plato, *Republic*	
3.414C-E	149
Pliny, *Ep* 9.21	82
Pliny, *Ep* 10.96-97	85
Ps.-Demetrius 1	63
Ps.-Demetrius 2	62
Quintilian, *Inst* 1.8.3	144
Quintilian, *Inst*	
3.3.12-15	66
Quintilian, *Inst*	
3.8.49-52	144
Quintilian, *Inst*	
6.1.25	144
Quintilian, *Inst*	
9.2.29-37	144
Quintilian, *Inst*	
11.1.41	144

INDEX OF MODERN AUTHORS

Aageson, J.W. 6, 7
Adams, A.W. 119
Aland, B. 209-11
Aland, K. 209-11
Aleith, E. 133, 135, 138, 142
Alt, A. 172, 185
Andresen, C. 191
Archer, R.L. 116
Ast, U. 192
Aune, D.E. 62, 71, 79, 81, 83, 86, 88, 118, 134

Backhaus, K. 87, 88
Badcock, F.J. 110
Baeck, L. 88
Balch, D. 91
Barnett, A.E. 130, 131, 133, 158
Barnikol, E. 192-94
Barrett, C.K. 184, 185, 201, 210
Barrett, D.P. 210
Barthes, R. 65, 66, 88
Barton, J. 31
Bassler, J.M. 5, 8-10, 12, 19, 22, 25, 40, 43
Bauer, W. 100, 130, 131, 150, 200, 216
Baumgarten, A.I. 200
Baur, F.C. 107, 132, 137, 151, 152
Beare, F.W. 206, 216
Becker, J. 70, 88, 129, 151, 155, 159
Beker, J.C. 10, 11, 15, 151, 153-59, 161, 162
Berger, K. 61, 62, 70, 83, 88
Best, E. 105, 107, 121
Betz, H.D. 60, 61, 70, 76, 83, 88, 182, 183, 185, 193, 194
Bienert, W.A. 136, 140
Bieringer, R. 76, 88

Black, J.S. 118
Blackman, E.C. 110
Blass, F. 106
Bloomquist, L.G. 79, 88
Boismard, M.-É. 45, 46, 51
Bolling, G.M. 198
Bornkamm, G. 182
Botha, J. 83, 89
Brown, R.E. 152
Brox, N. 41, 86, 88, 112, 131, 149
Bruce, F.F. 1, 30, 97, 100, 107, 124, 148, 151, 165
Bultmann, R. 77, 84, 89, 191, 192
Bünker, M. 63, 78, 89

Campenhausen, H. von 1, 38, 41, 96, 100
Carroll, J.T. 192
Carson, D.A. 112, 124
Charlesworth, J.H. 196, 200, 223
Cheyne, T.K. 118
Childs, B.S. 16, 17, 19, 27, 41, 99, 103
Clabeaux, J.J. 110
Clark, K.W. 201, 211-13
Clarke, K.D. 96, 208
Classen, C.J. 61, 66, 89, 90
Clemen, C. 189
Collins, R.F. 90, 93, 157-60, 162, 205, 206, 231
Comfort, P.W. 210
Conzelmann, H. 8, 15, 42, 131
Cope, L. 193
Cosgrove, C.H. 192
Couchoud, P.-L. 189

Dahl, N.A. 98, 123, 126, 156, 165

INDEX OF MODERN AUTHORS

Dassmann, E. 130, 131, 133, 139, 140, 142
Davies, M. 112
Davies, S. 140
Debrunner, A. 106
Deissmann, G.A. 61, 68, 70, 89, 118
Delobel, J. 193
Detering, H. 215
Dibelius, M. 8, 15, 42, 131
Dihle, A. 70, 71, 89
Donelson, L.R. 5, 8, 9, 11, 15, 16, 19, 20, 113, 139, 147-49, 166
Donfried, K.P. 150
Dormeyer, D. 61, 67, 79, 82, 89
Doty, W.G. 202, 203
Doughty, D.J. 190, 194, 219
Duff, J. 97, 119, 133
Dunn, J.D.G. 151, 154, 155, 158
Dupuis, J. 135

Eckart, K.-G. 194
Ehrlich, E.L. 192
Ehrman, B.D. 151, 158, 211
Eisenhut, W. 61, 65, 66, 89
Ellis, E.E. 18, 112, 116, 117, 124, 166, 172-76, 180, 182, 186, 209, 222, 229
Enslin, M.S. 126
Epp, E.J. 98, 99, 189, 201, 204, 207, 209
Eshbaugh, H. 202, 207
Evans, C.A. 18, 102, 112
Ewald, H. 172, 186

Farmer, W.R. 30, 201
Fee, G.D. 193, 194, 209, 228-32, 234
Feldman, L.H. 199
Ferguson, E. 97
Fieger, M. 180, 186
Finegan, J. 186
Fiore, B. 8, 15
Fitzer, G. 193, 228
Fitzmyer, J.A. 120, 124, 155, 190-94, 206
Friedrich, G. 194

Fritz, K. von 143
Fuhrmann, M. 64, 65, 89
Funk, R.W. 30
Furnish, V.P. 98, 113, 189-91, 194, 205, 206, 219

Gamble, H.Y. 5, 30, 32, 98, 99, 105, 108, 109, 112, 120, 204, 209, 214
Gaston, L. 207
Gnilka, J. 79, 81, 85, 90, 193
Goehring, J.E. 194
Goodspeed, E.J. 31, 103-106, 114, 115
Goulder, M.D. 97
Grant, F.C. 103
Grant, R.M. 199-201
Green, J.B. 27
Gregory, C.R. 1, 96
Groh, D.E. 208
Grossouw, W.K.M. 193
Guthrie, D. 101, 103, 109-12, 116, 125

Haefner, A.E. 148
Hagen, W.H. 191
Hahneman, G.M. 33, 97, 105, 133, 134, 138, 139
Hanson, A.T. 160
Harding, M. 133
Harnack, A. 32, 99-101, 103, 106, 109, 132, 136, 138, 139
Harris, J.R. 116
Harrison, P.N. 152, 184, 186, 191
Harvey, W.W. 133
Hawkins, R.M. 189, 220
Hawthorne, G.F. 116
Hedrick, C.W. 194
Hengel, M. 65, 90
Henne, P. 97
Hill, C.E. 98
Hillard, T.W. 97
Hills, J.V. 187
Hobbs, A.M. 97
Hoffmann, R.J. 132
Hommel, H. 65, 90
Hoppe, R. 84, 90

Horn, F.W. 193
Hübner, H. 71, 83, 90
Hughes, F.W. 73, 75, 90
Hurd, J.C., Jr. 102, 200

James, M.R. 138, 139
Jeremias, J. 180, 186
Jervis, L.A. 102
Jewett, R. 73, 75, 90, 151, 208
Johanson, B.C. 73, 90
Johnson, E.E. 192
Johnson, L.T. 5, 8-10, 12, 16, 19, 20, 38, 118
Joyce, P. 187
Junack, K. 170, 174, 186

Karris, R.J. 11, 192
Käsemann, E. 107, 192
Kasser, R. 139, 140, 142
Kearsley, R.A. 97
Keck, L.E. 104, 153, 155, 191, 192, 196, 205, 206
Kenyon, F.G. 119, 133, 170, 186
Kern, F.H. 159
Kiley, M. 121, 148, 149, 158
Kilpatrick, G.D. 208
Kim, Y.K. 97
Kitzberger, I. 72, 90
Klappert, B. 192
Klassen, W. 98
Klauck, H.J. 62, 63, 67-69, 73-76, 78, 79, 85-87, 90
Klein, A.F.J. 139, 140, 142, 143
Klein, G. 191
Knight, G., III 5, 26, 106
Knopf, R. 103
Knox, J. 31, 32, 103-105, 109, 110, 192, 215
Knox, W.L. 105
Koester, H. 129, 135, 136, 151, 158, 206, 208, 212
Koskenniemi, H. 59, 63, 91, 118
Kümmel, W.G. 84, 91, 102, 150

Lake, K. 100-103, 109
Lake, S. 100, 103

Lambrecht, J. 88
Lane, W.L. 134
Lang, F. 75, 77, 91
Lausberg, H. 65, 66, 75, 91
Layton, B. 160
Lemcio, E.E. 28
Lightfoot, J.B. 129, 130, 138
Lincoln, A.T. 132, 158
Lindemann, A. 45, 129, 131, 142, 160
Loisy, A.F. 181, 186, 189
Louw, J.P. 39
Lovering, E.H., Jr. 198, 204, 220
Lüdemann, H. 181
Lull, D.J. 23

MacDonald, D.R. 140, 190, 193, 234
McDonald, L.M. 1, 97, 135
MacDonald, M.Y. 11, 140
Macgregor, G.H.C. 170
McKnight, E.V. 64, 91
McLeman, J. 186
MacRae, G.W. 98, 99, 142, 163, 189, 204
Magne, J. 193
Malherbe, A.J. 42, 59, 63, 64, 91, 144, 149, 161
Mann, C.S. 201
Marshall, I.H. 5, 40, 42, 184, 186
Martin, J. 66, 67, 91
Martin, R.P. 105, 116
Martyn, J.L. 104
Maurer, K. 198, 199, 219, 220
Meeks, W.A. 215
Meier, J.P. 199
Meldelson, A. 200
Metzger, B.M. 1, 36, 96, 132, 138, 150, 195, 207, 210, 214
Miller, J.D. 5, 152, 184, 186
Milligan, G. 97
Mitchell, M.M. 78, 91
Mitton, C.L. 34, 99, 105, 132
Morton, A.Q. 170, 171, 186
Moule, C.F.D. 30, 90, 109, 110
Mowry, L. 214, 218

Muddiman, J. 183, 187
Müllenbrock, H.J. 90
Munro, W. 190, 192, 194, 195, 197, 201, 202, 206, 209, 220-22, 224, 226
Murphy-O'Connor, J. 14, 98, 115, 116, 118, 119, 123, 124, 192, 193, 204, 234

Neuner, J. 135
Niccum, C. 229
Nida, E.A. 39
Niebuhr, R.R. 30
Nielson, C.M. 34
Nixon, C.E.V. 97

O'Neill, J.C. 96, 106, 172, 176-78, 180, 182, 187, 190, 191, 193, 194, 200-202, 207, 208, 216, 219, 220
Oberlinner, L. 8, 22, 85, 91
Oesterley, W.E.O. 165
Olbricht, T.H. 73, 91
Olson, K.A. 200
Orton, D.E. 187
Ottley, R.R. 200

Pagels, E.H. 133, 134, 147, 167, 216
Paige, T. 112, 166
Patzia, A.G. 98, 99, 107
Payne, P.B. 229
Pearson, B.A. 194
Peters, M.K.H. 200
Petersen, N. 6, 212
Petersen, W.L. 197
Phillips, T.E. 126
Pickering, S.R. 97
Pink, K. 138, 139, 143
Pokorny, P. 149, 166
Porter, S.E. 29, 96, 102, 110, 112, 124, 126, 148, 187
Preisendanz, K. 177, 187
Price, R.M. 193, 204, 217, 218
Prior, M. 15
Probst, H. 77, 78, 92

Quinn, J.D. 33

Räisäinen, H. 182
Reed, J.T. 108, 124
Refoulé, F. 191
Reid, D.P. 116, 117
Richards, E.R. 116, 118, 125
Richardson, P. 102, 200
Rist, M. 134, 142, 145, 146, 148, 160, 164
Roberts, W.R. 59
Römer, C. 143
Roller, O. 125
Roloff, J. 84, 92
Rosenblatt, J.P. 27

Sanders, E.P. 142, 163, 200
Sanders, H.A. 174, 187
Sanders, J.A. 1, 27, 32
Sanders, J.T. 194
Sanford, E.M. 199
Schenk, W. 79, 84, 92, 192, 194
Schenke, H.-M. 112, 162
Schmidt, D.D. 194, 203, 204, 208
Schmithals, W. 107-109, 120, 123, 192
Schneemelcher, W. 130, 131, 136, 138, 139, 140, 142
Schneider, G. 61, 62
Schnelle, U. 71, 76, 92, 193
Schnider, F. 72
Schoedel, W.R. 129
Schoon-Janssen, J. 63, 72, 92
Schubart, W. 170, 187
Schweitzer, A. 181, 187
Schweizer, E. 84, 92
Sitterson, J.C., Jr. 27
Smith, M. 216
Snyder, G.F. 98
Souter, A. 1, 96
Speyer, W. 135, 141, 145-47, 164
Stendahl, K. 98
Stenger, W. 72
Stettler, H. 37
Stinespring, W.F. 18
Stirewalt, L.M. 144
Stowers, S.K. 12, 13, 118, 119, 199, 203

Strecker, G. 61, 71, 73, 79, 87, 92, 190
Streeter, B.H. 101, 102
Strugnell, J. 192
Sumney, J.L. 9
Sundberg, A.C., Jr. 33, 97
Swete, H.B. 200
Syme, R. 143, 146

Talbert, C.H. 191
Thompson, R.P. 126
Thornton, C.-J. 126
Thraede, K. 59, 63, 92
Thrall, M. 102
Titus, E.L. 193
Towner, P.H. 5, 14, 38, 186
Trilling, W. 75, 92
Trobisch, D. 30, 31, 95, 98, 103, 113-24
Trompf, G.W. 193
Trummer, P. 18
Turner, E.G. 171, 188
Turner, M. 27

Vallée, G. 163
van Spanje, T.E. 185, 188
Verner, D.C. 161
Vielhauer, P. 61, 63, 71, 72, 92
Vööbus, A. 216
Vouaux, L. 138

Walker, W.O., Jr. 96, 102, 126, 185, 188, 191-93, 207, 213, 235

Wall, R.W. 27-29
Wallace-Hadrill, D.S. 200
Walton, S. 107
Watson, D.F. 80, 93
Weiss, B. 104
Weiss, J. 103
Wendland, P. 61, 71, 93
Westcott, B.F. 1, 96, 133-35
White, J.L. 171, 188, 202
Wickert, U. 107
Widmann, M. 192, 193
Wiles, M.F. 215
Wilkins, M.J. 112
Wilkins, M.J. 166
Williams, C.S.C. 1, 96
Williams, R. 187
Wilson, S.G. 110
Winkelmann 65
Wisse, F.W. 194, 197, 198, 209, 213, 216, 217
Wolfe, B.P. 18, 25
Wolter, M. 81, 84, 93
Wood, C. 32
Wuellner, W. 74, 83, 93

Young, F. 8, 9, 39

Zahn, T. 99, 100, 101, 103, 109
Zeitlin, S. 200
Zeller, D. 83, 93
Zeller, E. 107
Zuntz, G. 99, 105, 106, 114, 121, 124